THE ECONOMICS OF FRANÇOIS QUESNAY

The Economics of François Quesnay

Gianni Vaggi
Associate Professor of History of Economic Thought
University of Pavia

Duke University Press   Durham 1987

First published 1987

Published by
The Macmillan Press Ltd

Published in USA by
Duke University Press, Durham

Printed in Hong Kong

Library of Congress Cataloging-in-Publication Data
Vaggi, Gianni.
The economics of François Quesnay.
Originally presented as the author's thesis
(Doctoral—Cambridge).
Bibliography: p.
Includes index.
1. Quesnay, François, 1694–1774.   2. Economics—
France—History—18th century.   3. Physiocrats.
I. Title.
HB105.Q5V34   1987   330.15′2   87–3549
ISBN 0–8223–0757–X

In memory of Maurice Herbert Dobb, 1900–76

Contents

Foreword

The revival of the analytical principles of classical political economy that has gathered pace since the mid-1960s has been based on the firm foundation of a logically coherent theory of value and distribution. It was the failure to provide this foundation which for many years confined the classical approach to being, at best, a repository of useful ideas on growth and technological progress (Smith's discussion of the division of labour and Marx's dissection of the labour process being good examples), or, at worst, identified with simple-minded devotion of the labour theory of value as the 'qualitative' expression of capitalist exploitation – the position to which Hilferding retreated in the face of Böhm-Bawerk's critique of Marx, so depriving the surplus approach of any quantitative significance as a theory of value and distribution. The publication of Piero Sraffa's *Production of Commodities by Means of Commodities* changed all that. Sraffa not only generalised the mathematical solutions to the surplus approach which had been advanced by Dmitriev and Bortkeiwicz, but also presented the analytical *structure* of the surplus approach with stark clarity. Moreover, Sraffa provided a critique of the neo-classical theory of the rate of profit and so of the entire neo-classical explanation of value, distribution and output – hence clearing the ground for the redevelopment of classical theory.

With the analytical core now secure, attention can be turned to the development of other facets of classical and Marxian theory and to the empirical insights which this theory provides. In stark contrast to the neo-classical approach, which reduces all economic activity to a single principle – the competitive resolution of individual attempts to maximise utility subject to the constraints of technology and endowment – classical theory is constructed from a number of analytically separable components. The core of the theory, the surplus approach to value and distribution, takes as data the size and composition of output, the technology in use (the conditions of reproduction) and the real wage (or, in some cases, the rate of profit). These data do not, however, lie outside the realm of economics (as, for example, the neo-classical economists' utility functions do). We need to provide theoretical explanations of their determination. Hence Smith, Ricardo and Marx advanced theories of the real wage and of the level of output (Say's law in the case of Ricardo), and Smith and Marx presented detailed analyses of technological change. Assembled around the core, these theories are the building-blocks of a general theory of the operations of the capitalist economy. There is in all this a clear danger of constructing a disjointed *ad hoc* collage of theories and empirical generalisations. This is avoided by enveloping the entire edifice in a general characterisation of the economic system: the clear specification, that is, of the capitalist mode of production. This serves both to cement the elements of the theory together and to eliminate propositions that do not fit.

Broadly, there are two jobs to be done in developing and extending the classical framework.

First, the classical theory itself must be developed and generalised. All the elements surrounding the core analysis of value and distribution – theories of output and employment, of accumulation, of technology, of the wage, of competition and so on – require reassessment and 'modernisation' in the light both of Sraffa's results and of the many changing facets of the modern capitalist system. This will involve both theoretical development *and* empirical analysis, for one of the important characteristics of classical theorising is the manner in which theory is grounded in the socio-economic data of the system under consideration – the institutional environment is an essential part of the theory.

Second, the rejection of the now discredited neoclassical theory throws open a wide range of problems in international trade, development economics, fiscal and monetary policy and so forth, into which the classical approach can provide new insights. In part these will lead to the refreshing task of debunking the policy prescriptions of orthodox theory which revolve primarily around the fundamental theorem of welfare economics and the supposed 'efficiency' of competitive markets. But there is also a positive job to be done. The reconstruction of economic theory will inevitably precipitate a reinterpretation of economic policy and problems.

The reappraisal of classical economics set off by Piero Sraffa's work is carried to the study of physiocracy by Gianni Vaggi. Vaggi demonstrates that important concepts of price and profit were present in the writings to Quesnay contrary to what has previously been believed. Quesnay did not, however, develop a coherent notion of profit related to the general process of competition which is to be found in Adam Smith's *Wealth of Nations*. It was, of course, the lack of the concept of a general rate of profit which prevented Quesnay from extending his analysis of the determination of surplus from his agricultural examples. Vaggi's work raises once again the question of just how influential was Smith's trip to Paris. The association between the theory of distribution and the concepts of natural market price were not present in his work before that visit.

Trinity College, Cambridge JOHN EATWELL

Preface

Over the period I have been working on this book I have greatly benefited from the advice of many friends and collegues, even though none of them his responsible for the opinions presented in this work.

I must first express my profound debt to the late Maurice Dobb and the late Ronald Meek. Dobb was my first supervisor during the completion of the Ph.D. thesis in Cambridge. His interesting suggestions and his kind rebukes remain among my most important and dear memories as a student. Meek provided many useful comments on a previous version of the work. Although I disagree with some of his opinions, this book is not meant to be a criticism of his interpretation of physiocracy. On the contrary, I try to offer, if possible, a continuation of the analysis of Quesnay's economics along the lines drawn by Meek's 1962 book.

Without the advice and the precise comments of John Eatwell I would not have been able to complete this book; certainly he is responsible of having pushed me to try to improve too many previous drafts. I would also like to thank Phyllis Deane and Peter Groenewegen, who examined my Ph.D. thesis; I learnt a great deal from their reports, which were the source of many modifications in the original work. Groenewegen also made many useful comments about the final outline of this book. Niccolò de Vecchi, Augusto Graziani, Giorgio Lunghini, Murray Milgate and Alberto Sdralevich provided useful remarks at different stages of the work. I would also like to remember the patience of my mother, of my wife Franca and my son Paolo.

Finally, I wish to thank the Consiglio Nazionale delle Ricerche, and the Ministry of Education, Rome, whose financial help made it possible to complete this research.

Pavia   GIANNI VAGGI

1 A Reinterpretation of Physiocracy

A INTRODUCTION

1.1 Why re-examine physiocratic economics? The problem of value

Few aspects of the history of economic analysis enjoy such a clear-cut and unquestioned interpretation as physiocracy.[1] The major elements chosen for praise are usually Quesnay's concept of net product, his study of the physical characteristics of capital – the different types of advances – and the presentation of a general description of the economy as a model of reproduction. Most of these features were remarked upon by Marx in the *Theories of Surplus Value* (see Marx, 1963, vol. I, pp. 308–10, and the rest of ch. 6), and in a chapter which he wrote for Engels' *Anti-Dühring* (see Engels, 1878, pp. 268–77). More recently, the physiocrats have been praised for being 'the first to proclaim the doctrine of free-trade' (Marshall, 1890, p. 625), for having anticipated a general equilibrium system (see Schumpeter, 1954, p. 242) and, above all, for the first use in economics of a rough input–output table (see Phillips, 1955, pp. 137–8; Leontief, 1951, p. 9; Maital, 1972, p. 505).

Despite the many notable achievements unanimously ascribed to Quesnay, however, there is at least one flaw. It is widely thought that Quesnay failed in one remarkable and important respect: he was unable to provide an analysis of the exchange value of commodities. The weakest aspects of physiocracy seem to be linked to this fact; the view of the sterility of industry and the absence of the category of entrepreneur's profit. Most historians of economic analysis use the *Tableau Economique* to demonstrate that physiocracy is unavoidably limited to the analysis of the *material* and *physical* aspects of commodity production.[2] Even Professor Meek's famous essay 'The Interpretation of Physiocracy' failed to modify this well-established view.[3] The opinion that this is a gap in the physiocratic theory of value has not been shaken either by the evidence of remarks such as: 'As the market value is, so is the revenue' (*Extrait des Economies Royales de M. de Sully*, Kuczynski and Meek, 1972, p. 9), or by the fact that one of the physiocrats' major contentions was the *bon prix* for the products of land.

In this book I put forward a different interpretation of physiocratic economics, starting from an analysis of what Quesnay and his disciples wrote about the theory of value and of prices. This approach will lead to a reconsideration of all their writings. Indeed, setting the problem of value inside the analytical structure of Quesnay's economics will throw new light on some aspects of his thought which have not yet been duly considered. It will emerge that some traditional views and opinions about physiocracy must be revised, and a new appreciation of its impact on political economy will be offered.

This interpretation of physiocracy is founded on three main propositions. First, it will be shown that the physiocrats put forward a detailed analysis of the laws of market exchange, from which they derived many interesting notions of price. All these concepts are linked, by means of precise logical relationships, in a single general scheme.

Secondly, these price categories play an essential role in the physiocratic theories of production and distribution of wealth, which also take on a new significance; in particular, it appears that wealth and revenue are considered by the physiocrats to be *value* categories as well as purely material magnitudes. The problem of the determination of the exchange value of commodities is an essential and important element of physiocratic economics. It is much more complex than is usually believed, leaving the way open for a reinterpretation of physiocracy. This will explain the existence of important ambiguities and contradictions in the way in which Quesnay and his disciples examine and justify their theories of the production and distribution of surplus. However, there will be no attempt to amend these 'mistakes'; many authors have already done this and have provided coherent mathematical formulations of the 'logical nucleus' of Quesnay's economics.[4] In this book I adopt a rather different approach: I try to explain the historical as well as the analytical reasons that led Quesnay to formulate a theory which presents some contradictions and inconsistencies. In fact, these shortcomings arise in particularly difficult and important aspects of physiocratic theory,[5] so even Quesnay's faults and contradictions provide an opportunity to present a more complete picture of physiocracy. In particular, a study of the limitations and flaws of Quesnay's analysis shows that he posed all the relevant questions, even though he failed to give the appropriate answers, concerning the causes of wealth and revenue in a market exchange economy; thus he set the stage for the English classical economists.

This last point brings me to the third and major aim of this re-examination of physiocracy, for my purpose is not limited to a revision of traditional interpretations. I aim to reconsider the role of physiocracy in the history of economic thought in the eighteenth century, a period which saw a growing interest in economic facts and analysis, leading to the formation and development of economics as a science. The emergence of aspects of physiocratic thought which have so far been rather neglected will lead to a reassessment of its contribution to the making of political economy, and throw further light on the historical and analytical features of the development of economic ideas from Sir William Petty to Adam Smith. In particular, Quesnay's contribution to value theory will be examined in the light of the Smithian dichotomy between natural and market prices. On the one hand, we shall investigate all the nuances of the physiocrats' break with the doctrine of mercantilism and of their predecessors, Petty and Cantillon in particular. On the other hand, we shall examine the various aspects which characterise Quesnay's anticipation of Smith, and which testify to the different stages in the evolution of economic ideas preceding the birth of classical economics.

Therefore, leaving aside any claim to completeness, an analysis of physiocracy is a useful starting point from which to re-examine the characteristics of the method, approach and discourse which go under the name of classical political economy. The existence of certain well-known common features in the theories of the classical economists is reaffirmed: the idea of net product and of reproduction, the existence of classes which have different functions in the production and distribution of wealth, the general interdependence of production and circulation of the social output. But it will also emerge that in physiocracy relative prices were already being used for the distribution of surplus. Furthermore, Quesnay's writings emphasise the internally dynamic character of political economy, a fact which emerges from his choice of the question of the *development* of France as the major object of his study; later, the main problems to be analysed were to be *growth* for Smith and *transition* for Marx, Quesnay and other classical economists are mainly interested in explaining the changes, modifications and evolution of economic systems.

These are the main aims of my reinterpretation of physiocracy, and they lead to major modifications and amendments of the traditional views of some aspects of physiocratic thought. In addition, there are four more specific issues which must be mentioned at the outset, since a new view is provided of their role and significance in physiocratic thought. First, it will be shown that Quesnay followed a particular method in his analysis of economic phenomena. In each piece of writing he examined a *single* well-defined topic. From this it follows that the *Tableau Economique* cannot be regarded as an exhaustive synthesis of the whole of physiocratic economics. It must be supplemented by all Quesnay's other economic writings, in particular by the articles he wrote for the *Encyclopédie*, from which the *Tableau* was constructed, and by the later works which explained and defended it.

Secondly, the *prix fondamental* appears as the most important concept of price among those used by Quesnay. This price is not simply equal to the physical cost of production of commodities, as is normally believed; it also includes a net element, rent, in the value of commodities. This fact has important consequences. It shows that the notion of *prix fondamental* links Quesnay's analysis of the process of formation of prices to his view of the economy as a system of reproduction. Moreover, this concept of price constitutes an important analytical stage in the transition from the early seventeenth-century theories of prices towards Smith's analysis of price determination in the *Wealth of Nations*.

A third matter which also appears in a novel light is the physiocratic argument in favour of free trade. This was not due either to a preconception in favour of international competition, or to their belief in the unlimited beneficial effects of free trade. Quesnay and his disciples simply wished to sustain the effective demand for French foodstuffs. They considered the possibility of exporting the products of agriculture to be one of the main features of their analysis of the process of development of the French economy. They believed that exportation would raise the prices of primary commodities in the domestic markets.

Fourthly, it will be shown that, contrary to widespread belief, Quesnay considered the profits of farmers as part of the net product of the country. These profits play an *essential* role in the process of economic growth, because they are regarded by the physiocrats as being the typical basis for the accumulation of capital in agriculture. The physiocrats believed that only by means of this process of accumulation could France become prosperous and wealthy.

1.2 The tradition

Since Smith described the physiocratic system as the 'nearest approximation to truth' (Smith, 1776, vol. II, p. 199), the importance of Quesnay's place in the history of ecomomics has been widely recognised. Quesnay's contributions have been associated with many specific issues, from the single tax on rent to *laissez-faire*, from the fight against mercantilism to the study of the general conditions of equilibrium of an economic system.[6] Recent discussion, following the publication of Sraffa's (1960) *Production of Commodities by Means of Commodities*, has underlined the existence of two major approaches to economics: marginalism and the theories of surplus.[7] This discussion has also led to a reinterpretation of Quesnay's work; from being simply an 'early writer', he has become the economist who first provided the analytical structure of classical political economy.[8]

This reconsideration of physiocracy has brought to light two new reasons for praising Quesnay's contribution to economic thought. He is often regarded as one of the first authors to try to put forward a *general systematic analysis* of social and economic events,[9] but his reputation rests, in particular, on the specific nature of the economic laws by which he related the systematic laws of circulation, distribution and expenditure of wealth to those of its production. Not only are all economic phenomena related to one another, but they are dependent above all upon the conditions of production of commodities.[10]

A second major reason for Quesnay's important position in the history of economic thought concerns the particular way in which he analysed the process of production. In physiocracy the view that the national economy is characterised by a process of reproduction, in which commodities are produced by means of labour and of other commodities, comes to the fore for the first time. In this theory an investigation of the material characteristics of the goods which constitute the inputs and output is essential in order to guarantee the technical and social process of reproduction of the economy.[11] Thus the physiocrats put forward a remarkable analysis of the conditions of production which bring about an output of agriculture higher than the capital employed; this study won them Marx's praise (see Marx, 1970, p. 554 n. 1).

From their view of the process of production the physiocrats derive the famous concept of *produit net*; that is to say, the difference between the output of agriculture and its inputs. This notion is the central point around which Quesnay organises his discussion of all economic matters, and it has always been regarded as one of his most important analytical achievements.[12] However, Quesnay is generally criticised for having examined only the physical aspects of the process of production and circulation of commodities.[13] In particular, his notions of wealth and surplus are simply of different quantities of agricultural products, and not value categories (see, for instance, Napoleoni, 1975, p. 12).

For this reason, few scholars have studied the problem of value in physiocracy. Most of them espouse, either explicitly or implicitly, one of the following three opinions. One group maintains that Quesnay's economics does not need a theory of prices at all, because all the relevant magnitudes which appear in the *Tableau* are physical quantities of agricultural products. According to this view, which we could label the 'all corn' interpretation of physiocracy, in agriculture output and input are homogeneous commodities. Therefore some commentators maintain that Quesnay could determine the size of the surplus directly in physical terms, instead of expressing all the magnitudes in *livres* (see Garegnani, 1960, pp. 5–6; Roll, 1938, p. 134). It is supposed that the output of the primary sector includes the same types of commodities as have been used as means of production during the year. There is a net product because it is assumed that for each commodity the quantity used as means of production must not be higher than the quantity produced, and for at least one commodity it must be smaller. One can easily determine the revenue by subtracting from the gross output the physical quantities of commodities which have been used up. In this situation prices are either completely irrelevant, or at any rate of no specific interest for the measurement of revenue. The net product is just a quantity of 'corn', a conventional term to indicate the composite commodity which constitutes the output of agriculture. Both from the point of view of positive investigation and from that of policy recommendations there is no need for a notion of price, either as a price level or as a relative price; value concepts do not play any analytical role in Quesnay's surplus theory. Manufacture cannot influence the size of the net product, which is entirely determined inside agriculture.[14]

Other authors believe that the output of the primary sector and its means of production are heterogeneous commodities. This view gained considerable support after the publication in 1955 of Phillips' article on the *Tableau Economique*. Phillips presents the *Tableau*

Economique as a sort of closed input–output table.[15] From his description of the *Analyse de la formule arithmétique du Tableau Economique* (see Meek, 1962, pp. 150ff.) as a Leontief model it is clear that the products of industry appear among the inputs of the primary sector; in agriculture, as in manufacture, there is no homogeneity between inputs and output. Moreover, the country's surplus is made up of one unit of 'corn' and one unit of manufactured goods; therefore, according to this view, its magnitude can only emerge in value terms, as the difference between the values of the gross annual product of agriculture and of its means of production. Therefore relative prices are required in order to determine the size of the national surplus. However, according to this second view, Quesnay bypassed the problem of the physical difference between the gross output of agriculture and its means of production, by adopting a *given system* of relative prices (see Ridolfi, 1973, pp. xiv–xvi, xxviii–xxxi). The supporters of this second approach believe that, for Quesnay, prices are determined by international competition and domestic prices must fall into line with the average prices of the international markets, and that this is the reason why Quesnay regards prices as fixed and constant (see Hishiyama, 1960, pp. 35–6). All the magnitudes of the *Tableau* are expressed in terms of value, but if prices are constant they are nothing but mere 'volume indexes. And it is as 'volume indexes' that one must interpret the numbers which appear in the *tableau*' (Ridolfi 1973, p. xxx).

Therefore, according to the 'fixed prices' interpretation, as with the 'all corn' interpretation, it is possible to ignore the question of price determination. Whether one reasons in terms of value magnitudes or considers purely material quantities, changes nothing in the analytical structure and results of physiocratic theory as far as production, distribution and expenditure of surplus are concerned.[16]

The followers of the third interpretation of the problem of prices in physiocracy share with the supporters of the 'fixed prices' approach the view that industry produces part of the means of production of agriculture. But for them the problem is not resolved by finding a standard of measurement which can allow the transformation of manufactures into corn and *vice versa*. Prices cannot be taken as constant, because the value magnitudes which appear in the *Tableau* do not represent mere accounting relationships. In fact, the milliards of *livres* used by Quesnay in the *Tableau* are thought 'to represent a conventional and handy expression of *physical quantities*' (Cartelier, 1976, p. 63, italics in the original).

According to these commentators, the heterogeneity of inputs and output, in both sectors, explains why Quesnay *must* adopt relative prices and build up a theory of price determination (see Salvati, 1980, pp. 38–40).[17] With given techniques of production, the relative price of iron and corn is determined by the following system of equations:[18]

$$\begin{cases} C_c p_c + I_c p_i + S = C p_c \\ C_i p_c + I_i p_i \qquad = I p_i \end{cases} \tag{1}$$

With $p_c = 1$, the exchange ratio of iron to corn is: $p_i = C_i/(I - I_i)$, and the value of the net product is:

$$S = \frac{(C - C_c)(I - I_i) - I_c C_i}{I - I_i}$$

The system with S and p_i as unknowns describes the physiocratic price theory, which has all the relevant features of the *classical system of prices* (see Cartelier, 1976, p. 57). In such a system relative prices can be determined on two conditions: first, the method of production of each commodity must be given; secondly, some particular rule must be fixed for the distribution of the net product. In physiocracy this rule says that all the surplus must be ascribed to the corn-producing sector. The *Tableau* is thus considered as an anticipation of the price theories of Ricardo and Marx, and more recently of Sraffa; this last approach seems to be based mainly on the fact that the outputs and inputs of the two sectors are heterogeneous commodities.[19] This argument is regarded as not only necessary but also *sufficient* to show that Quesnay actually had a theory of price determination.

I will show that all these interpretations provide incorrect descriptions of the physiocratic theory of price determination. In particular, they are unable to portray correctly the definitions of prices put forward by Quesnay and their role in physiocratic economics (see Chapter 2, particularly 2.7 and 2.8).

1.3 The role of value

By placing Quesnay's analysis of value in the context of his work as a whole, we see that it is intimately linked to many other features of physiocracy. The physiocrats' theory of prices clarifies and supports most of their contentions and policy proposals; it is one of the pillars of physiocratic economic thought. This opinion will be substantiated by our examination of particular aspects of Quesnay's analysis of value and prices, and by studying the way in which he relates these phenomena to those of production and distribution of wealth and surplus.

(a) Prices and markets

In physiocracy, markets and prices play an important role in the determination of the causes of the development and prosperity of nations, Quesnay introduces the notion of 'price in the sale at first-hand'; these sales refer to the exchanges of commodities which take place between their producers and the merchants. According to the physiocrats, the wealth of a country must be measured by evaluating the quantities of its agricultural products at their 'first-hand prices'. It will become clear that this notion of price plays an essential role in establishing the view that trade is a sterile activity. In fact, none of the exchanges which take place after the first sale can increase the wealth of a nation.

These issues pose the problem of the nature and role of the notions of price and of the analysis of markets in Quesnay's economic theory. It will be shown that he clearly saw the role of relative prices in the determination of the value of the net product. Furthermore, he did not consider prices as mere parameters, but devoted much effort to the examination of market forces and to the analysis of their influence on both monetary and relative exchange values. It emerges that all three current views about the role of prices in physiocracy (see 1.2 above) provide inadequate and incomplete descriptions of Quesnay's price theory.

The various concepts of price put forward by Quesnay were designed to give a complete and consistent description of all the relevant stages of production, exchange and consumption of commodities. We shall see that the physiocrats do not investigate the processes of production and circulation of commodities only in physical terms; for them commodity production is a phenomenon which takes place according to the rules of a market exchange economy. Quesnay distinguishes between the price received by the producer – the current price, and the price paid by the consumer – the retail price. With these notions of price, and with the help of numerical examples, he explains the ruinous consequences of merchants' activities on the whole economy. Consumer, farmers and landowners would benefit from the abolition of the exclusive privileges of traders and foreign trade.

In his analysis of markets Quesnay introduces new notions, but he also borrows from mercantilist literature and from Cantillon categories which, in the middle of the eighteenth century, were accepted as part of the 'state of knowledge' in economics. It is with the category of *fundamental price*, however, that Quesnay clearly abandons earlier views of the exchange value of commodities, which mostly incorporated the idea that price depended on the physical costs of production (see Chapter 3, 3.8). The fundamental price has traditionally been identified with the technical cost of production of commodities, that is to say with the sum of the value of subsistence wages, raw materials and the wearing out of fixed capital (see Chapter 3). I will show that, according to the physiocrats, the *prix fondamental* of the products of land also includes an element, rent, which is part of the net product of the country. Thus in the physiocratic theory of reproduction rent is an income which must be accounted for in the surplus from the point of view of the system as a whole, but it is also an item of expense for agricultural entrepreneurs. Quesnay's fundamental price is the key analytical category which relates market phenomena to the process of reproduction of the economy. On the one hand, this concept is a benchmark for the market prices of commodities; on the other, the fundamental price has a precise relationship with the technical and social aspects of the process of production of commodities. Hence this notion is an important element in the analytical bridge between pre-physiocratic price theories and Smith's analysis of the natural price of commodities.

(b) The theory of value and the production and distribution of wealth

Besides being an interesting set of concepts in themselves, price categories are not isolated elements of physiocratic economics; Chapters 4 and 5 will show that these notions are employed by Quesnay in his analysis of the origin and distribution of surplus and wealth. The examination of price categories leads to a new interpretation of the physiocratic doctrine of the exclusive productivity of agriculture. Traditional opinions which explain this aspect of physiocracy by appealing to the idea of the 'gift of nature' do not bring out the fact that Quesnay defended his theory of the origin of surplus directly in value terms. He tried to show that market competition allows the existence of a value surplus, over costs, in the prices of primary commodities, while the market value of the products of industry is always equal to the expenses incurred in their production. Hence the net product of agriculture also depends on the existence of a permanently high effective demand for the products of land. The need to secure such a high demand explains Quesnay's efforts to persuade aristocrats to spend their revenue purchasing French foodstuffs. Similarly, the physiocrats' argument in favour of the free export of corn does not spring from a belief in the unlimited benefits of free trade; it is rather an attempt to secure a large foreign demand for the primary commodities of France.

Moreover, it becomes clear that Quesnay does not consider *all* the activities directly linked to the exploitation of soil to be productive; only those occupations that employ more advanced techniques of production, requiring large investments in fixed capital are productive. He considered that labour employed in the primary sector was always productive, provided it was assisted by the appropriate amount of capital.

Price categories are even more important if we are to form an accurate picture of the physiocrats' analysis of the distribution of surplus. Despite the unanimous belief of other writers, I will show that the physiocrats considered farmers' profits to be a share of the nation's surplus. Quesnay has a precise notion of profit upon alienation, which is given by the difference between the *bon prix* and the fundamental price of agricultural products. Thus the concept of *bon prix* is also clearly defined. From this we can see how the physiocrats envisaged the process of economic development that would lead France to prosperity. This process is based on the accumulation of capital in agriculture via the *necessary* step of the reinvestment of farmers' profits. I will also show that Professor Meek's view that in physiocracy profits are only a *temporary* share of the net product, is based on an unsatisfactory interpretation of the reasons that led Quesnay either to underestimate or to ignore the existence of farmers' profits in some of his writings. This was due mainly to the physiocrats' political preoccupation with the need not to displease the dominant classes.

(c) The physiocrats' contribution to political economy

An examination of the nature and analytical role of market and prices in physiocracy shows that Quesnay and his disciples singled out some fundamental elements of the developing capitalist mode of production; for instance, the importance of large investments in securing the productivity of agriculture and the link between profits and accumulation of capital. Although Quesnay detected and analysed many important aspects of the capitalist mode of production, he did not, and certainly could not, see all its features. The physiocrats' writings are still influenced by features of feudal society; and the coexistence of old and new strands of thought in their interpretation of the working of economic systems brings to light the existence of 'inconsistencies' and 'flaws' in physiocracy itself. Quesnay wants a free trading system to *coexist* with the surplus in a single sector of the economy; a rise in the prices of foodstuffs *should* benefit not only the farmers but also the workers and the poor people who consumed them. Moreover, the physiocrats claimed to demonstrate that no antagonism would exist between farmers, who had to increase the fixed capital and improve the methods of cultivation, and landlords, who by law and custom received the net product. In order to solve these contradictions they invoked the appropriate *ad hoc* workings of market competition. These particular market mechanisms were intended to guarantee the coexistence of all the major features of the physiocratic process of growth with a rise in the standard of living for all social groups.

The use of the notion of competition did not help Quesnay and his disciples to reconcile the contrasting elements of their theories into a simple analytical scheme. But the 'errors' of an author can reveal important features of his thought. The study of the historical and analytical reasons for the existence of these flaws in physiocratic economics can make an important contribution to our understanding of its methodology. The ambiguities in Quesnay's arguments derive mainly from the fact that he refused to allow his method of investigation, which was based on abstraction and simplification, to lead him too far from contemporary history. For Quesnay the particular situation in France represented the source of the problem and a test for any solution. This peculiar 'taste for history' is not limited to physiocracy; it is typical of the whole of classical political economy.

Historical conditions alter rapidly, and this was particularly true in Quesnay's time. The concepts and arguments of physiocracy reflect the contradictions of a period of fundamental change. Quesnay fails to provide a mathematically coherent model of the contrasting forces of an epoch of transition: the old political order represented by the power of the aristocracy, and the new economic phenomena typical of capitalist production. But the existence of contradictions in physiocratic thought does not mean that it is impossible to appreciate its analytical structure, its link with the past and its value for the future.

The physiocratic contribution to classical economics is not limited to methodology; from this reinterpretation it emerges that Quesnay provided the analytical structure that characterises political economy. Certainly he lacked some categories – for instance, the notion of a rate of profit as a percentage on the capital invested – but the ground-plan in which all these concepts will later be inserted is already here. In fact physiocracy contains contradictions and 'errors' because, although it singled out the most important issues and questions for the analysis of a capitalist economy, it lacked some of the concepts necessary to provide satisfactory answers. However, the analytical structure of Quesnay's economics already *logically requires* the use of some of the most important analytical categories developed by his famous successors.

First, in order to support their view of the accumulation of capital, the physiocrats would need the notion of a normal rate of profit on the capital invested, a concept introduced by Turgot (see Meek, 1973, p. 22; Groenewegen, 1971, pp. 333–4). Secondly, Quesnay could not fully appreciate the importance of the division of labour in the process of production for the distinction-between productive and sterile activities, and for the analysis of increases in productivity. This was brought out later by Smith. Thirdly, we know now that Ricardo developed an appropriate explanation of the distribution of surplus between the landlords and the capitalist entrepreneurs. Thus he dealt with one of Quesnay's major worries, which was also one of the weakest aspects of his theory. Finally, it is true that there are many weaknesses in Quesnay's analysis of the determination of the exchange value of commodities, and of its relationship with the processes of production and circulation of wealth. Nevertheless, his 'faults', and inconsistencies constitute part of the foundations on which Marx grounded his economic analysis. Like Quesnay, Marx intended to provide a theory of the origin of surplus-value based on capitalist production, and to relate this theory to the determination of the prices of production of commodities.

Thus we can see that, paradoxically, Quesnay's contradictions and ambiguities underline his merits as a founder of the theories of surplus. His 'errors' revealed to his successors all the most important aspects of classical political economy.

1.4 Outline of the work

Before going on to examine the physiocrats' analysis of market and prices, I will attempt to clear up some misunderstandings which seem to characterise the current interpretations of physiocracy. The major problems concern Quesnay's methodology and the role of the *Tableau Economique*, which is often identified with his entire economic work.[20] Since Quesnay does not openly discuss the issue of price formation in the *Tableau*, most interpreters have come to the conclusion that this question and that of the analysis of market mechanisms have no role in physiocracy.

However, a careful analysis of Quesnay's methodology shows that the *Tableau* cannot be regarded as a faithful and complete *synthesis* of the whole of physiocratic thought. Quesnay did not write a single complete treatise on economic subjects (as many other authors did); instead he wrote several articles, each dealing with a specific topic. The particular answers he gives to these specific economic questions are the elements of a larger, more complex system of thought. In order to provide a satisfactory interpretation of physiocratic thought, all the different aspects of Quesnay's economics must be analysed *together* and confronted with the leading themes and contentions of physiocracy. It will become clear that the main purpose of the *Tableau* is to analyse a specific aspect of the economy: the effects on gross and net products of different policy measures, and in particular of changes in the circulation and employment of the social output. In order to carry out this examination, Quesnay has also to investigate some aspects of the problems of production, distribution and disposal of national output. Thus, in the *Tableau* he studies the reciprocal effects of variations in some economic magnitudes in the process of circulation of commodities between classes, and does not examine other important aspects of physiocratic economics.[21]

In Chapter 2 I shall provide textual evidence to support the view that Quesnay and his disciples regarded wealth and revenue as *value magnitudes* as well as physical quantities of agricultural products.[22] This derives from the heterogeneity of the inputs and the output of agriculture, and from Quesnay's description of the role of relative prices.

Chapters 3–5 present the major contentions of my interpretation of physiocratic economics. Chapter 3 describes the various price concepts that Quesnay uses and his analysis of the laws of markets. He distinguishes between the price which is received by the producer, the current price, and that which is paid by the consumer, the retail price. Quesnay uses these notions of price to explain the damaging effects of the activities of professional traders on the welfare of both consumers and producers. These two classes (and the landowners too) would greatly benefit from the reduction in the power of the merchants that would result from introducing free competition in domestic and international trade. I shall also argue that the most important of Quesnay's notions of price is that of the *prix fondamental*. Against the traditional view, I shall maintain that, in the case of primary products, this concept is not equal to the technical cost of cultivation, but also includes an item, rent, which is part of the net product of the economy.

In Chapter 4 I shall examine the way in which Quesnay used his theory of value in the analysis of the production of surplus. It emerges that he did not consider the net product simply as a 'gift of nature'. In fact Quesnay defends his view of the exclusive productivity of agriculture and of the sterility of manufacture in value terms. Many interesting price concepts are employed to support this doctrine. Moreover, his distinction between productive and unproductive activities makes original use of several pieces of economic theory, for example, his notion of effective demand, his analysis of free trade and his discussion of the productivity of capitalist agriculture.

Quesnay also uses price theory to investigate the distribution of surplus and the accumulation of capital in the primary sector. In Chapter 5 I shall show that for the physiocrats the farmers' profits are the essential element that gives rise to economic development by securing the reinvestment of part of the annual surplus. Contrary to general belief, for Quesnay these profits constitute an important systematic share of the net product, which is not limited to the rent of the proprietors and the revenue of the crown.

Finally, in Chapter 6 I shall draw together my central conclusions on the content and significance of Quesnay's analysis and his contribution to the development of the theories of surplus. My study of the nature and analytical role of market and prices in physiocratric thought shows that Quesnay and his disciples singled out some fundamental aspects of classical political economy. However, some of their contentions and results seem either unsatisfactorily supported or even mutually contradictory. The major flaws appear in the doctrine of the existence of surplus in a single sector of the economy – agriculture; in the particular notion of profit used by the physiocrats; and in the role they assign to market competition both in domestic and in international trade.

Quesnay gave the wrong answers to the right questions. Some of the inconsistencies in his economic theory uncovered very important problems for the development of economics as a science. In particular, he raised some fundamental issues for the definition of the analytical structure of classical political economy. Turgot, Smith, Ricardo and Marx provided better solutions to many of the problems raised by Quesnay, but he certainly paved the way for them.

B   QUESNAY'S METHODOLOGY AND THE *TABLEAU ECONOMIQUE*

1.5 The object of physiocratic analysis: the prosperity of France

My examination of Quesnay's approach to economics may be divided conveniently into three areas: the problem he wanted to study, the method of analysis he adopted and the solutions he suggested. Quesnay's principal aim was to discover ways in which the wealth of a country could be increased. He chose this field of investigation because of economic and social conditions in France at the time (see Landry, 1958, pp. 11, 39–47; Eltis, 1975b, p. 327), which he regarded as not only characterised by a delayed process of development, but also on the verge of imminent ruin. The physiocrats considered France to be an underdeveloped country. It suffered from definite features of backwardness and immiseration (see Meek, 1968, p. 46). There was an endemic shortage of foodstuffs and famines were a recurring phenomenon (see *Fermiers*, Groenewegen, 1983, p. 14). Quesnay himself remarked that the population of France had fallen from 24 million to 16 million between 1650 and 1750 (see *Grains*, Meek, 1962, p. 83). The nobles and the clergy also suffered from serious financial problems; the revenues from their landed estates decreased sharply during the same period, as Mirabeau laments in his

Mémoire sur les états provinciaux (see Mirabeau, 1758, pp. 50–1).[23]

Financial conditions in France had been under severe strain for several decades. In the face of continually rising expenditure on the military as well as on supporting the Court at Versailles, public receipts were permanently inadequate.[24] The fiscal system, based on the *fermiers généraux*, was grossly inefficient; huge expenses were incurred in raising a very inadequate revenue.[25] By the middle of the eighteenth century the problem of French finances was worse than it had ever been.[26] In this environment, it comes as no surprise to find that Quesnay's objects of analysis are the mechanisms which influence the wealth of the country. He tries to provide a logical apparatus from which to derive useful recommendations for the economic policy of the government, 'so that the sovereign authority, always guided by what is self-evident, should institute the best laws and cause them to be scrupulously observed, in order to provide for the security of all and to attain to the greatest degree of prosperity possible for the society' (*Maximes générales du gouvernement économique d'un royaume agricole*, Meek 1962, p. 231).

For Quesnay, as for Smith, the level of national income per capita is the best indicator of the economic prosperity of a country (see Fox-Genovese, 1976, pp. 97–8; Meek, 1968, p. 45). Thus only an analysis of the nature and origin of revenue and wealth can point the way towards the general welfare of the country. An explanation of the causes of the value of the net product was thus the central theoretical subject of the physiocrats, and measures to ensure its increase their main practical concern.[27]

1.6 The method: abstraction and simplification

The backwardness of the French economy raised several more specific questions – the main economic issues of the time. Which sector of the economy should be helped? Should foreign trade be controlled? What type of taxation should be implemented? Quesnay was convinced that economic behaviour and activities could not be studied or explained other than on the basis of an abstract general analysis of the working of the economy.[28] Economic events are not mere accidents; there are general laws which link together and regulate the actions of men: 'in nature everything is intertwined, everything runs through circular courses which are interlaced with one another' (*Sur les travaux des artisans*, Meek 1962, p. 204).

But Quesnay did not simply believe that everything depended on everything else: on the contrary, he thought that economic facts should be understood and explained on the basis of specific relationships of cause and effect connecting the actions of individuals. Economic events are the result of the working of objective laws, which describe the systematic order of society (see Neill, 1948, p. 172). To the physiocrats this is the *natural order* of things, and the regularities that it demonstrates are *natural laws*, which represent a normative guide for men and governments (see *Despotisme de la Chine*, I.N.E.D., 1958, vol. II, p. 934; *Analyse*, Meek, 1962, p. 154). Quesnay's efforts were thus directed into putting forward a general causal model of the economy which included a definition of wealth and shed light on the causes of its increase according to natural laws. In fact, the precise interrelationships of the economic magnitudes in the natural order describe the only way in which nations and people can become powerful and prosperous; that is to say, by adapting their actions and their economic policy to these very laws (see Johnson, 1937, pp. 221–2).

The natural order does not necessarily hold its way, however; natural laws are normative rules, but they can be disobeyed by men and by the rulers of nations (see Zagari, 1972, pp. 6–7, 20–5).[29] People can disrupt the working of the natural order, and the physiocrats saw this as the main cause of poverty in a country. Natural laws are at work in society, but they are not powerful enough to be effective under any circumstances (see Fox-Genovese, 1976, pp. 10, 124, 252).[30] People in general, and statesmen in particular, 'should be given instruction in the general laws of the natural order which constitute the form of government which is self-evidently the most perfect' (*Maximes générales*, Meek, 1962, p. 231).

At the beginning of the dialogue *Sur les travaux des artisans*, Quesnay describes the method that must be followed in order to build up a general model of the natural order of society. His reasoning is so clear that it is worth quoting him at length. Referring to natural events, he says:

> the fact that these different movements are necessarily interconnected means that things can be understood, differentiated, and examined only through the medium of abstract ideas . . . each relation can be differentiated only through the causes and effects which characterize it; the more we set out to arrive at precise distinctions, the more we are reduced simply to a few causes and a few effects by means of which, without losing sight of the concate-

nation as a whole, we get a clear picture of the principal parts through their different functions in the general order of nature. Here, where we are confining ourselves to the physical order which is the most advantageous for men combined together in society, and where we are making an overall examination of the employments of men which conduce to public welfare, we differentiate them on the basis of their most noticeable and distinct causes and effects, in order to subsume them under primary general classes. It is only through the medium of such abstractions that we can examine and appraise the mutual relations between these different classes of men and work in the social order, and give them the designations which conform most closely to their functions, in order to express ourselves in exact terms in the detailed working-out of economic science (Meek, 1962, p. 204).

Therefore, in order to study the system of natural laws, one must use a method of simplification and abstraction. For Quesnay the scientific method is a process that, at least in the first instance, does not try to explain *all* aspects of the economy at the same time. His method of analysing only one aspect at a time certainly implies that other characteristics of economic reality are probably neglected, although they can affect some of the variables considered in the problem under investigation. But Quesnay believed that this process of abstraction and simplification was the only method by which scholars could unveil, one by one, all the relationships of cause and effect among the variables, in order to provide a general description of the working of the natural order (see Meek, 1962, p. 370).

Sur les travaux des artisans also sheds light on another typical feature of Quesnay's method: he is always concerned not to lead his work too far from reality, by means of too many simplifications. In order better to appreciate the content of his writings, one must keep in mind this characteristic of his literary style. In fact he explains that 'the more we set out to arrive at precise distinctions, the more we are reduced simply to a few causes and a few effects'. However, he immediately adds that this purpose must be achieved 'without losing sight of the concatenation as a whole'. He is not satisfied with understanding single aspects of the economic order of society, which can be detected by isolating them from the remaining features of the economy, but always aims at an overall picture of the functions of each part within the system as a whole. This means that he sometimes does not adhere strictly to his method of abstraction and simplification. The boundaries of the subject under examination are always being penetrated by other aspects of the economy – aspects which, according to his methodological rule, should be abstracted from, at least in the first instance. Often Quesnay seems so afraid that his analysis will depart too far from economic reality that he crowds the stage with many different problems at the same time.

Quesnay's methodology is an original mixture of rationalism and empiricism,[31] and he was certainly influenced by authors like Locke[32] and Descartes.[33] The physiocrats implicitly adopted what has been called the 'economic interpretation of history' (see Weulersse, 1910a, vol. II, p. 132). According to this view, our understanding of society must be based on the fundamental needs of human beings and their attempts to satisfy them (see Einaudi, 1958, pp. ix–xi). Societies are formed according to the specific ways in which people succeed in solving the problem of subsistence (see Meek, 1962, p. 376).[34] Political and juridical institutions reflect the economic relationships between individuals, the latter being differentiated according to their role in the process of production, distribution, expenditure and consumption of wealth (see Fox-Genovese, 1976, p. 47; Weulersse, 1910a, vol. II, pp. 37–40, 106–8).

Therefore 'the needs and the desires' of people are 'the principle and the effect of society' (Mirabeau, 1764, vol. II, p. 16), which is thus founded on the mutual economic interests of men.[35] Quesnay made a fundamental contribution by putting the analysis of social and economic activities on a materialistic basis. This taste for investigating the material aspects of life made him an extremely careful observer. And if deism and materialism coexisted in Quesnay's mind, certainly in 1760 it was materialism, not deism that constituted the novelty' (Weulersse, 1910a, vol. II, p. 117).[36]

1.7 The answer: exclusive productivity of agriculture

Quesnay's answer to the problem of the prosperity of France is simple and derives from his views on the origin of wealth and revenue: the theory of the exclusive productivity of agriculture (see Weulersse, 1910a, vol. I, pp. 243–4). Having adopted the view that only the primary sector can yield wealth and revenue, Quesnay and his disciples identify the major cause of the misery and backwardness of France as the decline of its agriculture: from the middle of the seventeenth century the cultivation of the soil had become less and less profitable (see Beer, 1939, p. 42). From this general principle physiocracy derived well defined recommendations concerning contemporary economic issues and offered specific advice. The physiocrats' economic policy derived from their political economy. 'Natural laws' showed that only the primary sector could yield a surplus. Administrators must implement measures to raise its productivity. The welfare of individuals would follow; the financial problems of the country would be solved; wealth and prosperity would be assured for the whole nation.

A first group of recommendations was addressed to the public administrators. These concerned the two major economic issues of the time: the fiscal system and the corn trade. The *impôt unique* was intended to free farmers from several types of taxes which ultimately prevented any planning of production and investment.[37] The physiocrats also wanted to change the fiscal system which was based on the *fermiers généraux*, a kind of tax collector (see Mirabeau, 1760c, vol. I, pp. 102–4).[38] A fiscal reform along physiocratic lines would, it was claimed, raise both the fiscal revenue of the nation and farmers' incomes. On the other hand, the physiocrats thought that trade was being hampered by *droits* and import quotas (see Depitre, 1910b, pp. xv–xviii), which imposed a limit on the sales of French farmers. Free foreign trade should be designed to establish the most favourable market conditions for French primary goods (see Chapter 4, 4.6).

A second group of recommendations was addressed to landlords and all the other classes that received part of the annual net product of the country. They must avoid buying manufactured goods, mainly from foreign merchants, and shift their pattern of expenditure in favour of the products of French agriculture.

A third piece of advice was directed primarily at agricultural producers. First, the amount of cultivated land must be increased and farmers must use their gains to cooperate with the state in extending cultivation by means of drainage schemes (*défrichements*) (see Sée, 1967, pp. 33–6). Secondly, agricultural entrepreneurs must raise the capital invested in tools and instruments, livestock and houses, and all the items which form part of the equipment required for the efficient cultivation of land (see below, Chapter 2, 2.6). Thirdly, the increase in such capital should be accompanied by modernisation of the methods of cultivation. With few exceptions (in the north of the country), the techniques of production employed in France were extremely old-fashioned and highly inefficient. The *jachère* system was still in use in almost all the provinces. This required that land should be left uncultivated for either one year in every two, or two years in every three; there were cases in which land was cultivated for only one year in every eight, and even for only one year in every twenty (see Sée, 1967, pp. 33–4). A reduction in the number of fallow years and the introduction of a system of crop rotation were thought to be of prime importance.

In France in the middle of the eighteenth century no other group of thinkers on economic subjects showed the same degree of homogeneity and solidarity as *les économistes*; as a group they were labelled a *secte*.[39] Yet there were different opinions on economic matters, and other writers were also influential both in the administration and in literary circles. Vincent de Gournay (1712–59) was the most admired of these; he and his followers shared with the physiocrats the view that France would benefit greatly from freedom in both foreign and domestic trade.[40] Gournay and his school, and not the physiocrats, were the true supporters of *laissez-faire*; they did not limit their advocacy of free trade to the products of the land, but wanted to extend the system to all commodities. Gournay never accepted the idea of the exclusive productivity of agriculture.

The *Abbé* Galiani, ambassador of the King of Naples at the Court of Versailles, was also quite influential in Paris, especially in the late 1760s. He always opposed physiocracy, and founded his critique on an alternative explanation of the fundamental causes of wealth and prosperity of nations. Galiani believed that these were mainly the products of the manufacturing sector, and strongly attacked the physiocrats' doctrine of the exclusive productivity of agriculture (see Chapter 4, 4.2).

Finally, there were the supporters of the idea that the wealth of a nation was determined by the size of its population. They did not constitute an organised group, but their influence was widely diffused among the scholars of the time (see Landry, 1958, pp. 12–13; Weulersse, 1910a, vol. II, p. 268). Mirabeau himself had been a convinced *populationiste* (see Weulersse, 1910a, vol. II, pp. 269, 275), and had become famous with the publication of the first three parts of *L'Ami des hommes* in 1756 (see Weulersse, 1910a, vol. I, p. 53), where he dealt with economic matters in a way fully consistent with *populationiste* views. In a letter to Rousseau in 1767, he claimed to have been converted to physiocracy as the result of a conversation with Quesnay at the end of July 1757 (see Schelle, 1907, pp. 225–35; Hect, 1958, p. 256).

1.8 The literary genre used by Quesnay

The neglect of the problem of the particular literary form used by Quesnay to express his opinions helps to explains some of the confusions in the interpretation of his thought. Economists had quite early become used to treatises, in which the author gave a systematic presentation of all the relevant matters. Steuart's *Inquiry into the Principles of Political Oeconomy* and Smith's *Wealth of Nations* are two examples of this genre, which was used by many other economists. In Quesnay's time the literary form of the tract had already been used by Locke and Petty in the English tradition. In France there were no such outstanding examples, but even there economics already included the contributions of writers who expressed their views by means of long essays.[41] The most influential of these was Cantillon's *Essay sur la nature du commerce en général*, a work originally written in English.[42] Mirabeau was one of the first French authors to present his views by means of long treatises, such as the *Théorie de l'impôt* and the *Philosophie rurale*.

Unlike Mirabeau, Quesnay was not a man of letters, and he did not choose to put forward his views in the form of a treatise. He presented his opinions by means of short pieces, which mainly took the form of articles.[43] The choice of this literary genre was not casual or accidental; Diderot and D'Alembert had asked Quesnay to contribute to the *Encyclopédie*, so that from the outset he discussed economic matters by writing articles on single well-defined subjects. *Fermiers* and *Grains* appeared in 1756 and 1757 respectively, but Quesnay also wrote three more pieces for the *encyclopédistes*: *Hommes, Impôts, and Intéret de l'argent*.[44] This particular way of presenting his ideas characterised Quesnay's entire economic work. After his collaboration on the *Encyclopédie*, he wrote three successive *Tableaux* in the schematic form of a zigzag. In subsequent years he collaborated closely with Mirabeau, and their work was presented in the *Philosophie rurale*. Quesnay then embarked on a second period of intense writing on his own between the end of 1765 and the end of 1767. He published this work in the form of articles in two periodicals controlled by the physiocrats: the *Journal de l'agriculture, du commerce et des finances* and the *Ephémérides du citoyen*.

Quesnay's articles were designed to convince his readers of the correctness of his opinion on a specific subject (see Zangheri, 1966, p. x). There is, however, a major difference between the articles of the late 1750s and those of the 1760s. The earlier writings had to provide an exposition and illustration of the main principles of physiocracy; they were intended to convince the ruling classes and the administrators that physiocratic recommendations were based on sound foundations and would benefit the whole nation. In the second half of the 1760s, however, physiocracy was bitterly attacked, particularly on the question of the exclusive productivity of agriculture, and most of Quesnay's later articles were written to defend and justify his views. In these works his *vis polemica* emerged in all its toughness, particularly where he used another literary genre very much in vogue in those days: the dialogue.

The use of the literary form of article influenced Quesnay's way of writing on economic matters; he concentrated on one problem in each piece and hence handled the most relevant economic questions one at a time. Whether he was explaining his views or defending them, Quesnay's efforts were completely absorbed by the particular issue under discussion. At the same time, he thought that economics should provide a general picture of the working of all the aspects of the natural order; therefore he stated, in each article, the particular hypotheses on which the following investigation was based. These assumptions both defined the limits of the subject under analysis and allowed an easier identification of the connection of the argument of the article with those of other writings.

Quesnay's particular way of presenting his opinions adds further difficulties to our interpretation of his economic thought. A correct interpretation can only result from a joint examination of *all* his economic works, since they are logically connected and complement one another. Only by investigating the nature of these interrelationships can one get a clear picture of the overall content of physiocratic economics. However difficult, this task cannot be ignored without running the risk of misinterpreting Quesnay's economics and overlooking some of its important features. Most commentators have ignored the physiocratic analysis of the laws of markets and of price determination, since these topics do not play a prominent role in some of Quesnay's most famous writings, such as the different *Tableaux* and the *Analyse*. They have therefore been regarded as either irrelevant, or at least as unrelated to the main physiocratic issues.

A final difficulty for the interpretation of Quesnay's works arises from the fact that, although he intended to present his views on one problem in each work, he did not always stick to this rule. In some works the hypotheses are vague and the reasoning becomes less straightforward; Quesnay is quite clear on the analysis of each single point, but he moves easily from one problem to another. Therefore one must try to identify and link together in a logical sequence all the remarks, comments and passages which, although they refer to the same topic, may appear in different works.

1.9 The different *Tableaux*

The *Tableau* so attracted the attention of Quesnay's contemporaries and of historians of economic ideas that the many other physiocratic writings have been neglected. Indeed some interpretations are based on the idea that the whole of physiocratic thought can be grasped through this single work. The identification of Quesnay's economics with the *Tableau* seems to be founded on two parallel arguments: first, that no relevant features of physiocracy are lost by concentrating on this work, secondly, that the *Tableau* is the logical inner nucleus of Quesnay's economics, its 'rational core' (Herlitz, 1961a, p. 17; see also Fox-Genovese, 1976, p. 258).[45]

Quesnay's method of investigation, and the way in which he presented his results and recommendations, clearly contradict the idea that a single work, however important, can be taken to represent the whole of physiocratic economics. There is a fundamental unity among all Quesnay's works. Although different writings deal with different economic questions, when they are carefully examined and considered together, they can all be regarded as chapters of a single 'book' whose subject is the analysis of the production and circulation of wealth and surplus. The crucial position of the *Tableau* in this 'book' is unquestionable, but it is still only one of the elements that go to make up a complete picture of physiocratic economics.

These considerations are also important in establishing the role of price and value categories in Quesnay's economics. The fact that these problems are not discussed in the *Tableau* does not permit a reader to dismiss their importance. Certainly, among Quesnay's works the *Tableau Economique* represents a major effort to give a general description of the working of the economy. But it is also intended to illustrate some more limited aspects of the economic system.

It must be noted that Quesnay used the title *Tableau Economique* for a number of schemes which he used during ten years of economic investigation.[46] These schemes are dissimilar both in the figures adopted and in the form in which the relationships are expressed.

Quesnay uses two basic forms of *tableau*: one is the zigzag, so called because of the characteristic descending lines which repeatedly cross the page (see Kuczynski and Meek, 1972, section 3).[47] The other is the 'arithmetical formula of the *Tableau Economique*', which appeared in 1766 in *Analyse de la formule arithmétique du Tableau économique*, published in the *Journal de l'agriculture* (see Meek, 1962, p. 158). Between these two schemes there are several other *tableaux*, namely those in the *Philosophie rurale*, the best known being the *Précis des résultats de la distribution répresentée dans le Tableau*. This work helps to provide an explanation of Quesnay's transition between the early *tableaux* and the 'formula' (see Gilibert 1977, pp. 31–52).

Notwithstanding the formal differences, there are some evident uniformities between all the *tableaux* which reveal that each is just a different way of expressing the same ideas. In all the *tableaux*, Quesnay analyses the phenomena related to the distribution, expenditure and circulation of surplus and of social product.[48] In a letter to Mirabeau, written at the end of 1758, Quesnay says that in writing the *Tableau* he had 'the purpose of displaying expenditure and products in a way which is easy to grasp' (Meek, 1962, p. 108). In another letter to the same friend, Quesnay makes it clear that the *Tableau* examines the following two aspects of the economy: 'for in the zigzag wealth is regarded in relation to men and men relatively to wealth; and this relationship is one of the main subjects of the *Tableau*. A second subject is the process of the distribution of revenue, which ensures that the revenue is returned together with men's subsistence' (ibid. p. 116). Thus one of the main purposes of the *Tableau Economique* is the analysis of the employment of that part of annual output which must be used to secure the reproduction of the economy on the same scale. This part of the social product must circulate according to the technical characteristics of the process of production.

However, the shares of the net product that accrue to the landlords, to the clergy and to the sovereign, can be freely spent in many different ways. Both the zigzag and the formula examine the effects of alternative ways of employing the annual revenue (see Eltis, 1975a, pp. 181, 190; Herlitz, 1961a, pp. 13–14; Phillips, 1955, p. 138). This investigation must make clear the appropriate pattern of expenditure. Hence the *Tableau* is a scheme that describes the distribution of the surplus between the classes and explains the effects on future production of its circulation through the expenditure of the proprietors and the sovereign.[49] As well as examining the effects on the future wealth of the nation of different ways of employing the surplus, in the *Tableau* Quesnay also studies the relationships between the modes of expenditure of the revenue and its distribution among the classes of society (see Mirabeau, 1760b, p. 194). As a scheme of circulation of wealth, the *Tableau* must demonstrate to the dominant classes in the country the benefits they will obtain from spending most of their revenue on home produced foodstuffs (see *Explication du Tableau Economique*, Kuczynski and Meek, 1972, pp. i–ij). Quesnay wants to convince the ruling classes that certain apparently dangerous measures ultimately increase the revenue of the landlords and of the country thanks to the natural laws which relate these actions to the surplus.

Quesnay saw the *Tableau* as an important guide for the formation of economic policy in France and, in particular, as a scheme for the analysis of the circulation of the social product. The *Tableau* gives a quick view of the way in which, via the process of circulation, different policy measures affect the wealth of the country. This interpretation is supported by the fact that he consistently uses the *Tableau Economique* as a model for his analysis of the effect of the distribution of revenue (see Gilibert, 1977, p. 9). It is an analytical tool which allows an immediate appreciation of the economic consequences of the behaviour of the landlords and the administration (see Fox-Genovese, 1976, p. 218). The *Premier* and *Second problème économique* are typical examples of Quesnay's use of the *Tableau*.

In the first, he analyses the effects of an increase in the price of corn (see Meek, 1962, pp. 168–9). The second discusses the advantages of abandoning all forms of indirect taxation in favour of a single tax on rent (see ibid., pp. 186–8).[50] In both cases Quesnay wants to show how clearly and easily one can appreciate the effects of different economic policies on the wealth of the country by using the *Tableau Economique*.[51] In fact at the beginning of the *Premier problème économique* he states: 'we shall take a very complicated case, which will make clearer the application of the calculation and rules of the *Tableau Economique* and throw light on a number of questions relative to the question which has been put forward' (Meek, 1962, p. 168). Then he uses the *Tableau* to show how the extra revenue that results from an increase in the prices of agricultural products is distributed between the productive and the sterile class (see ibid., pp. 170–1).

1.10 The 'state of bliss' in the *Tableau Economique*

That the *Tableau Economique* is neither a general comprehensive textbook of physiocracy nor its rational core can also be seen by analysing the hypotheses that Quesnay develops in order to describe the distinctive features of the economy investigated in the *Tableau*. The assumptions he makes are remarkably similar in all writings, and represent the features of an economic system which has already reached a sort of 'state of bliss'.[52] At the beginning of the *Analyse*, Quesnay presents the hypotheses underlying the whole work:

> Let us assume, then, a large kingdom whose territory, *fully culti-vated by the best possible methods*, yields every year a reproduction to the value of *five milliards;* and in which the permanent mainte-nance of this value is ensured by the *constant prices* which are current among trading nations, in a situation where there is unre-mitting *free competition in trade* and *complete security of property* in the wealth employed in agriculture (Meek, 1962, p. 151, italics added).

This passage contains four assumptions. First, and most important, the primary sector uses the best techniques of production. Large-scale cultivation has been extended to all lands, which, in turn, are exploited by rich farmers (see *Extrait*, Kuczynski and Meek, 1972, p. 14). These farmers, acting as capitalist entrepreneurs, make large investments in agriculture (see ibid., pp. 6, 15; *Analyse*, Meek, 1962, p. 160). The employment of these huge stocks of capital, or 'ad-vances' as Quesnay calls them, and the use of large-scale methods of cultivation are the distinguishing features of a prosperous agricultural country. For Quesnay, a wealthy agricultural country is one 'where the annual advances are able, with the aid of the fund of the original advances, to produce 100 per cent' (*Explication*, Kuczynski and Meek, 1972, p. vi). This ratio is exactly the same in all three versions of the zigzag and in the formula. Two other ratios distinguish a modern and efficient agriculture; one between revenue and annual production (2:5), the other between the annual advances of the sterile class and those of the productive one (1:2). The hypotheses about the technique of cultivation are a crucial step for the under-standing of the *Tableau*, because they represent the structural re-lationships which exist in a prosperous economy.

A second assumption concerns the security of property, not such a well-known issue, but one which was highly important for Quesnay. This was not simply a matter of guaranteeing the right to ownership of the soil; for the physiocrats it was essential that the wealth that had been invested in the exploitation of land should be secured against any form of retaliation, either from the landlords or from the administration. The *avances foncières* of the proprietors and, above all, the *avances primitives* of the farmers provide the resources needed to implement and maintain the best techniques of cultivation; hence they must be protected against any possible disruption (see *Extrait, ibid.*, pp. 7–8).

A third assumption concerns the existence of free trading conditions, particularly in foreign trade, for the products of French agriculture (see ibid., p. 8). For Quesnay this is one of the most important ways of securing prosperity, not only for landlords and cultivators, but for the whole country (see below, Chapter 3, 3.6).

The fourth assumption states that in the *Tableau* prices are regarded as constant. Quesnay acknowledges the existence of prices, but in this work he analyses some relationships among economic magnitudes which, according to him, can be more easily examined and illustrated without introducing the complication of price variations. The widespread opinion that price concepts have no role to play in physiocracy does not seem to take into account that the very existence of a hypothesis about prices in the *Tableau* underlines the fact that value categories *are* regarded as important by Quesnay. After all, the magnitudes of the *Tableau* are expressed in value terms, and the 'fixed prices' assumption is not a subterfuge to avoid the problem of price determination. On the contrary, according to Quesnay's methodology this hypothesis defines the limits of the analysis of the *Tableau* and indicates a point of connection with other writings.

As a matter of fact, in the *Tableau* Quesnay assumes that all the appropriate economic policies *have already been implemented;* therefore natural laws have *already* established so to speak, the natural levels of prices (see *Du Commerce,* I.N.E.D. 1958, vol. II, p. 829–30). Moreover, in order to express the magnitudes of the *Tableau* the market values of primary products, as well as being stable and constant, must also be permanently high, because only such high prices can appropriately be used to measure the wealth of the country (see Mirabeau 1760b, p. 135; also below, Chapter 2, 2.3). Certainly if Quesnay does not try to explain what determines these stable and high prices, all his theoretical work is built on very fragile foundations.

Despite his methodological purpose and attention to the actual economic problems of France, this would amount to assuming a *deus ex machina* a *bon prix* of '18 livres per *setier* for corn' (*Analyse*, Meek 1962, p. 153), without saying anything about how it could be attained or about the reasons why it would be beneficial to the country. One of the hypotheses that make up the pillars of the *Tableau* would remain unexplained, and the reader would not know which measures should be taken in order to reach the proper price level which characterises the state of bliss. The use of the *Tableau* for economic policy purposes would be greatly endangered.

But there are several further assumptions that are common to the various versions of the *Tableau*. A fifth concerns the existence of a single tax, which falls on the two milliard *livres* of the annual revenue of the landlords (see *Analyse*, Meek, 1962, p. 153). This is the famous *impôt unique*, which guarantees that the entire burden of taxation, inclusive of the *dîme* of clergy, is a fixed proportion of the revenue of the country. Hence 'taxes are not destructive . . . and they are imposed directly on the net product of landed property' (*Extrait* Kuczynski and Meek, 1972, p. 4).

A sixth assumption concerns the expenditures of the landlords, who are supposed to spend half their revenue on agricultural produce and the other half on manufactured commodities (see *Explication*, ibid., p. i).[53] Quesnay wants to secure a prosperous market for the products of French agriculture. Thus he recommends that the classes which receive the revenue should spend a constant and high proportion of it on the purchase of agricultural products (*luxe de subsistance*), instead of buying the commodities of the sterile class (*luxe de décoration*) (see *Extrait*, ibid., p. 12 *Explication*, ibid., pp. i – ij).

This recurring theme in physiocratic writings introduces the seventh assumption. The proprietors, the sovereign and the Church neither save nor hoard money in any form; there are no 'monetary fortunes, which steal a portion of the revenue away from circulation, distribution, and reproduction' (*Extrait*, ibid, p. 4). This is not a trivial and minor assumption if one remembers the intellectual milieu to which Quesnay addressed his writings. Mercantilist views were still very powerful, and certainly their supporters must have been horrified by Quesnay's statement that '*monetary fortunes are a clandestine form of wealth which knows neither king nor country*' (ibid., p. 13, italics in the original). Money must not be either hoarded or saved, but has to be invested in 'the operations necessary for the prosperity of the kingdom (ibid., p. 18) Quesnay addresses these words to the sovereign, to the *Intendant Général*, and to all the administrators; they must favour the investment of monetary funds in the productive sector and oppose the formation of financial rents, such as interests on 'contracting loans' (see ibid., p. 14).

1.11 The exclusive productivity of agriculture: a necessary complement to the *Tableau*

Our examination of Quesnay's assumptions has shown that the prosperous agricultural country described in the *Tableau* has little in common with the French economy in the middle of the eighteenth century. The *Tableau* presents a hypothetical situation which embodies the main characteristics of the natural order of society. If one wants to identify a specific country with the kingdom described in the *Tableau*, it must be England, where most of the policy recommendations of the physiocrats had already been put into effect.

Although the physiocrats saw the *Tableau* mainly as a picture of an ideal economy, they also used it as 'a sort of conceptual standard with reference to which the effects of various policies on the actual contemporary economy could be judged' (Meek, 1962, p. 378). These policies must move France out of its backward economic conditions into a state of prosperity like that already achieved by England. The assumptions that lie behind the various *Tableaux* are really nothing more than Quesnay's specific solutions to this general problem. They show the measures that must be taken in order to initiate and regulate the process of development which can bridge the economic gap between a poor France and a wealthy England.

Among several assumptions that underlie the analysis of the *Tableau*, those concerning the conditions of production are particularly important. Quesnay says that the figures of the *Tableau Economique* imply that annual advances yield a revenue of 100 per cent a 'golden ratio', which indicates the predominance of large-scale cultivation, as in England (see *Extrait*, Kuczynski and Meek, 1972, p. 21). However, in the *Tableau* itself Quesnay does not examine the process of production, and does not explain why or how a modern agricultural sector, which employs large means of production, is the only part of the economy capable of yielding a net product (see below, Chapter 4, 4.3). In the *Tableau* both the methods of production and the scale of output must be regarded as data, as must the amounts of wealth and surplus which circulate among the classes; the ratios between the advances and the outputs of the two sectors are given (see Fox-Genovese, 1976, pp. 279–81).

In the various *Tableaux* there are several places where Quesnay confirms that the conditions of production are to be taken as data (see, for instance, *Analyse*, Meek 1962, p. 153). In the *Analyse*, Quesnay warns readers that these data are entirely dependent upon the particular stage of development of the conditions of production of the primary sector;

> 'the different states of prosperity or decline of an agricultural nation offer a host of other cases, and consequently other sets of *data*, each of which serves as the foundation of a special calculation which is in all strictness applicable to it. The data with which we began, according to the most constant rule in the natural order, fix at *five milliards* the total reproduction which the *productive class*, working with *two milliards* of annual advances causes to be annually regenerated in a territory such as that we have described. According to this hypothesis the annual advances reproduce 250 per cent' (ibid., Quesnay's italics).

Political societies can pass through different stages, either of progress or of backwardness, which are characterised by different technical and social conditions of production; that is to say by different sets of data; and each set can be applied only to its own particular case.[54] In the earlier zigzag there are many passages that indicate clearly that the methods of production are taken as given (see *Extrait*, Kuczynski and Meek, 1972, p. 2 note b and p. 6).

The figures in the *Tableau* refer to a situation in which large-scale farming is employed throughout the country. However, in this work Quesnay does not explain the technical and social relationships that justify the existence of the agricultural surplus. There is no examination of the reason why in agriculture 600 *livres* of annual advances give an output of 1500 *livres*, while the 300 *livres* annually advanced by the sterile class yield an output which is worth only 300 *livres*.[55] The existence of this net product is a datum.[56]

Of course, while it is true that the conditions of production are taken as given in the *Tableau*, this does not mean that they are thought to be an uninteresting topic. On the contrary, Quesnay is convinced that an investigation of the sources of wealth and revenue is necessary in order to give appropriate advice to the rulers of France. Depending on the answer to this question, different economic policies must be implemented. 'It is in a knowledge of the true sources of wealth, and of the means of increasing and perpetuating them, that the science of the economic administration of a kingdom consists' (ibid., p. 22). For Quesnay, the analysis of the origin of surplus and wealth is a necessary pre-requisite for the *Tableau* to be a meaningful and useful representation of Physiocratic contentions. By following his method of dealing with one problem at the time, he dedicates some specific works to the study of production. Furthermore, in the writings that accompany the *Tableau* he clearly indicates where this examination can be found. In the *Explication* he advises readers to go back to the articles *Ferme*, *Fermiers* and *Grains* of the *Encyclopédie* in order to find the analysis of the productive process and of the relations between the different types of advances and output in different conditions of cultivation (see *Explication*, ibid., p. vi). [57, 58]

Quesnay's theory of production is characterised by his view that only the conditions of production in the primary sector allow the means of production to reproduce themselves *plus a revenue*. The process of production of the sterile class produces no more than what was employed at the beginning of the year. The *Tableau Economique* can usefully be employed as an instrument of physiocratic economic policy only on the basis of the specific view of the origin of wealth according to which, by the laws of the natural order, revenue and wealth can only be produced by the primary sector. Without the theory of the exclusive productivity of agriculture the *Tableau* would provide no support for physiocratic contentions concerning taxation, trade policy and the pattern of expenditure.

The theory of the origin of wealth and surplus is a fundamental aspect of physiocracy, and Quesnay explains it in two stages. First of all, wealth does not derive from the exchange of commodities (*le commerce de revendeur*), but from their production (see *Observations sur l'intérêt de l'argent par M. Nisaque*, I.N.E.D., 1958, vol. II, p. 766, and below Chapter 2). Secondly, only agriculture produces a net product, while manufacture does not add anything to the value of its advances. It is this second point that came under the fiercest attack from the critics of physiocracy. Quesnay was aware that his view of the genesis of surplus was the cornerstone of physiocratic policies, and his last economic works are devoted mainly to defending the idea that a surplus can only originate in agriculture. In these later writings he tackles the problem of the origin of wealth and surplus mainly in value terms and makes great use both of price concepts and of the analysis of market mechanisms (see Chapter 4: 4.4).

2 Value and Wealth

In this chapter I will show that the physiocrats did not regard wealth and revenue as mere collections of *physical* quantities of primary goods, as is usually believed.[1] For Quesnay the amount of consumable agricultural produce is the basis of the prosperity of the people, but only the *value* magnitude of wealth can be used to compare the economic power of France with that of other countries. In order to become part of the nation's wealth products must pass through markets, where they are exchanged according to certain monetary prices. Quesnay contends that a specific concept of price – that which rules the 'sales at first hand' – must be employed to measure the country's wealth. He uses this particular idea of price to deny the quality of 'productive' to those exchanges that take place after the first sale of a product, which he calls 'resale trade'.

The size of the agricultural surplus, which indicates the growth potential of the nation, is measured by the difference between the value of output of agriculture and the value of its inputs. In fact the physiocrats regarded the products of cultivation and their means of production as heterogeneous commodities. In particular, the advances of agriculture are made up not only of primary products, but also include manufactured goods. Therefore one must know the relative prices of manufactured commodities and foodstuffs in order to measure the net product. Moreover, these exchange ratios are not regarded by the physiocrats as being constant over time; on the contrary, they believe that relative prices must change in favour of the products of the land.

2.1 *Telle est la valeur vénale, tel est le revenue*

This statement comes from the *Extrait des Economies Royales de M. de Sully* (part of the third edition of the *Tableau*), and the text continues: '*Abundance plus valuelessness does not equal wealth. Scarcity plus dearness equals poverty. Abundance plus dearness equals opulence*' (Kuczynski and Meek, 1972, p. 9, italics in the text)[2]. This will certainly look rather strange to a reader who is used to the traditional interpretation of physiocracy, according to which Quesnay considered only the material aspect of wealth. It is not so much because Quesnay speaks of 'price' and 'value' that this passage is puzzling, but because of the relationship he seems to establish between these concepts and those of wealth and revenue. That the abundance of agricultural commodities is an important element in judging the 'opulence' of a country is a well-known feature of physiocracy. However, Quesnay gives the prices of these goods the same weight as their physical quantities in the determination of wealth. Moreover, this passage is neither peripheral nor unimportant: it is part of the comments Quesnay wrote to accompany and explain the *Tableau* (see Meek, 1962, 235; also *Grains, ibid.*, p. 84).

Indeed the idea that *both* the abundance of products *and* their high value are the source of wealth and revenue is a point upon which Quesnay frequently insisted. In the *Questions intéressantes*, he discusses the situation of two countries with the same quantities of products, but with different prices, and says that the country with higher prices is richer and more powerful than the other (see I.N.E.D. 1958, vol. II, pp. 661–2). The same is true for landlords: 'the exchange value of foodstuffs yields them more revenue in one country than in the other' (ibid., p. 662). Quesnay concludes: 'so are not those who obtain more revenue from their foodstuffs effectively richer than the others?' (ibid,).[3] Passages in which he underlines the importance of considering wealth and revenue in value terms can also be found in one of his best-known works: the *Analyse de la formule arithmétique du Tableau Economique*, where he says this about primary commodities: 'the more they are sold at high prices, the more net product cultivation yields' (Meek, 1962, p. 164).

From this it seems clear that the physiocratic concept of wealth cannot be defined in simple material terms; it also requires the examination of the market values of commodities. Quesnay explicitly says that *both* the quantities of primary products *and* their monetary prices are needed to evaluate the wealth of a country. In chapter VII of *Philosophie rurale*, which is traditionally ascribed to him,[4] Quesnay writes: 'in order to evaluate the annual wealth of a nation . . . it is necessary to examine together, first the quantity of the products, secondly their monetary prices' (Mirabeau, 1764, vol. I, p. 340). Here national wealth is a sum of values, the result of multiplying the quantities of agricultural products by their prices. The physical and value aspects of wealth are recognised throughout Quesnay's economic work. Sometimes he emphasises the technical and physical aspects of the production of wealth, and the importance of improving methods of cultivation. However, the existence of advanced techniques of production, and hence an abundance of agricultural goods, is a necessary but not sufficient condition to guarantee a country's wealth and prosperity. It is also essential that there exist the possibility of selling the products at a good price: *bon prix* (see Chapter 5, 5.3).

The problem of prices and the analysis of the technical conditions of production quite often appear in the same writings. The two aspects of wealth are always linked in Quesnay's mind. In *Grains* he writes that 'only an easy sale at a good price can preserve abundance and profit' (I.N.E.D., 1958, vol. II, p. 461). And immediately after this sentence he analyses the conditions of production of large- and small-scale farming. Even more striking is the case of the fifth and sixth sections of chapter VII of *Philosophie rurale*, where Quesnay analyses the methods of cultivation of certain primary commodities: corn, livestock, woods and fields (see Mirabeau, 1764, vol. I, pp. 358–71). For each he considers the relationship between the expenses of cultivation and the gross output, but a few pages earlier he dedicates two paragraphs to explaining that '*la valeur vénale constitue les richesses*' (ibid., p. 338). Finally, the *Prémier problème économique* is entirely dedicated to an examination of the effects on the revenue of the country of an increase of one-sixth in the prices of its products (see Meek, 1962, pp. 168, 170, 172–3, 180 note 3).

Prices and the techniques of cultivation reflect two of Quesnay's principal preoccupations: to improve the conditions of production in agriculture and to ensure that the products will be sold at a proper price. The fact that both the abundance of products and their market values are regarded as the basis of the wealth of a country is an important outcome of Quesnay's investigation into political economy, but it is also a necessary foundation for his economic policy recommendations. Therefore, the question of the selling price of agricultural goods cannot be considered as a marginal or unimportant aspect of physiocracy. Contrary to traditional interpretations, Quesnay and his disciples believed that prices could affect the wealth of a country.

The physiocrats were interested not only in wealth, but also in revenue, i.e. that part of the annually produced wealth which is freely disposable without detriment to further production (see Mirabeau, 1764, vol. I, p. 350)[5]. Thus the net product is the only part of annual production that can be employed in many different ways (see *Premier problème économique*, Meek, 1962, pp. 179–80). In order to measure the annual revenue, one must know what are the techniques of production - the link between the inputs and the outputs of agriculture. The surplus, in physical terms, is given by the difference between the gross output and the commodities that must replace the means of production, including the necessary consumption of the workers.

But, according to the physiocrats, prices too play an important role in differentiating revenue from wealth. Mirabeau writes: 'the revenues of the nation are not simply made up of the products of the territory of the country; it is also necessary that these products have a market value which exceeds the price of cultivation expenses. Only this surplus can yield either a revenue or a net product' (Mirabeau, 1764, vol I, p. 339; see also p. 337). The net product is a value concept and its size in given by the difference between the price at which an agricultural good is sold and the value of the expenses that have been incurred in its production.[6]

The existence of a physical surplus of agricultural products over the means of production is a necessary condition for the existence of a net product, but the physiocrats believed that it was not sufficient to guarantee that the country actually had a revenue. Only a comparison between the *values* of output and inputs could determine the size of the country's surplus. Exchange values therefore come into the picture, and Quesnay gives a precise description of the prices that affect the size of the net product; they are, of course, the prices of the products of agriculture, which must be compared with the prices of their means of production. In fact, as he writes in *Hommes*,

> even that produce which is necessary for men's needs is not, merely by virtue of its exchangeability, regarded as a profitable form of wealth if its market value does not exceed the value of the work and the other costs which its production demands (Meek, 1962, p. 89)

In order to secure the existence of a surplus the price of an agricultural product must exceed a well defined level, that of the unit cost of production of the commodity in question. Only at prices above this level there is production of new disposable wealth. Thus the very notion of surplus, the nucleus of physiocratic economics, acquires a precise and complete significance only in terms of value. Of course the definition of revenue in value terms has important implications for the distinction between productive and sterile activities (see Chapter 4, 4.4).

Before proceeding further in our analysis of the physiocratic concepts of wealth and revenue, we must clear up a possible misunderstanding about the role of prices in the determination of the size of the net product. There are in fact many passages in which the physiocrats point out that high prices are a powerful incentive to investment in agriculture. High prices of the products of land induce farmers to use all available means in order to increase their production, including improving the methods of cultivation (see Mirabeau, 1764, vol. I, p. 338; see also below Chapter 5, 5.3). Technical progress increases the material difference between outputs and inputs and the net product grows in physical terms. In this case prices affect wealth and revenue only indirectly, since they act like a catalyst in a chemical reaction. Hence one should not worry too much about value categories; prices only play the role of stimulating agricultural production.

However, for Quesnay this is not the *only* way in which prices influence the prosperity of a country and the size of its surplus. In *Grains* he quite unambiguously states that 'not only is the proper price favourable to the progress of agriculture, but it is also in the proper price itself that the wealth which agriculture procures consists' (Meek, 1962, p. 84). In this passage, Quesnay rejects the idea that prices act as mere catalysts; on the contrary, they are placed *on the same level* as the quantities of the products, as one of the *two* elements that *determine* the value of the annual wealth of the country.

2.2 The material conditions of production and the marketability of the products of land

One reason for Quesnay's fame in the history of economic thought lies in the strength with which he fought the mercantilist view that the wealth of a country should be measured by the amount of money lying in its coffers (see Johnson, 1937, pp. 616, 619). However, in eighteenth-century France, mercantilist views were already losing ground, while different opinions were coming into fashion, views that have been grouped under the name of *populationnisme*. The *populationniste* believed that the only true wealth of a nation was the number of its inhabitants; people made a country opulent and rich.[7] The main way in which France could increase its economic power was, according to this school of thought, by adopting laws and policies designed to increase its population.

The physiocrats fought this view as strongly as they fought mercantilism. In opposition to both streams of thought, Quesnay maintained that the quantities of consumable agricultural products, and not money and people, were what could bring prosperity to a country.[8] The first preoccupation of rulers must be to implement policies which increase the physical quantities of agricultural commodities produced and consumed each year. However, according to the physiocrats not only should France increase output of the primary sector [9] but, in order to raise the surplus, this had to be combined with measures to reduce the quantities of products needed as means of production of that output.

These considerations are not shaken by our reinterpretation of the physiocratic concepts of wealth and revenue as value magnitudes. But material production describes only one aspect of the genesis of wealth; the other concerns the possibility of selling the products through exchange on the market. In *Hommes* Quesnay gives one of the clearest explanations of his notion of wealth: '*exchangeable wealth is that which is exchanged with monetary wealth*, in accordance with the price which constitutes its market value. Wealth is marketable or exchangeable only to the extent that its possessors are able to sell it and that it is sought after by purchasers' (Meek, 1962, p. 89, italics in the original). Hence the products of agriculture are not wealth in themselves, but must have the additional quality of being exchangeable against money; that is to say they must be *richesses commerçables*.

For Quesnay wealth is something that can be exchanged according to the rules of a market economy in which exchanges occur in monetary terms. He seems to believe that, in order to be considered 'exchangeable wealth', a commodity must possess two qualities. First, the 'possessor' of the good must be 'able to sell it'. He is a free man and the goods he has produced are his own private property; it is up to him to decide what he wants to do with them. The free and complete alienability of goods is a fundamental characteristic of a market exchange economy and so is the conjunction of the features of possession and property in the same person of the producer. Quesnay speaks of 'the right to the necessary freedom' in order to have a circulation of commodities according to natural laws, where exchanges take place with 'equality between equal men' (*Despotisme de la Chine*, I.N.E.D., 1958, vol. II, p. 926).

The second condition for a product to be exchangeable wealth is that there must be a market for it; there must be somebody who wants to buy it. A good which cannot be sold by the producer because nobody requires it cannot be regarded as wealth. What matters is not that a product is actually exchanged against money, but the existence of this possibility if and when the producer decides to sell it. Then the commodity can enter the sphere of circulation as a marketable item. The French term *richesses commerçables* expresses very clearly the idea that in order to acquire the quality of wealth a product must become an object of trade.

Therefore agricultural goods must be *commerçables*; it is only by the possibility of being sold, and by the price at which exchange can take place, that they acquire the characteristic of wealth. But, in addition, the quantity of wealth which is created through the sale of the good depends on the value which it realises in exchange for money on the market. 'Exchangeable wealth therefore constitutes wealth only in proportion to its price' writes Quesnay in *Hommes* (Meek, 1962, p. 90). In chapter VII of the *Philosophie rurale* he confirms that a commodity must have two qualities to be considered part of national wealth: 'the country requires that the soil produces as much as possible, and that the products become wealth by means of the highest possible market value; because its wealth and revenue derive from this value' (Mirabeau, 1764, vol. I, p. 337). Thus it is clear that, for Quesnay, the wealth of nations is measured by the exchange value of their products; an idea which was to be fundamental in English classical economics.

2.3 First-hand markets and the measurement of wealth

The marketability of products is an essential requirement for them to be considered as part of the wealth of a country. But Quesnay does not refer to the process of circulation of commodities in general; he has in mind a specific act of exchange, the so-called 'sales at first-hand', a term which is peculiar to physiocratic thought[10]. Apart from its old-fashioned flavour, the expression *vente de la première main* refers to a market in which exchange takes place between the farmer who has produced the good and the merchant who first buys it. (In the case of manufactured commodities the role of the seller is taken over by the artisan.) Hence when Quesnay says that the market value of a product affects the wealth of the country, he refers to a specific concept of price and not to a generic and vague idea of market value; it is the selling price which is received by the farmer. This particular price is the one by means of which the annual wealth of a country may be calculated. For the physiocrats annual wealth is measured by the 'overall annual receipts of the productive class in the sales at first-hand' (*Réponse au mémoire de M. H.*, I.N.E.D., 1958, vol. II, p. 750).

Therefore, in order to discover the factors that influence the revenue of a country, one must examine the forces which affect the monetary earnings of farmers. In the *Analyse*, in a passage where Quesnay defines the productive class as the people employed in agriculture, he also clearly indicates the dividing line between productive and sterile activities, within the process of circulation of commodities:

> We include within this class all the work done and all the expenses incurred up to the sale of the products at first-hand; it is through this sale that the value of the annual reproduction of the nation's wealth is ascertained. (Meek, 1962, p. 150)

The concept of the 'first-hand market' provides one of the analytical devices that allowed the physiocrats to distinguish those economic deeds and actions that can influence wealth and revenue from those that cannot. For the physiocrats, all the economic activities which occur before and during the first sale affect the value of agricultural products and hence the size of the revenue of the nation. On the other hand, the economic activities which take place after the sales at first-hand cannot influence the size of the annual wealth of the nation. This does not imply that these later activities are either irrelevant or unrelated to the welfare of the people or to the possibilities for development of the nation. But as far as wealth is concerned, it can only be increased up to the point at which the products are sold 'at first-hand', and it is precisely by means of these sales that it is possible to measure the value of the annual production of the nation's wealth (see Le Trosne, 1777, pp. 938, 959).

Quesnay further qualifies this notion of prices in the sales at first-hand: not only must they be the prices of first-hand markets and be higher than the unit cost of production of the products, but in order to be used for the evaluation of revenue and wealth 'first-hand prices' must be permanent and stable. In *Grains* Quesnay explains that only permanent dearness and abundance constitute the wealth of a country (see Meek, 1962, p. 84); in fact 'a transitory dearness would not bring about a general circulation of wealth in the whole nation' (ibid., pp. 84–5).

Thus, according to Quesnay, it would be wrong to take any price which is observed in sales at first-hand as an appropriate element for the evaluation of the wealth and revenue of the country. A temporarily high price cannot be used as the basis for such an evaluation, even if it is a price of sales at first-hand and covers the expenses of cultivation. Quesnay seems to believe that in such a case only part of the population benefits from the existence of the high price, and hence that this kind of situation cannot be seen as corresponding to an increase in the general wealth of the country. The particular market value that affects the country's wealth and revenue is the price level which *permanently* rules first-hand markets.

Here Quesnay rejects the mercantilist view that high and favourable prices are, by themselves, sufficient to give wealth both to individuals and to countries. In fact he links wealth and revenue directly to the existence of stable and normal prices for the products of land. The requisites of stability and permanence in these market values are clear indications of Quesnay's belief that these prices are the outcome of the working of systematic forces which display their effects in first-hand markets. Chaos and chance have no role to play in an inquiry into the causes and measurement of the nation's wealth. Quesnay does not intend to study temporary and erratic phenomena, but the permanent and normal features of the economy.

This analysis of the physiocratic concepts of wealth and revenue, and of 'first-hand prices', reveals two important problems in Quesnay's theory of markets and prices. First, although the concept of stable and permanent prices in sales at first-hand leads the physiocrats to an investigation of the forces that operate in this particular market and provoke the day-to-day movement of prices, we must also study the relationships, if any, between price fluctuations and the physiocratic analysis of the way in which a stable level of first-hand prices can be attained. Secondly, Quesnay points to a specific threshold for the price of a product above which it yields a revenue: the unit cost of production. We must therefore examine whether there is a precise relationship between this latter notion and that of stable and permanent prices. Only by considering these two questions can we know when a 'first-hand price' can be used correctly for the measurement of a country's revenue, and hence give a precise meaning to the physiocrats' notion of wealth (these two issues will be examined in Chapter 3).

2.4 The sterility of trade

The concept of first-hand sales helps to clarify the physiocratic view of the circulation of commodities. In particular, it establishes the fact that wealth can only be obtained in the process of production of goods, including their first sale, and not in the following exchanges. Commodities are exchanged between various people and in many different markets before they are consumed. But as far as the measurement of wealth is concerned the only type of circulation of commodities that matters is that of the first act of sale and purchase (see Herlitz, 1961b, p. 126). And in *The Tableau Economique avec ses explications* Mirabeau writes: 'here by circulation we mean only the purchases at first-hand' (Mirabeau, 1760b, p. 148).

The idea that trade is a sterile occupation is necessary for the physiocrats to prove that only the primary sector can produce a net product. In order to maintain that only a particular sector of the economy is productive, they must first show that a net product cannot arise from the trading activities of merchants and dealers, who simply exchange commodities among themselves and with consumers. By the middle of the eighteenth century the idea that trade affected the prosperity of a country was widespread among scholars and in literary circles in both England and France. Quite often trade was considered to be the primary source of wealth, both for the individuals and for nations. Mercantilism had dominated economic thought for a long time and was still very powerful; it constituted a compulsory point of reference for anybody who wanted to put forward ideas on economic policy.[11]

With the gradual transition of capitalism from what might be called its mercantile stage to the industrial one, the influence of mercantilist ideas began to decline. In France Vincent de Gournay and his school began to advocate free competition in both domestic and foreign trade.[12] But they did not deny that trade could be a source of wealth for a nation. The idea that a country could grow rich mainly by improving the techniques of production of its products, without even trying to 'beggar its neighbours' by distorting commercial relations in its favour, was a new one in 1760. The idea that trade *cannot* originate wealth had never been proposed before Quesnay; not even by authors like Cantillon, who were not Mercantilists and who never particularly stressed the influence of trade on the welfare of nations.

According to Quesnay, in trade there is always an exchange of commodities of equal value; wealth could not spring out of trade because nobody would be prepared to exchange one commodity for another of inferior value. In the *Dialogue sur les travaux des artisans*, Quesnay says that *'trade is only an exchange of value for equal value'* (Meek, 1962, p. 214, italics in the original). If men behave rationally and cheating is ruled out, no one can receive commodities whose value is higher than that of the commodities he has sold. And since trade can take place only in so far as the values of the commodities exchanged are equal, wealth and revenue cannot be affected by people's reciprocal sales and purchases (see Le Trosne, 1777, pp. 903, 954; Bloomfield, 1938, pp. 721–2).[13]

This notion of the sterility of the activities of merchants and dealers does not imply that the physiocrats ignored the role of money as a medium of exchange. They clearly were *not* thinking of eighteenth-century France as a 'barter economy', in which trade was carried on in kind. Barter still existed, but money was now the main form in which people obtained their incomes and the commodities they consumed. For example Mercier defines 'to sell' as 'the exchange of commodities against money' (Mercier, 1767, p. 257, his italics). The circulation of commodities, by means of several sales and purchases, can take place only through the money which is used by buyers and sellers to exchange their commodities (see ibid., p. 258). Money is nothing more than a medium of exchange, *un gage intermédiaire* (see Baudeau, 1767, vol. I, p. 179). Its total amount cannot be increased by the sales and purchases of people. As with money, the products exchanged exist before they start to circulate among individuals. The process of resale circulation of commodities cannot affect their physical quantities and the money prices at which they are sold 'at first-hand'; hence it does not affect the wealth of the nation.

On the basis of this notion of wealth, it is no surprise to learn that Quesnay and his disciples opposed the activities of merchants and of all those who interposed themselves as middlemen between the first producer and the consumer (see also below, Chapter 3, 3.4). The physiocrats distinguished the sales of the products of agriculture–'sales at first-hand'–from the various resales. After the first act of purchase a commodity enters a different type of circulation which Quesnay called *le commerce de revendeur* (see *Intérêt de l'argent*, I.N.E.D., 1958, vol. II, p. 776). This is regarded as a sterile occupation. Mercier de la Rivière divided acts of exchange into two categories: 'a man *trafique* when he *buys and resells* the commodities which originally belong to other men; a man *commerce* when he obtains from his own land the commodities which he exchanges against some other values' (Mercier, 1767, p. 269, his italics). While *trafiquer* has a negative connotation, *commercer* is judged positively, because it can have beneficial effects on the prices of the products of land (see below, Chapter 4, 4.4 and 4.5).

Resale trade has a negative influence on the wealth and revenue of a nation, because merchants and middlemen have to be maintained at the expense of the productive class out of the commodities it has produced. They 'manage to keep for themselves a share of the wealth of other men' (ibid.). Resale trade increases the costs to the nation, because the people it employs can survive only at the expense of workers in the primary sector. They receive a 'salary' which does not correspond to the production of new agricultural goods, which would be part of the country's wealth. Resale trade thus constitutes a deduction from the nation's annual wealth.[14]

The physiocrats' denial of any productive role of resale trade was not grounded on an ethical judgment, but derived from their general view of the distinction between productive and sterile activities. The expressions they use to describe trade are not always as negative and destructive as is sometimes believed. Quesnay and his disciples realised that resale trade can sometimes be thought of as a necessary occupation,[15] because it helps to satisfy the wants of the people by reallocating commodities among them. Merchants transfer commodities from one province to another and then make it easier for different individuals to find the commodities they want to buy.[16]

However, even in those passages where Quesnay refers to traders and merchants in a positive way, he stresses the difference between productive and necessary activities. The usefulness of an occupation is quite distinct from its ability to create new wealth; resale trade may be necessary, but it is certainly unproductive. In the *Réponse au Mémoire de M. H.*, Quesnay clearly distinguishes necessary from productive activities: 'the action of exchange does not produce anything; it is only necessary to satisfy the need which is itself the cause of exchange. One must then distinguish what is only necessary from what is productive' (I.N.E.D., 1958, vol. II, pp. 757–8).

Hence Quesnay does not deny the role of people's needs in giving rise to, and stimulating, exchanges and trade (see below, Chapter 3, 3.1). But he separates these two aspects of his economic analysis quite clearly. On the one hand he studies the relationships between wants and commodities: trade, the phenomenon of circulation of commodities after they have left the producers. On the other hand, he analyses the production of wealth and revenue and the factors that affect their magnitude. The first is the realm of 'want and exchange', the second that of 'value and production'. The line which divides economic phenomena into these two groups is defined by the markets for sales at first-hand and by the associated concept of 'permanent' prices. The prices of the products of land are determined on this market; once commodities have 'crossed' the line and reached the stage of resale trade, their values cannot be modified.

2.5 The heterogeneity of input and output in agriculture

We have seen that the physiocrats regarded national wealth not simply as a set of physical items, but as a value magnitude. I will now explain why they *had to* consider wealth and revenue in value terms. In fact, according to Quesnay, there is no sector of the economy in which the output and its means of production are made up of the same commodities. Thus relative prices are necessary to measure the net product of agriculture, which for the physiocrats is the social surplus of the whole country. Indeed Quesnay's investigation into the composition of the means of production in agriculture provides overwhelming reasons for rejecting the 'all corn' view of physiocracy (see above, Chapter 1, 1.2) because the input and output of agriculture are heterogeneous commodities.

Each year agriculture requires two milliard *livres* of *avances annuelles*, in order to produce five milliard *livres* of products (see *Analyse*, Meek, 1962, pp. 151–4). These are primary products, retained by the cultivators at the end of each year to be employed in the next productive cycle. Annual advances are circulating capital, because they are used only once and at the end of the productive process they must be entirely replaced.[17] But agriculture also requires the original advances, *avances primitives*: all the commodities, tools and equipment which have been advanced by the farmer before the first productive period, in order to be able to start cultivating the land (see *Explication*, Kuczynski and Meek 1972, p. vi). For Quesnay the original advances 'ought to be regarded as if they were a fixed property which should be preserved with great care in order to ensure the production of the taxes and the revenue of the nation' (*Extrait*, ibid., p. 5). Quesnay regards these advances as a sort of fixed capital, which is used in production for several years (see *Maximes générales*, Meek, 1962, p. 232). The part of these advances which wears out in production must be replaced with newly produced goods, so that the stock does not decrease. The value of this share of the original advances which must be replaced yearly is one milliard *livres*.

For the physiocrats this milliard of 'interests' on the original advances is made up of commodities which are produced not in the primary sector, but by the sterile class.[18] At the end of each productive cycle the farmers must buy one milliard *livres* of manufactures in order to replace the fixed capital which has been consumed.[19] Therefore the two sectors are technically interrelated; each must buy part of its inputs from the other (see Fox-Genovese, 1976, p. 284; Phillips, 1955, p. 143; Eagly, 1961, pp. 56, 57).

Textual evidence heavily supports an interpretation of physiocracy in which industrial activities contribute to the process of production of the primary sector. To quote a famous passage from the *Analyse*:

> Thus the annual expenditure of the productive class is *three milliards*, made up of *two milliards* of products which it retains for its consumption, and *one milliard* of goods which it has purchased from the sterile class. These *three milliards* form what are called THE RETURNS of the *productive class*, *two milliards* of which constitute the annual advances which are consumed for the labour directly involved in the reproduction of the *five milliards* which this class causes to be annually regenerated, in order to restore and perpetuate the expenses which are destroyed by consumption. *The other one milliard* is taken by this same class out of the proceeds of its sales for the interest on the advances of its enterprises. (Meek, 1962, p. 154, Quesnay's italics)

For Quesnay the manufactured commodities which restore the original advances are even more important than the agricultural products which constitute the annual advances for the undertaking and improvement of the process of production. In fact, one fundamental cause of a country's prosperity is the abundance of its original advances and the extent to which they are preserved. Quesnay writes in the *Analyse*:

> The fund of wealth employed in cultivation which constitutes the original advances is subject from day to day to a wearing away which demands continual repairs, absolutely necessary if this important fund is to remain intact and not to move progressively towards complete annihilation, which would destroy cultivation, and consequently the reproduction, and consequently the wealth of the state, and consequently also the population. (ibid.)

Therefore the products of industry are necessary to maintain the stock of the original advances of agriculture, for part of the means of production of the primary sector must be purchased by the farmers from the manufacturers. Thus the advances of agriculture are made up of heterogeneous commodities, and in order to calculate their overall size one needs to know the relative prices of the products of land and of manufactured goods.

2.6 The composition of the *Avances Primitives*

Notwithstanding Quesnay's unambiguous statements in the *Analyse*, some commentators have argued that he considered the *avances primitives* to be made up of agricultural products. For instance, Meek says that Quesnay 'visualised these "interest goods" . . . as consisting essentially of agricultural produce of various kinds, livestock for replacing losses, stocks of seed, etc., to meet emergencies and subsistence for men employed to repair buildings, machines, etc.' (Meek, 1962, p. 279, n. 5; see also Eltis, 1975a, pp. 189, 197). Notice that the authors must not be confused with the supporters of the 'all corn' interpretation. Although they believe that the replacement needs of fixed capital can be satisfied entirely inside the primary sector, they do not deny the importance of industry; agriculture buys one milliard of products from the sterile class for the consumption of its own workers (see Meek, 1962, pp. 275, 283; Napoleoni, 1976, pp. 17–18). The role of industry in providing inputs to the primary sector is not questioned: the manufactured commodities bought from agriculture are not considered as luxuries, they are part of the necessary means of subsistence yearly required by farmers and peasants (see Meek, 1962, p. 286).

However, a brief examination of the structure of the *avances primitives* provides interesting indications of the way in which the physiocrats viewed the social and technical organisation of the process of production in agriculture. In the *Analyse* there is no indication that the peasants' consumption includes commodities which have been purchased from industry. It appears difficult to maintain that the milliard *livres* received by agriculture from industry is made up entirely of consumption goods, on the contrary it includes industrial products destined for the replacement of the *avances primitives* which wear out annually. Meek correctly singles out livestock as an important constituent of the *avances primitives*, but the importance of livestock, and of the associated manure, must not obscure the fact that the fixed capital of agriculture also includes instruments, tools, machines and other items of equipment which are provided by the sterile class (see Boudeville 1954, pp. 459–60, 464–5). The physiocrats always associate livestock, and particularly horses, with machines and instruments, as the most relevant items of the original advances (see for instance Baudeau, 1767–70, vol. XI, p. 140; vol. XII, p. 144). This is confirmed by an examination of Quesnay's long list of the total expenses that a farmer incurs for the cultivation of 40 *arpents* of land with one plough and four horses. Among the annual costs we find 'the expenses of the wheelwright, harness-maker, ropers, canvas, farrier, for shoes, harness, the awles of the cart, tyres for the wheels, etc.' (*Fermiers*, Groenewegen, 1983, p. 14). And the 'interests' which must restore fixed capital are listed as follows: 'for the interests on the stock for outlays on the purchase of horses, ploughs, carts, and other landed advances, which have been sunk and from which other livestock is subtracted, can be estimated at three thousand *livres*' (ibid., p. 15; Quesnay's italics; see also Baudeau, 1767–70, vol XI, p. 140, vol. II p. 144).

For the physiocrats the fact that the replacement of the original advances includes both manufactured commodities and livestock is a typical feature of the most advanced methods of cultivation (see Mirabeau, 1760b, pp. 126–7, 135). Large-scale cultivation, which employs horses instead of oxen, requires the availability of ploughs and of all the other tools and equipment which allow the superior power of horses to be fully exploited. If farmers do not provide an adequate number of ploughs and carts and do not care about their maintenance any type of technological progress in the methods of cultivation is severely hampered. Horses and manufactured instruments are technically connected inputs in the process of production of the primary sector.

The milliard of 'interests' can be considered as being composed of commodities designed for two different uses, namely to replace fixed capital and to provide some types of consumption goods, but of these two functions the first absorbs the larger share.

This interpretation of the items which make up the fixed capital of agriculture fits well with the physiocrats' view of the 'ideal' condition of cultivation: the capitalist exploitation of land in England and in the northern provinces of France (see Woog, 1950, pp. 42, 44, 51, 62 note 2). In these regions the farmers' demand for manufactured goods is the major factor in the development of the iron industry.[20]

2.7 The relationship between industry and agriculture

Our investigation into the role of the products of industry as means of production for the primary sector has made it clear that Quesnay and his disciples regarded industry as a true and proper sector of the economy, a fact which is clearly shown in the 'formula' of the *Tableau Economique*, where the share of industrial output, even if smaller than that of agriculture, is very large (two-sevenths, almost 30 per cent of overall annual production).[21] Mirabeau underlines the degree of development of the industrial sector by remarking that, like agriculture, it requires some kind of fixed capital; two milliards of original advances are necessary for the process of production (see Mirabeau, 1760b, p. 178).[22, 23]

It is important to note that in France in the middle of the eighteenth century many industrial activities were still part of agriculture. These occupations were known as *industrie rurale*, or *campagnarde*, and were widespread in several regions of France (see Bairoch, 1963, p. 295). Such industry consisted mainly of the production of clothes, using raw materials taken directly from agriculture (see Sée 1967, p. 128). All these occupations were actually carried out either by peasant families or by peasants who had become artisans. The latter were still closely linked to agriculture, both because they received from it all the necessaries of life and because farmers were the main buyers of their products.

It is not surprising to find Quesnay describing industry as a large economic sector; in fact in his ideal economy agriculture is characterised by large-scale cultivation which requires huge advances, including manufactured products. The very need for tools and instruments of production in modern capitalist agriculture provides a major impulse to industrial activity.[24] Quesnay recognised that the introduction of new methods of cultivation required the use of new types of equipment and of agricultural machines (see *Questions intéressantes*, I.N.E.D. 1958, vol. II, p. 631).[25]

This brief examination of some features of manufacturing industry in the France of Louis XV should help to refute a possible objection by those interpreters of physiocracy who believe that in agriculture input and output are the same commodities. In fact, one could say that in order to measure the net product of agriculture, it is not necessary to know the relative prices of industrial and primary commodities, *even if* manufactured goods appear among the inputs of agriculture. It is enough to extend the definition of the primary sector to include *all* the activities that give rise to a commodity which is employed in any way as an input in the production of some product of land. By definition, this sector of the economy is self-sufficient. One can assume that the instruments of cultivation are produced by the peasants when they are not working in the fields, in the evenings and during the winter. As Molinier says: 'hence a good part of industrial production is the result of the accessory occupations of the peasants' (Molinier, 1958b, p. 101).[26] The primary sector is completely closed as far as its input requirements are concerned; its means of production *must not come* either from other countries or from other parts of the economy. Only this can ensure that the surplus can be measured directly in physical terms. Farmers do not buy their means of production on the markets. Among the inputs of 'enlarged agriculture' are physically heterogeneous commodities, but there are no relative prices, because these goods are not marketed, but are produced and exchanged inside agriculture.

All this provides a much less naive view of physiocracy than the traditional 'all corn' interpretation. However, here too no price theory is needed to determine the net product of the economy. But this interpretation, which is based on the idea of *industrie rurale*, must be rejected because it gives an inadequate description of the physiocrats' analysis of markets and industry. In fact, it implicitly assumes that there are no markets at all for the products of manufacture. Of course commodities are exchanged: farmers buy instruments of production from 'farm artisans' and give them raw materials and necessaries. However, these transactions have nothing to do with the exchanges which take place in markets; they are not sales and purchases against money, nor is it possible to speak of barter, which would in any case imply the existence of exchange ratios determined in specific markets. The situation resembles that of a large peasant family, some of whose members cultivate the soil and produce the necessaries of life, while others keep in good order the various kinds of equipment necessary to continue production on the land.

Moreover, the idea that there is a single 'enlarged primary sector' which includes industrial activities makes it difficult, even impossible, to distinguish between productive and unproductive occupations. Another major aspect of Quesnay's economics is thus eliminated. The activities directly linked to the cultivation of the soil and the occupations of artisans are two sides of the same productive process, hence there is no reason to divide them into 'productive' and 'sterile'. Therefore, according to this view, the physiocratic contention in favour of the consumption of the products of land would be completely meaningless. Moreover, the question of the choice of a pattern of consumption by the landlords could not even be posed, because they receive their rents directly in terms of agricultural products.

Although the physiocrats intended to favour agriculture and opposed the policies that protected the industrial sector,[27] they recognised that manufacture was a separate branch of the economy. In particular, Quesnay considered that the exchange values of the products of industry were determined in different markets from those of primary commodities. The relative prices of the products of land and those of manufacture are the exchange ratios between their monetary prices, which are determined in separate markets. Quesnay had a clear view of the formation of relative prices: 'marketable goods . . . have a market value, which is relative and reciprocal for any good against the other ones, and in particular against a kind of wealth that we call money' (*Questions intéressantes*, I.N.E.D., 1958, vol. II, p. 652 note 11; see also Du Pont 1772, p. 374). People buy and sell commodities not for money itself, but in order to obtain other goods they need; however, according to Quesnay, these desires must in general be satisfied by means of exchanges against money on the markets. Money is the medium which facilitates the exchange of all types of commodities, because it is used 'to establish the measure of the reciprocal value of the goods which constitute wealth' (*Impôts*, ibid., p. 584).

The physiocrats set out to describe the features of a market exchange economy in which relative prices are established through markets. In chapter 1 of Le Trosne's *De l'intérêt social,* under the heading '*Définition de la valeur*', there is another passage which clearly shows the physiocrats' view of the role of money and the nature and importance of relative prices. For Le Trosne value has three related features. First, value is a social characteristic of commodities and not simply a technological one; it derives from the activities of men, who try to satisfy their needs by means of market exchanges (see Le Trosne 1777, p. 889). Secondly, 'the value consists in the exchange ratio which exists between any one thing and any other' (ibid.). Relative prices, not simply monetary ones, are the true measure of value. However, thirdly, in a market exchange economy the relative prices of commodities are known only by their exchange against money, 'the price is the expression of value: they are not separate in exchange, everything is reciprocally the price of a commodity; in the sale the price is in terms of money' (ibid.). In the process of exchange the monetary price is the necessary form of the value of commodities; in order to find the relative prices of commodities one must first know their monetary prices.

2.8 Changes in relative prices

We have seen that for Quesnay and his followers there were two major sectors in the economy and that their exchange relationships took place on markets by means of monetary prices. This introduces a major topic of physiocracy: the question of changes in relative prices which derive from changes in the regulation of foreign trade (see Chapter 4, 4.6). When we analyse this question it becomes clear that, although they regarded relative prices as an important feature of a market exchange economy, the physiocrats did not consider these values to be fixed and constant. In the *Tableaux* prices are given, because this is an *ad hoc* hypothesis used to study some effects of the modes of expenditure of revenue (see above, Chapter 1, 1.10). But at the same time changes in relative prices are regarded as important means of achieving wealth and prosperity.

The physiocrats emphasised that, in order to secure the prosperity of France, the prices of its products must be kept high relative to those of other countries. In *Hommes, à propos* of the average prices of foodstuffs on international markets, Quesnay wrote: 'it is the market value relative to your neighbours which makes up your wealth' (I.N.E.D., 1958, vol. II, p. 536; see also p. 556). The prosperity of a country is influenced by its terms of trade. Since France had a large agricultural sector, the physiocrats advocated raising the monetary prices of French foodstuffs; in fact this was regarded as the best way of improving the exchange ratios of home products against foreign ones. If the rulers implemented the economic policy necessary to raise the prices of the products of land, the surplus too would increase. Nations, said Quesnay, 'have a great interest in this price [that of their output] rising as much as it can; because the increase of this price raises the net product' (*Remarques sur l'opinion de l'auteur de l'Esprit des lois*, ibid., p. 783).

Rarely do the physiocrats say that the prices of manufactured commodities varied in the same direction, and by the same percentage, as those of the products of agriculture (see for instance, *Premier problème économique*, Meek, 1962, pp. 170–1, and *Grains*, ibid., p. 73). Therefore the exchange ratios between the products of the two sectors should not vary, whatever happens to their monetary prices. However, it should be noted that in these passages Quesnay was not discussing the process of price formation, but simply trying to defend his view of the sterility of manufacture. For this purpose he used the argument according to which industry only 'reshapes' the products of soil, without adding anything to their value (see *Premier problème économique*, ibid., p. 175; see also Le Trosne, 1777, pp. 937, 939).[28]

According to Mercier de la Rivière, the stability of relative prices could perhaps be justified in a closed economy, where exchanges with other countries can be neglected. In this case 'it will be absolutely irrelevant that products experience either a high or a medium increase in terms of money' (Mercier, 1767, p. 227). However the physiocrats did not consider the case of a closed economy as either relevant or interesting; in general a nation buys from and sells to its neighbours, even if only on a small scale. In an open system, foreign trade affects the home exchange ratios and their variations have important consequences for the wealth of the country. Normally, when a country like France sells its products to other nations, the relative prices of home foodstuffs must rise against those of foreign industry, but this is also bound to affect domestic relative prices, which cannot remain constant. Suppose that the introduction of free foreign trade modifies the exchange ratio of corn to foreign manufactured goods. In this case the idea of constant relative prices inside the economy brings about a paradoxical result, because French corn has *two* different prices relative to the products of industry; one in France and the other on foreign markets. This conflicts with the physiocratic assumption that free competition in domestic and foreign markets establishes the same prices everywhere (see below, Chapter 3: 3.5).

But the idea that exchange ratios are constant does not accurately describe the physiocrats' view of prices even in a country with no external trade.[29] The physiocratic notion of relative prices is not confined to the case of foreign trade. Inside the country, market forces establish the monetary prices and hence the exchange ratios of commodities. Article IX of a subsection of *Questions Intéressantes* (entitled *Grains*) is completely devoted to the advantages for the country of having high prices of foodstuffs relative to those of other goods, and Quesnay concludes that 'the prosperity and the power of states will be partly dependent upon the market value of necessaries considered relative to the prices of other commodities' (I.N.E.D., 1958, vol. II, p. 636). Hence administrators must try to increase the prices of French foodstuffs relative to those of both home and foreign manufactured goods.

In particular, the physiocrats advocated the reduction of indirect taxes on primary products and the abolition of all types of fiscal barriers between the provinces of France. All these duties reduce the prices of the produce of the soil relative to those of manufactured commodities, hence the value of the net product decreases. Farmers must use more of their goods to obtain the same quantities of manufactured commodities in order to replace their inputs.

Le Trosne examined the negative effects on surplus that derive from a distortion of the relative prices of the inputs and outputs of agriculture. He discussed the case of a tax which modifies the exchange ratios of commodities inside a country (see Le Trosne, 1777, p. 900). Before any disturbance occurs, the price of the products of land is at its natural level of 20 *sous*, that is to say 1 *livre*, *par mesure*; the value of the gross output is 5000 *livres*, that of the *réprises* ('returns') is 3000 *livres*, and that of the surplus is 2000 *livres*. Then fiscal policy causes a reduction of one-fifth in the prices of primary products. Therefore there is a change in their exchange ratios against other commodities. However commodities are not exchanged directly through barter, but are sold and purchased on markets, which show the change in the money values of commodities. The farmers receive less money for the same quantity of output, because 'the value of each measure, which ought to be twenty *sous*, will be only sixteen *sous*'. Therefore the farmers 'are obliged to give a larger quantity, for a fixed quantity of other products'. The conclusion of the passage shows that, for Le Trosne, a change in the monetary prices of agricultural products affects their exchange ratios with the commodities which make up that part of the returns which has to be bought outside agriculture and, in consequence, influences the surplus.

The farmer must restore his returns, which were previously equivalent to 3000 measures, that is to say 3000 *livres*. But after the reduction in the price of his products from twenty to sixteen *sous* the farmer still needs a value of 3000 *livres* for his returns, hence, at sixteen *sous* per measure he must keep 3750 measures (remembering that 1 *livre* = 20 *sous*). 'Therefore only 1250 measures will be left for the net product, and they will no longer have a value of 1250 *livres* but of 1000. Because of the reduction of one-fifth of the first-hand value, the revenue, which should have been 2000 *livres*, is actually diminished by half' (ibid., italics added).[30] Therefore the change in relative prices affects the profitability of cultivation. Indeed, it changes the ratio of the net product to the means of production in agriculture, which is one of the major indicators of the degree of development of a country (this ratio moves from 2:3 to 1:3). Moreover, the value of agricultural surplus decreases.

Finally, some comments on the interpretation of the *Tableau Economique* as a 'classical system of prices' (see Chapter 1, 1.2). This approach sees industry as a complete and proper sector of the economy with a market for its products, and recognises the importance of relative price variations. However, despite its advantages over other interpretations, it still results in an incomplete and inaccurate description of physiocratic economics. In particular, it fails to examine in detail what the physiocrats actually said about market mechanisms and price determination.

The inadequacies of this interpretation are best shown by a paradoxical result implicit in it. By solving the system of equations set out on p. 8 above, we see that industry seems to 'count more' than agriculture; the so-called sterile sector affects the values of both unknowns, while agriculture only influences the size of surplus! The second equation of system (1) (see p. 8) determines the unit price of iron in terms of corn:

$$p_i = \frac{C_i}{I - I_i}$$

which depends only on the techniques of production in the iron sector. The surplus, S, depends on the techniques of production of both sectors. The two unknowns are determined in a logical sequence; one first finds p_i from the second equation, then, by substituting its value into the first equation, one obtains the value of the net product.

However, these results certainly do not accord with the idea of a 'physiocratic system of prices' as a variation of the classical system of prices. Hence the exchange ratio and the value of the net product must be determined at the same time, and the value of both unknowns must be affected by both equations. However, in system (1) (p. 8) p_i is not influenced by methods of agricultural production, and this gives rise to a paradox. The second equation, which represents the process of production of the industrial sector, directly influences the relative price, and indirectly, through its influence on p_i, influences the value of the surplus S. Technical changes in manufacture determine a variation in the values of both variables p_i and S. On the other hand, the first equation, which describes the productive process of the primary sector, plays a role only in the determination of the size of the surplus.[31] Therefore, neither state intervention in the primary sector nor technical progress in cultivation can influence the relative prices of foodstuffs and manufactured goods. But this result conflicts with the physiocrats' analysis of increases in the price of wheat (see below, Chapter 4, 4.4–4.7). The idea that the *Tableau* is a 'classical price system' confines Quesnay's value theory to a sort of straitjacket, and fails to take account much of the physiocratic analysis of the role of prices and values.

3 The Theory of Prices in Physiocracy

A THE LAWS OF THE MARKET AND THE CURRENT PRICE

3.1 Value in use and value in exchange

We have seen that Quesnay considered the gross and net output of the economy as value magnitudes, and not simply as physical quantities of agricultural products. Assumptions about the existence of the appropriate level of exchange values of foodstuffs are implicit in the *Tableau Economique*, where the measurement of national product requires the use of prices of 'sales at first-hand'. It is now time to investigate what Quesnay said about the working of market forces and the specific concepts of price he adopted.

Since Quesnay's purpose was to relieve mankind, and the French people in particular, from miserable economic conditions, it is no surprise to find that his analysis of markets and prices is part of a general conception of man and society. For Quesnay, nature is not dominated by chaos, but displays an inner order; the study of its regularities is the major purpose of a social scientist. Thus, as Quesnay stated in *Le Droit naturel*, in human societies there is a 'physical law, to mean *the regular course of all physical events in the natural order*' (Meek, 1962, p. 53, Quesnay's italics).

According to the physiocrats, the economic laws of society result from the actions of individuals seeking the satisfaction of their wants and desires; 'the union of these two causes . . . is the principle and the result of society', wrote Mirabeau in the *Philosophie Rurale* (Mirabeau, 1764, vol. II, p. 16). Production and exchange of commodities originate because of the wants of people; individuals require their necessaries of life and desire the highest degree of enjoyment. Man 'is forced to take care of his subsistence and is led towards pleasure' (ibid. p. 15). But, above all, needs are the stimulus to economic activity and constitute the fundamental motive for the origin of societies:[1] 'for subsistence is the primary object of all societies' (Quesnay's notes, from Manuscript M. 778, no. 1, at the *Archives Nationales*, in Meek, 1962, p. 66). The economic system is designed to produce and allocate commodities that will satisfy people's wants and desires.

The physiocrats studied the way in which people organise themselves to solve the problem of subsistence, since from this feature of human activity derive the customs, habits and political order of civil societies. Mirabeau wrote: 'one must consider the principles of public matters and the roots of the whole of mankind, *subsistence*. All the moral and physical parts which strengthen the society derive from, and are subordinated to it' (Mirabeau, 1764, vol. II, pp. 9–10, italics in the original). The level of cultural and scientific activity of a country depends on its means of subsistence, as do all sectors of the economy: agriculture, trade, and industry (ibid., p. 11).

Therefore, for the physiocrats, as for many other scholars of the eighteenth century, 'the foundation of society is the subsistence of men' (*Le Droit naturel*, in Meek, 1962, p. 55).[2] The development and working of societies are explained by the category of 'mode of subsistence'; which is the way in which humanity organises itself in order to accomplish its 'three original needs; (1) that of its subsistence; (2) that of its conservation; (3) that of the perpetuity of its species' (Mirabeau, 1764, vol. II, p. 13). However, in any society people compete against one another for their survival and enjoyment; 'everybody tries to acquire goods for himself' (ibid., p. 12), rather than for other people. Each man tries to satisfy his needs while minimising his expenses and toil (see *Sur les travaux des artisans*, Meek, 1962, pp. 212–13).[3] Natural law suggests the most convenient system for co-ordinating the contrasting interests of people, in conformity with 'the order of distributive justice' (*Le Droit naturel*, ibid., p. 51).

According to Quesnay the general principle, which prevents confrontation and procures harmony, is the fact that everybody obtains a share of the products of the country according to his efforts in production; thus 'the right of *everybody to everything* is reduced to the share which each of them can procure for himself' (ibid., p. 47, italics in original). Hence, not only are societies founded on the subsistence of individuals, but they are also characterised by the way in which commodities are distributed within them. In fact, 'civil laws establish the rules for the distribution of the product and the wealth of a country' (Mirabeau, 1764, vol. II, p. 10). And manmade laws must be in harmony with natural ones in securing 'the reproduction and the regularity of the annual circulation of the wealth of a Kingdom's territory' (*Le Droit naturel*, in Meek, 1962, p. 55). The laws which regulate the distribution of wealth are a way of satisfying people's wants, but they are also intimately related to the reproduction of the whole economic system.

The satisfaction of wants and the search for enjoyment are the foundations on which the processes of production and exchange of commodities are built; but the distribution and reproduction of wealth must take place through the market, and in order to explain the determination of the exchange values of commodities Quesnay distinguishes their *use value* from their *exchange value*.[4] For the physiocrats the first term refers to the particular physical characteristics of a commodity, which make it suitable for the satisfaction of a particular need. Of course, the same commodity will be enjoyed quite differently by different people, depending on the way in which they feel that it can satisfy their own needs and desire. Hence for Quesnay, in a normal trading situation, exchange is always advantageous both to the buyer and to the seller; an individual will never exchange one commodity against another unless he is convinced that he will gain utility thereby. Hence 'one must always assume that it (exchange) is always profitable to both' contracting parties (*Sur les travaux des artisans*, ibid., p. 214; see also Le Trosne, 1777, p. 905).

Therefore, according to Quesnay, the use value has a precise role to play; the products of land become wealth only in so far as there are people who want them. Products must be able to satisfy the needs and wants of men, otherwise they cannot be considered as wealth (see *Hommes*, ibid., p. 88).[5] For Quesnay, as for other predecessors of Smith (see for instance Hutcheson 1754–55, vol. II, p. 53), the use value of a good does not normally affect its price; it is only a 'prerequisite' for its marketability (see Fox-Genovese, 1976, pp. 232, 279). It is a *necessary, but not sufficient*, condition for deciding whether any particular commodity is part of the national wealth.

The use of value of a product is a condition for its exchangeability, but the amount of wealth which is measured in the exchange depends only on the market value of the commodity: 'the value of all items of wealth, regarded from the point of view of their exchangeability, consists only in their price' (*Hommes*, Meek, 1962, p. 90). Therefore only the exchange value of a commodity can be used as a measure of the amount of wealth embodied in it, which does not depend on its use value. Quesnay believes that goods can be ranked according to their use values; some are more important than others. In *Hommes* he considers the famous example of food and diamonds (ibid.).[6] But this ranking of commodities does not affect their price; the most important goods can be free, so that everybody can obtain them without having to pay a price. This is the case of air and water 'and all other goods . . . which are in a very plentiful supply and available to everyone' (ibid., p. 89; see also Cannan, 1893, p. 4). There is no market for these goods, even though they are essential to life and are very much sought after: they are goods but not wealth' (ibid.).[7]

3.2 The systematic forces of a market exchange economy

We have seen that for the physiocrats the use value of a commodity is only a 'prerequisite' of its exchange value, because it ensures that it can be sold on the market. There is no quantitative relationship between *valeur usuelle* and price; these are two distinct features of the commodity, which are by no means regulated by the same laws.[8] Quesnay is quite unambiguous on this point in a passage in the article *Hommes*, which is worth quoting: 'we should not confuse the price of items of exchangeable wealth with their use value, for these two values rarely have any connection with one another' (Meek, 1962, p. 90).[9]

Therefore the wants and desires of people do not influence the use value of commodities, which is always the same, but above all needs cannot affect their exchange ratio on the market. Moreover, price variations do not depend on the will of the contracting parties and on the particular level of satisfaction they believe they will obtain in consuming the commodities (see Le Trosne, 1777, p. 891; Sewall, 1901, pp. 88–91).[10] People who exchange commodities act only in view of their own satisfaction and self-interest, but this fact does not lead to arbitrary values of prices, depending on the reciprocal strength of buyers and sellers. These two contrasting forces are checked and regulated by the market. Quesnay believes that, if a market exchange economy is allowed to work according to the laws of the natural order, it reconciles the different interests of the exchangers, because none of them can fix a price according to his own interest (see *Sur les travaux des artisans*, Meek, 1962, p. 215). Hence 'the price of exchangeable products depends neither on the buyer nor on the seller' (ibid.). Certainly their opposite interests give rise to the market, but 'the seller and the buyer, taken separately, are not the arbiters of the prices of products' (*Réponse au mémoire de M. H.*, I.N.E.D., 1958, vol, II, p. 752). For the physiocrats the market is a meeting place for all the people who want either to purchase or to sell a commodity; it is the behaviour of the two sides which gives rise to those regularities in the determination of prices which can be regarded as laws.

Thus, according to the physiocrats, both buyers and sellers are subject to the laws of the market, which fix a price *independent of their wills*:

> the price of exchangeable products depends neither on the buyer nor on the seller. The one is obliged to buy at a price higher than that at which he has an interest in buying, and the other is obliged to sell at a lower price than he would like. Thus there are *other decisive conditions* determining prices which force them to sacrifice their interests in their sales and purchases (*Sur les travaux des artisans*, Meek, 1962, p. 215, italics added).

On many occasions Quesnay mentions the factors which affect the prices of commodities; the clearest passage can be found in the *Réponse au mémoire de M. H.*, where he writes: 'with respect to the products nobody ignores that general causes of their current price are their scarcity and plenty and the high or low degree of competition between sellers and buyers' (I.N.E.D., 1958, vol. II, p. 752).[11]

Therefore there are two main forces which influence the prices of commodities: supply, that is to say the quantity which has been produced during the year, and competition. This is a very general remark, but Quesnay provides a more detailed analysis of the determination of prices. He gives a precise description of the working of scarcity and of competition, and of the situations in which prices depend either on one or the other of the two causes. This examination is part of Quesnay's overall study of the process of circulation of commodities between the classes of society. In fact, for him the market not only reflects the opposite actions of buyers and sellers, but it is also the instrument which regulates the contrasting interests of all classes, by means of the determination of the exchange value of commodities. But the analysis of this part of Quesnay's value theory requires a careful definition of the various notions of price he introduces and of their mutual relationships.

3.3 The distinction between current and retail price

Quesnay uses many concepts of price, whose precise definition is not always easy to isolate, because it requires long, and sometimes pedantic, analysis of the philological context. Thus, it might be useful to the reader to have at the outset a brief definition of two of the major concepts of price used by the physiocrats. Quesnay often speaks of *prix du vendeur* and of *prix de l'acheteur*, which we shall call current and retail price respectively (see for instance *Hommes*, I.N.E.D., 1958, vol. II, pp. 532–3; *Lettre de M. Alpha*, ibid., p. 942). The current price is the price that the merchants pay either to the artisans or to the farmers, the direct producers of commodities, and it coincides with the concept of price in the sales at first-hand. Thus it is the price to be used for the measurement of national wealth.[12] The retail price refers to the market value which is paid by the consumer to the tradesman on the retail market. The two notions refer to different acts of exchange, and the merchants are the middlemen between the two markets. We shall see that these price notions provide empirical background and give a precise meaning to the main political issues and policy recommendations of physiocracy. For example, the concept of current price is used by the physiocrats to indicate the price established in first-hand markets by international competition, which is used in the *Tableau* for the evaluation of wealth and of revenue.[13]

Quesnay calculates the current and retail price with the aid of numerical examples derived from two tables, which can be found in the articles *Hommes* and *Grains* respectively (I.N.E.D., 1958, vol. II, pp. 532, 462):

The two tables refer to trading conditions in France in the middle of the eighteenth century when exports of corn were highly restricted. The poor economic situation of the country is reflected in the first two columns of the tables. The first describes the annual variations of agricultural output per unit of land.[14] Call x_j the quantity of corn produced in year j on each *arpent* of land.[15] The second column gives the unit prices of corn obtained by the cultivator when he brings the output to market and sells it. Hence they are the prices of first-hand markets, and y_j refers to the price of a *setier* of corn in year j.

Therefore the figures in the first two columns are precisely the two sets of data which must be used to measure the wealth of the nation: the prices of the sales at first-hand and the quantities of agricultural products (see section 2.3).[16] In fact the figures in the third column are given by the product $x_j \cdot y_j$, i.e. the gross monetary revenue accruing to the farmer from the sale of the output of each *arpent*. It is easy to find the quantities of corn which are actually purchased each year on the market by consumers who are able to pay for the product at its

Table 1   *État des prix du blé France, où l'exportation des grains est défendue*

Années	Setiers par arpent	Prix du setier	Total par arpent	Prix, taille et fermage par arpent
		£	£	
abondantes	7	10	70	
bonnes	6	12	72	
médiocres	5	15	75	74 £
faibles	4	20	80	
mauvaises	3	30	90	
	25	87	387	370 £

Table 2

Années	Setiers par arpent	Prix du setier	Total par arpent	Frais par arpent	Reste par arpent
Abondante	7 set.	10 liv.	70 liv.	60 liv.	10 liv.
Bonne	6	12	72		12
Moyenne	5	15	75		15
Faible	4	20	80		20
Mauvaise	3	30	90		30
TOTAL pour les cinq années	25	87	387		87

varying current price. Given the amount of cultivated land, which is fixed and corresponds to a number, K, of *arpents*,[17] the value of the overall output is $K \cdot x_j \cdot y_j$.

The figures in the two tables have precise links with Quesnay's analysis of the working of market mechanisms. With these calculations he intends to explain the difference between the values of the current and the retail price. In particular, he wants to prove that the buyer's average price is always higher than that of the seller, *just because of* the huge variations in the price of corn. In effect, he calculates that the price of a *setier* of wheat is '17 *liv. 8 s.* This has been approximately the ordinary price in the sales of our corn at Paris for a long time: but the common price for the farmers, who are the sellers, is only approximately 15 *liv.* 9 *s.*, because of the variations in the harvests' (*Grains*, I.N.E.D., 1958 vol. II, p. 462, note 1 to the table). Quesnay uses the term *prix commun* to indicate the average price between different years, in which the output of corn per *arpent* is assumed to vary from a very high level to a very low one.[18]

The average price of a *setier* of corn, p_a, is defined as follows: 'the common price of the buyer, who purchases the same quantity of corn every year for his own consumption, depends entirely on variations in prices over many years' (*Hommes*, ibid., p. 531).

p_a is an average value which takes into account changes in the price of corn in sales at first-hand, but is not affected by the quantity which is sold on that market. In fact, although p_a derives from the figures in the second column, which refer to current prices in sales at first-hand, it is clearly the price paid to the merchant by the consumer on a different market, the retail one. But the consumers need approximately the same amount of corn each year. Therefore, the quantity exchanged on the retail market is always the same (ibid.) and does not affect the average price paid by them. Quesnay gives a precise formula to calculate the retail price: 'a man consumes 3 *setiers* of wheat each year, that is to say 15 *setiers* in 5 years, for which he pays 261 *liv.*, or 3 times 87 *liv.*' (ibid., p. 532). This is the sum of the different prices of wheat over five years, as indicated in the second column of the two tables. '261 *liv.* divided by 15 *setiers* gives 17 *liv.* 8 *d.* for the price of each *setiers*. This has been the ordinary common price in France for a long time' (ibid.). Therefore p_a is the sum of the prices divided by the number of years:

$$p_a = \frac{\sum_1^5 y_j}{5} = \frac{87 \ livres}{5 \ setiers} = 17 \ livres \ 8 \ sous$$

The *prix commun de l'acheteur* is an average of the current prices over five years, but it is not weighted by the quantities produced and sold each year; it depends only on the different levels of the current price in the five years. On the other hand the quantities exchanged on first-hand markets vary over the five years, hence they influence the average current price of corn, which is paid by the merchant to the farmer in that period: 'the common price of the seller, who does not harvest and sell the same quantity of corn every year, depends on the different prices and the different quantities of corn sold at different prices over a number of years' (ibid., p. 531). Therefore the average current price is a weighted average of the prices in the sales at first-hand, where the weights are the quantities of corn produced and exchanged each year. p_v is:

$$p_v = \frac{\sum_{1}^{5} {}_j x_j \cdot y_j}{\sum_{1}^{5} {}_j x_j} = \frac{387 \; livres}{25 \; setiers} = \quad 15 \; liv. \; 9 \; s. \; 7 \; d. \; 1/5\text{th}$$

(ibid., p. 532; by mistake Quesnay wrote: 15 *liv.* 9 *d.* 7, 1/5ᵉ').

3.4 Conflicts in the circulation of commodities

With his numerical examples Quesnay provides further specifications for the working of market laws and the process of price formation. In particular, he explains both the huge fluctuations in first-hand prices and their difference from those paid by consumers. Moreover, Quesnay's analysis of the process of circulation of commodities provides a much more precise description than is traditonally believed of his view of the economic classes in the France, and of their roles in the production and exchange of commodities. The well known threefold classification of individuals, as belonging to the productive or to the sterile class, or as proprietors, is only a first approximation to the many groups envisaged by the physiocrats.

An important feature of Quesnay's investigation of the market exchange economy is the fact that the cultivators do not sell their products directly to the final consumers. Merchants manage to interpose themselves between the producers and the consumers of commodities. Their activity is not limited to the mere transportation of products from one province to another and from the countryside to the town; nor does it constitute a sporadic and unusual phenomenon. On the contrary, professional traders occupy the most active and powerful role in the process of circulation and exchange, as described by Quesnay in the following passage:

> the cultivator and the manufacturer, who sell to the merchant similarly turn to account the money they receive from the merchant by regenerating exchangeable products. The proprietor uses the money he receives from his farmer to purchase the foreign

commodities which the merchant has imported; and the merchant returns this money to the farmer who sells him the products yielded by his cultivation (*Hommes*, Meek, 1962, pp. 92–3).

Merchants are the necessary links between farmers and artisans, who produce the commodities, and landlords and other consumers who want to buy them; hence they operate on both retail and first-hand markets.

However, the merchants take advantage of their privileged position in the process of circulation, and gain at the expense of both consumers and producers. Referring to two individuals who want to exchange wine and corn, Mercier de la Rivière calls the merchant the '*agent intermediare* who keeps for himself ten measures on your corn and the same on my wine' (Mercier, 1767, p. 278). Tradesmen operate only in their own interest, 'which is always that of buying as cheap as possible and selling as dear as possible' (*Lettre de M. Alpha*, I.N.E.D., 1958, vol. II, p. 947). The interest of professional traders are opposed to those of the majority of citizens, and their profits must not be accounted for as revenues for the nation, since they are simply the result of buying and selling commodities which already exist. Quesnay says that even the profits of the merchants in foreign trade damage the people of a country, because they increase the prices of the commodities imported. 'Then the increase in the fortunes of these merchants represents a deduction from the circulation of the revenue, which is detrimental to distribution and reproduction' (*Extrait*, Kuczynski and Meek 1972, p. 3; see also *Grains*, Meek 1962, p. 73 and *Maximes Générales*, I.N.E.D., 1958, vol. II, p. 955). Hence, all the gains of tradesmen are an additional burden both on the producers and on consumers, because they are interposed between the price of the sales at first-hand and the retail price of a commodity. The activity of tradesmen has negative effects on the revenue of both the cultivators and the sovereign, hence their activity is detrimental to the distribution and reproduction of revenue.

The concepts of current and retail price clarify the economic mechanisms which allow merchants to exploit their position as middlemen and to make a gain. The third column of each table gives figures for the gross revenue per *arpent* of the producers; hence they are also the annual costs of the merchants.

$\sum_{1}^{5}{}_{j} x_j \cdot y_j = 387$ *liv.* are the overall expenses involved in the purchase of 25 *setiers* of corn over five years. And p_v is the average unit cost of a *setier* of corn to the merchant. Therefore before selling corn to the consumers they can calculate its average current price over the last five years, which tells them the level of retail price below which they make a loss. Hence p_v is one of the magnitudes on which professional traders base their economic decisions. In fact, according to Quesnay, the merchant can take advantage of the fact that he operates in two markets, because he has the possibility of building up stocks, that is to say he is not compelled to resell the goods he buys immediately, but can wait for the best time. Merchants can 'close their granaries hoping for an increase in prices' (*Grains*, I.N.E.D., p. 494, note 23). Thus, in years of plenty they are not eager to buy corn, because they still have it in their granaries; this implies that there is a lack of competition between French merchants, so that the current price is brought down to a very low level; thus tradesmen can buy most of their stocks at a very convenient price. In years of scarcity, stocks allow tradesmen to limit their demand and to prevent the establishment of even higher current prices, which would be more profitable to the farmers.

Unlike the cultivator, the merchants can gain from their activity because they are the masters in both markets, being the only ones who can take decisions about their behaviour as both sellers and buyers. But they cannot behave in exactly the same way in the two markets. In the sales at first-hand, tradesmen as well as farmers are subject to the working of systematic market forces and cannot decisively influence the current price. They can only modify the quantities in stock and calculate the average cost before resale.

But on the retail market, where they are confronted with a stable demand, merchants have a major influence on prices. In fact, in order to gain from fluctuations in the current price, they must follow a very simple and straightforward rule: to fix a retail price which is the simple average of the first-hand prices over the previous five years. Given the inverse relationship between the quantities of a product sold and its current prices, the average cost to the merchant, p_v, which is a weighted average, overrates the importance of the lower values of the current price; hence it is always smaller than the simple average p_a. This happens because merchants are wealthy enough to build up stocks, which allow them to leave a period of time between their purchases and their sales; thus they can decide their price policy on retail markets. Therefore there is a clear difference between the *prix commun de l'acheterur* and the *prix commun de vendeur*; p_v is a notional magnitude in the book-keeping of the merchants, while p_a is the actual market price in the exchange between tradesmen and consumers.

The farmers can also calculate p_v, at the end of a five-year period during which they have experienced different prices in sales at first-hand of their corn; the average current price is the average return to the cultivator on each *setier* of corn. However, they cannot derive from this any indication of their future behaviour as sellers: 'the average price, made up from that of several years, is not a guide for him; he does not at all share in this compensation' (*Fermiers*, Groenewegen, 1983, p. 14). The balancing of prices between bad and good years has an important influence on the economic conditions of the cultivators, but they cannot react by influencing current prices, because 'they cannot await more favourable times to sell their wheat' (ibid.). They cannot store the surplus in order to wait for the next market to take place; the entire output *has to be sold*, either during or at the end of the period of production: 'for the cultivator has either to sell at whatever the price happens to be or to give up cultivation for the market' (*Second problème économique*, Meek, 1962, p. 195). Poor farmers cannot decide when to sell their output, because it is only by its immediate sale that they can obtain the financial means necessary to carry on production. The cultivators must accept the current price in sales at first-hand; if it does not cover their expenses they can only decide to cease their activity.

It must be noted that for Quesnay farmers are unable to keep stocks of the products of land, not so much because of the physical qualities, that is to say, the perishability of agricultural commodities, but because they are too poor to be able to stock them. Only rich farmers can postpone selling their wheat until the price rises (see *Grains*, I.N.E.D., 1958, vol. II, p. 469; see also Mirabeau, 1764, vol. I, pp. 372–3). But this is an exceptional situation, where the direct producers of commodities are rich enough to take advantage of price changes. It is more usual for cultivators to suffer from price variations. Poor farmers must sell their products as soon as they can, at whatever price they can obtain; they need money to pay wages to the peasants, to buy tools and equipment from the artisans and to pay rent. The sale of the entire annual output is essential in order to carry on cultivation, since farmers do not have enough financial means and stocks of products.

Apart from the poverty of the cultivators, another cause of huge fluctuations in the current price of corn is the lack of freedom in foreign trade. Quesnay is mainly worried by the possibility of a fall in the current price of corn, but the relationship between the quantity of a commodity sold on the market and its price also works in the other direction:

> in a state which has no external trade at all, either of export or of import, the price of produce cannot be subject to any rule or any order. It necessarily follows the variations of scarcity and abundance in the country, and the state has to put up with excessively low or excessively high prices, both of which are equally disastrous and inevitable (*Hommes*, Meek, 1962, p. 93).

The major problem of a country where exports of corn are forbidden is that its total demand is limited to its internal consumption. Thus with a given level of demand there is no incentive to increase annual production, because this leads to a fall in the price (see *Grains*, I.N.E.D., 1958, vol. II, p. 461). To sum up: the huge variations in current prices have two major causes: (a) the poverty of the producers, the farmers; (b) the lack of competition among buyers, the merchants, which derives from the existence of restrictions on foreign trade. For these two reasons the price for sales at first-hand is highly influenced by annual production.[19]

3.5 Competition as the panacea

Quesnay's analysis of the process of circulation of commodities explains the relative stability of the retail price of corn in France and its coexistence with huge variations in the current price.[20] This steadiness is a positive thing, but it is not in itself sufficient to characterise an economy where exchanges take place according to natural laws. The real problem for France is fluctuations in first-hand prices. For the physiocrats, the power of merchants increases this instability and prevents a reduction in the gap between current and retail price. If farmers could build up stocks, this would automatically equalise the values of a commodity's market price in different years. They could then postpone the sale of a product until its price started to rise; so the increase itself would be less, because there would be a larger quantity for sale on the market. In abundant harvests the cultivators would not be obliged to sell their entire output, but could leave part of it in their granaries, thus preventing a sharp fall in prices.

Unfortunately, most farmers are too poor to have stocks, so Quesnay must find other measures to limit the power of merchants. And here we see that the notions of current and retail price provide the analytical basis for one of the most important physiocratic contentions: the establishment of free competition in foreign trade. The price mechanisms in the two markets illustrate the dangerous effects of the exclusive power of merchants, both for the producers and for the consumers. According to the physiocrats this power can only be restricted by increasing the degree of competition among them, and this result is achieved by introducing free competition in foreign and domestic trade (see *Grains*, I.N.E.D., 1958, vol. II, p. 494, note 23).

According to Quesnay, in a market exchange economy prices are not necessarily influenced by sudden changes in annual output; on the contrary they are influenced mainly by the conditions and the rules of trade. 'Good or bad harvests do not simply regulate the price of wheat, freedom or constraints in the trade of this commodity are principally the determinants of its value' (*Fermiers*, Groenewegen, 1983, p. 18). It is competition, or the state of trade as Quesnay frequently calls it, that plays the dominant role in determining the market value of commodities.[21]

However, competition exerts its overwhelming influence only if the country has all the features of a competitive system which works according to the natural order of society. Thus, exchangers must all have the same opportunities and nobody can enjoy a particularly favourable market position. Wise rulers must implement the highest possible degree of competition by removing existing obstacles to its working; 'it is the greatest *possible* competition with no restrictions, either on the times of sale, or on the thing, or on people, which is *the one and only* rule of trade; the only *justice* that one must ask from rulers' (*Lettre de M. Alpha*, I.N.E.D., 1958, vol. II, p. 941, italics in original). Positive laws must ensure that there are no restrictions and exclusive privileges in the exchange and circulation of commodities. In particular, Quesnay wants to oppose the power of corporations and guilds, and to abolish the exclusive privileges of merchants, who are considered by him to be the major obstacle to national prosperity. This situation can be overcome by increasing the number of people who are allowed to trade; the existence of a large number of competitors reduces the power and the profits of merchants. If they try 'to sell a product at too high a price and to buy it too cheaply, another trader arrives, willing to offer a better deal in order to be preferred' (ibid., p. 947).

Quesnay intends to secure a large number of purchasers for the products of French agriculture, by means of freedom in foreign trade:

> for it is only through the greatest possible degree of competition, open to all the merchants in the world, that a nation can be sure of securing the best price and the most advantageous market for the products of its territory, and of preserving itself from the monopoly of the country's merchants (*Maximes Générales*, Meek, 1962, p. 259).

In this passage Quesnay envisages a direct relationship between the degree of competition and the market value of the product: the greater the former, the higher the latter. But if there are only a few merchants, either because of their wealth, or because they have been granted exclusive privileges, they can easily gain at the expense of all other parties, since they exploit their unique position (see *Lettre de M. Alpha*, I.N.E.D., 1958, vol. II, p. 940).

Besides abolishing exclusive privileges, another obvious fact can make the economy more competitive; the existence of an efficient system of communications, both inside and outside the country. Therefore the government must build up 'roads, canals, navigable rivers, harbours' (ibid., p. 941; see also *Du Commerce*, ibid., p. 830). An extended system of communications encourages the existence of a large number of competitors on each market; in fact it is easy to carry goods from one place to another, thanks to 'the reduction in the expenses of transportation' (ibid., p. 824).

To sum up: according to the physiocrats, in a competitive economy there must be no legal privileges and a good system of transportation. These two characteristics are needed to guarantee the existence of a third, and most important, feature: a large number of traders. If the rulers ensure the existence of the characteristics of a competitive system, free competition brings about all the positive effects which are inscribed in the natural order of society.[22] Therefore the greatest possible degree of competition on the market is regarded by Quesnay as a major remedy for the ills of the economy. It is the main positive influence on the level of first-hand prices, overshadowing the effects of scarce and abundant outputs. Even more important, competition reduces the rewards to the selfish behaviour of buyers and sellers, since it 'regulatés without violence, but despotically, the rights of these two groups of people' (Mercier, 1767, p. 207); thus only competition can reduce the power and profits of professional traders.

3.6 Foreign trade and the stability of prices

According to the physiocrats the most important effect of a competitive trading system is the equalisation of prices in all markets for the same product. Competition tends to establish a single price for each commodity, in whatever province or town it is marketed. The tendency towards the unification of prices and markets had already been described by Cantillon (see Cantillon, 1755, pp. 11–13), but in Quesnay's economics it has the specific task of preventing the establishment of powerful and wealthy merchants, who can take advantage of differences between prices in different places.

The effects of a competitive system are even more important in international trade; foreign competition equalises the prices of commodities in all the trading countries: 'for on the assumption of freedom of external trade the price will always be regulated by the competition of the neighbouring nations in the produce trade' *Grains*, Meek, 1962, p. 87; see also Du Pont, 1764, p. 14).[23] With no barriers to foreign trade and easy communications, domestic prices quickly adjust to the international ones and 'corn always commands a more equal price', because 'the slightest price advantage in a country attracts the commodity to it, and equality is continually re-established' (*Extrait*, Kuczynski and Meek, 1972, p. 8, note b).[24]

The process of equalisation is based on the activities of merchants, who try to exploit differences between prices in different countries: 'the free competition between the merchants who transport the products from a country to another in order to resell them, produces an increase of the price in the country where it is too low and diminishes it in the country where it is too high' (*Du Commerce*, I.N.E.D., 1958, vol. II, p. 817, see also pp. 829, 832). If there are abundant harvests in France, the home tradesmen will carry corn to countries where production has been lower and the market value is therefore higher. Foreign merchants compete with domestic ones in the purchase of internal output and the degree of competition among buyers, on French first-hand markets, is much higher than before. If French merchants are not prepared to pay higher prices to the cultivators they risk reducing their stock too much and having no corn to sell to the consumers. In a situation of scarcity, free importation of corn prevents the current price from rising too much, because domestic merchants can buy the same commodities from foreign producers, and foreign merchants bring their corn to the country because of its higher price.

Therefore, besides equalising relative prices among different nations, unobstructed trade and easy communications reduce the huge variations of the current price; this exchange value becomes much more stable than before. Foreign trade evens out differences in the agricultural output of different countries; in the same year some nations have plenty of products, while harvests in other countries are poor. Thus, thanks to 'this general intercommunication and these successive and mutual alternations of abundance and scarcity, prices always remain at an intermediate level', in contrast with the previous huge variations (*Hommes*, Meek, 1962, p. 95). Free and unobstructed trade is part of the natural order of society; hence when a country makes its commercial rules and laws conform with natural ones, it immediately reaps a benefit. Good and bad harvests have much less influence on prices, and there will be no more shortages and famines.[25]

For Quesnay contemporary England provides the best example of the benefits of *laissez-faire*, and in particular of the free exportation of corn. The following table is an example of how he sees the level of corn prices in England, where it can be freely imported and exported (*Hommes*, I.N.E.D. 1958, vol. II, p. 533)[26].

Table 3 *État des prix des blés conformément aux effects de l'exportation en Angleterre*

Années	Setiers par arpent	Prix du setier	Total par arpent	Prix, taille et fermage par arpent chaque année
		£	£	
abondantes	7	16	112	
bonnes	6	17	102	
médiocres	5	18	90	74 £
faibles	4	19	76	
mauvaises	3	20	60	
	25	90	440	370 £

Stability in the prices of foodstuffs is regarded by the physiocrats as one the main causes of the wealth and prosperity of England, because 'the nation neither suffers harvest failure, nor years of low value' (*Fermiers*, Groenewegen, 1983, p. 13).

However, for Quesnay free trade in the products of land is not simply a way of eliminating famines and guaranteeing a stable supply of foodstuffs for French consumers. For the reduction in the range of fluctuation of the prices received by farmers in sales of their products also raises the average value of the current price of corn from its previously low level. For instance, in England the *prix commun du vendeur* is 17 *livres* 12 *sous*, while the *prix commun de l'acheteur* is 18 *livres*.; the difference between the two is much less than in France, and the total gain made by merchants over the five years is 10 *livres* (in France is 48, for the same amount of corn): 450 *livres* (18 *livres* times 25 *setiers*) minus the 440 *livres* they must pay to the farmers. Thus, freeing the exports of the products of land reduces the profits of the merchants, and, with a small increase in the retail price, leaves a price for the cultivators which is much higher than before.

According to Quesnay the benefits of free foreign trade for the products of agriculture are not limited to farmers and the primary sector; on the contrary they spread over the whole French economy and reach all the different groups of people. In fact, the low level of the current price, resulting from the prohibition of corn exports, has destructive effects both on the gains of the cultivator and on the productive capacity of the agricultural sector; 'because the low price of wheat in preceding years . . . made him neglect his cultivation' (ibid., p. 14.; see also *Maximes Générales*, Meek, 1962, p. 256). Farmers abandon cultivation, or at least are not encouraged to increase their *avances primitives* and to introduce new methods of production. The stability of first-hand prices and the increase in their average level enable cultivators to raise their productive advances and to introduce the cultivation methods typical of large-scale farming (see below Chapter 5, 5.3). Thanks to the 'regularity in the corn price', the farmer, 'being not compelled to withhold his wheat from the market can always provide the expenses necessary for cultivation' (*Fermiers*, Groenewegen, 1983, pp. 13–14). The rise in current prices of agricultural products will then provide a fundamental incentive for raising the advances employed in the cultivation of soil. Moreover, it will stimulate the farmers 'to cultivate idle lands and to improve lands of inferior quality' (Du Pont, 1774, p. 14). A prosperous agricultural sector, characterised by the existence of rich farmers, yields higher outputs and surpluses for the country and is the main reason for general wealth and prosperity.[27]

B   THE FUNDAMENTAL PRICE OF COMMODITIES

3.7 A benchmark for the current price

The categories of current and retail price highlight some new and interesting features of the physiocrats' analysis of market exchange and the circulation of commodities. Quesnay's often neglected theory of value and prices constitutes another logical step in the development of economic theory which took place in the second half of the eighteenth century and led to the formation of classical political economy. His analysis of market forces and price determination contributed to this change in two ways. First, thanks to the introduction of free foreign trade, the market ceases to be regarded mainly as a place of struggle and confrontation among classes. Quesnay underlines the aspects of conciliation of interests and of overall welfare, which are inherent in competitive markets. It must be remarked that for Quesnay the market does not cease to be the place where the wealth and output of the economy are distributed, but the whole society benefits from competition, because all classes gain at the expense of the merchants.

A second important aspect of Quesnay's price theory concerns the current price; international competition greatly reduces its fluctuations and the quantity produced each year is rendered less important for the determination of prices in sales at first-hand. Competition becomes the most relevant factor in the process of price formation; it unifies the market value of a commodity in different countries; first-hand markets cease to be a place of instability where damage is done to the nation, and become an instrument of stability, prosperity and order. But even according to natural laws the market value of commodities fluctuates from year to year; it is the task of this chapter to examine whether and how, according to the physiocrats, these price movements tend towards any specific level, which then fixes the current price of commodities. Quesnay's analysis of price determination goes further than saying that stability of the current price depends on international competition and natural laws. In this case the influence on prices of scarcity and abundance of products would simply be replaced by the almighty, but vacuous, word 'competition'. On the contrary, Quesnay thoroughly investigates the nature of this stable level of prices in sales at first-hand; he examines the factors which determine its value, and the forces which relate it to day-to-day changes in the current price.

In physiocratic analysis, the value of the current price changes continuously, while the *prix fondamental* is remarkably stable. But these two notions are connected, because Quesnay does not accept the idea that the current price fluctuates erratically. He believes that the process of price formation is influenced by natural laws, and not by chaos. Therefore the fundamental value of a commodity defines the stable and permanent level of the current price in sales at first-hand. In *Hommes*, discussing a situation in which there is free competition in international markets, Quesnay writes:

> as result of this general intercommunication and these successive and mutual alternations of abundance and scarcity, prices always remain at an intermediate level, determined by the average fundamental price in these countries which are joined together by trade (Meek, 1962, p. 95).

Therefore the level at which the current price finally settles is not the result of the opposing forces of supply and demand, but is regulated by the fundamental price of commodities. This is the most important notion of price introduced by Quesnay, because it provides a benchmark for all the other price concepts used by the physiocrats, and illustrates their view of the value of commodities. In effect, an examination of the elements which determine the fundamental price of products reveals the features of Quesnay's theory of value. In particular, the analysis of this notion is necessary to see whether Quesnay regarded as privileged the influence on prices either of supply and demand, or of cost of production.

Before examining Quesnay's definition of fundamental price it may be useful to have a quick look at the state of value theory before the physiocrats. This should help to locate their contribution in the development of history of economics. It should also allow us to evaluate Quesnay's theory of price in the light of his role as a precursor of Smith's analysis of the value of commodities.

3.8 The 'physical costs' theory of prices

Most pre-physiocratic economists believed that the forces that went under the traditional headings of 'supply' and 'demand' affected the market values of commodities (see for instance: Sewall, 1901,

     The Economics of François Quesnay

pp. 39–40; Hollander, 1973, pp. 29–33). While it was believed that 'supply' and 'demand' could explain the fluctuations of prices, it was also felt that they did not determine the particular level around which these fluctuations were occurring. This was ultimately determined by other forces. As early as Montchrétien's *Traicté de l'oeconomie politique* of 1615 we find a distinction between the price of a commodity, which fluctuates, and its value, which is always the same (see Beer, 1939, pp. 37–8; Montchrétien, 1615, p. 257).

Seventeenth-century scholars gave the question of the 'true value' of commodities much more importance than that of variations in market prices. For most of the century the central problem was that of determining the just price of goods,[28] which was identified mainly with the amount of expenses and labour which had to be incurred in order to obtain a certain quantity of them (see Beer, 1939, pp. 121–2). The costs and expenses incurred in the production of a commodity constituted a sort of standard, to which the market values had ultimately to conform (see Bowley, 1973, pp. 67–9). Another concept was that of *valeur intrinsique*.[29] Each commodity has a *valeur intrinsique* which must not be confused with the 'vibrations' of its price (see Steuart, 1767, vol. 1, p. 202). The notion of intrinsic value and the abandoning of the scholastic discussion of the 'justness' of prices lent strength to the view that the causes of the true value of commodities would not be found in the forces of supply and demand.

Other expressions were adopted to indicate the underlying value of commodities; Sir James Steuart also spoke of 'real value', by which he meant the cost of production of a commodity (see ibid, pp. 159–61). Boisguillebert, one of the forerunners of physiocracy, in his *Dissertation sur la nature des richesses, de l'argent at des tributs*, says that commodities have a sort of necessary price (see Routh, 1975, p. 58), which is the lowest possible level covering the expenses and the profits of the merchant, thus preventing any loss (see Boisguillebert, 1707–14, p. 404).

It is widely believed that before Smith and his notion of natural price the various 'real', 'intrinsic' and 'necessary' values of commodities were merely different expressions for the physical costs incurred in their production, including all material expenses which were necessary to obtain them (see Meek, 1962, pp. 334, 352).[30] The precise specification of these expenses varied widely from author to author; from Hutcheson's vague ideas concerning the 'difficulty of acquiring, or cultivating a commodity' (Hutcheson, 1754–5, p. 54; see also Scott, 1900, pp. 235–37) to Petty, for whom the expenses of production were nothing more than the amounts of land and labour which had been used up as inputs (see Bowley, 1973, pp. 84–6).

Petty, and later Cantillon, gave the physical costs view of prices a clear and more precise significance.[31] Cantillon made a sharp distinction between the market price of a commodity and its intrinsic value, which 'is the measure of the quantity of Land and of Labour entering into its production, having regard to the fertility or produce of the Land and to the quality of the Labour' (Cantillon, 1755, p. 29). He accepts and specifies Petty's indication that 'all things ought to be valued by two natural Denominations, which is Land and Labour' (Petty, 1662, p. 44). The physical costs explanation of prices is based on the simple idea that each commodity requires labour and natural resources (land) for its production. The value of the tools and equipment consumed in production can be reduced to the quantities of land and labour necessary to make them. Land and labour alone are the common constituent elements of all commodities. In order to have a single figure for the instrinsic value of a commodity, Cantillon must find an appropriate ratio which transforms the quantities of labour into a corresponding amount of land. This is possible because 'the value of the day's work has a relation to the produce of the soil' (Cantillon, 1755, p. 41). Therefore the quantity of labour necessary to produce a commodity can be substituted 'by the quantity of land of which the produce is allotted to those who have worked upon it' (ibid). The value of a commodity is determined by the amount of land which, either directly or indirectly, has been used in its production.

Cantillon's suggestions for determining the intrinsic value can be elucidated as follows. Suppose that L and l are the amounts of land and labour used in the production of one unit of commodity A; r is the rent per unit of land measured in terms of a composite commodity, corn, made up of agricultural products; rL is the quantity of corn necessary to produce one unit of A; $\bar{w}$ is the real wage rate, in terms of corn, which is assumed to be at a subsistence level.[32] Wages are entirely made up of agricultural commodities (in fixed quantities and proportions); thus $\bar{w}$ is the necessary consumption of each worker. In order to find the intrinsic value of A, p_A, one must transform the value of labour (in terms of corn), $\bar{w}l$, into the equivalent quantity of land. With given techniques of production in agriculture, the quantity of corn $\bar{w}l$ consumed by the workers in the production of one unit of A is:

$$\bar{w}l = \bar{w}l_w + rL_w$$

l_w and L_w are the quantities of labour and land necessary to produce the amount $\bar{w}l$ of corn, with $l > l_w$. The expression

$$\bar{w} = r\,\frac{L_w}{l - l_w}$$

shows the 'Par, or Equation between Land and Labour', which was regarded by Petty 'as the most important consideration in Political Arithmetic' (Cantillon, 1755, p. 43; see Petty, 1662, pp. 44–5). This equation gives the value of one unit of labour directly used in the production of A, which is in proportion to $\dfrac{L_w}{l - l_w}$; this is the amount of

land necessary to produce the quantities of goods given to workers as the wage for one unit of labour. The intrinsic value of commodity A is

$$p_A = rL + \bar{w}l = rL + l\,\frac{rL_w}{l - l_w} = r\left(L + l\,\frac{L_w}{l - l_w}\right)$$

The expression in parentheses is the quantity of land which is directly and indirectly required to produce one unit of the commodity. The intrinsic value of the commodity is in proportion to this quantity of land (see Herlitz, 1961b, pp. 113–14).

3.9 The determination of the fundamental price

We can now investigate Quesnay's precise definition of the concept of fundamental price and its innovative aspects, if any, with respect to the state of the theory of prices in the middle of the eighteenth century. In particular, it is interesting to see whether the physiocratic theory of value is a modification of the physical costs explanation of prices. Indeed the fundamental price has normally been identified by commentators with the technical cost of production of commodities (see for instance Meek, 1962, p. 389; Salleron, I.N.E.D., 1958, vol. II, p. 529, note 14; Cartelier, 1976, p. 51). It will be shown that for the physiocrats the fundamental price of agricultural products also includes a net element, rent, as well as the technical expenses of production.

Quesnay gives a clear-cut definition of the notion of fundamental price; in the article *Hommes* he writes:

the fundamental price of commodities is determined by the expenses or costs which have to be incurred in their production or preparation. If they are sold for less than they have cost, their price sinks to a level at which a loss is made (Meek, 1962, p. 93).

Two elements define the fundamental price. First, it is the sum of the expenses incurred by producers. Secondly, this price is also seen as the particular level of the current price below which producers make a loss (see Du Pont, 1774, pp. 7–8). In order to single out the component parts of the *prix fondamental* it is essential to consider both the features assigned by Quesnay to this category.

The first aspect, the cost of production, does not present many problems. Quesnay distinguishes the *prix fondamental* of the products of land from the *prix fondamental* of manufactures, because farmers and artisans incur different types of expenses in production. The costs to the artisan are made up of two basic items: (a) the raw materials, (b) subsistence goods for himself and for the workers he employs (see *Sur les travaux des artisans*, Meek, 1962, p. 213).[33] The *prix fondamental* of primary products is also equal to the expenses incurred by farmers for the cultivation of land. As in the case of manufactured commodities the cost of production of agricultural goods includes workers' wages. But Quesnay's analysis of the means of production of agriculture shows that the other expenses do not only include raw materials (see above Chapter 2, 2.5 and 2.6).[34] These are part of the annual advances, but there are also the original advances, which may be regarded as a kind of fixed capital. Each year one tenth of the value of the original advances must be accounted for as a cost by agricultural entrepreneurs, as a sort of annual charge necessary to preserve the stock of original advances from wear and tear and from deterioration. An initial difference between the fundamental price of manufactured commodities and that of the products of land arises from the fact that in agriculture there is fixed capital; hence the cost of production of commodities must include its depreciation allowance.

In attempting to establish the precise analytical content of the notion of fundamental price, almost all commentators have focused attention on the first element of the definition: the physical cost of production. The second, the price level at which the producer makes no losses, has been greatly overshadowed. This fact has led to frequent misunderstandings of the physiocratic notions of fundamental price. In fact, because the second aspect has been neglected, this concept has been identified with the physical cost of production of commodities in the strict sense of the word (see for instance Schelle, 1907, p. 313; Higgs, 1897, p. 124), which in the case of primary products includes wages, raw materials and the replacement of equipment used up in production (see Sewall, 1901, p. 88). According to this interpretation Quesnay takes a physical costs approach to the question of price determination. His price theory can be regarded as a variation of the 'land theory of value' of Cantillon,[35] and 'fundamental price' would be a different way of referring to *valeur intrinsique*. The physiocratic contribution would then be of little interest in the history of price theory.

In defining the *prix fondamental* as the technical expenses of production, most interpreters of physiocracy do not regard rent as part of the fundamental price of the products of agriculture. For instance Meek writes that 'in the case of agricultural produce, the 'market value' was higher than the 'fundamental price' by an amount equal (roughly) to rent' (Meek, 1962, p. 389); thus rent is not part of the fundamental price. However, the second element of Quesnay's definition of fundamental price says that it is the level of current price at which producers make neither losses nor gains. This is the minimum selling price for producers, and cannot be identified simply with the physical unit cost of production of commodities.[36] We shall see that the major difference between the fundamental price of the products of industry and that of primary commodities does not consist in the depreciation of fixed capital, but in the fact that, as well as material costs, the fundamental value of the products of land includes rent. Traditional interpretations have failed to bring out that in the case of the products of land the fundamental price is made up also of a *net element*, rent, which is part of the surplus of the economy.[37] By taking into account the two elements it is therefore possible to give a new and precise interpretation of the important analytical role played by the concept of fundamental price in Quesnay's analysis of the process of reproduction of society. As will be shown, an analysis of this price notion brings to light a new interpretation of the dual aspect of rent in physiocracy, as both cost and revenue.

Since this is a novel view of Quesnay's notion of fundamental price, one must carefully examine both the direct textual evidence and the way in which he uses this concept, especially in relation to those of current and retail price. In *Hommes* Quesnay gives a definition of *prix fondamental*. He writes: 'the necessary expenses for production of foodstuffs establish their fundamental price and the price degenerates into a loss when it falls below this fundamental price' (I.N.E.D., 1958, vol. II, p. 555).[38]

Of course, the cultivators suffer a loss when the current price fails to cover the sum of wages, raw materials and the consumption of fixed capital for the production of one unit of product. But the farmer can make a loss even if the current price is higher than this unit cost of production in the strict sense of the word, i.e. without rent. This happens if the difference between the current price and the technical cost of production is less than the rent that the cultivator must pay the proprietor on each unit of product. In fact farmers must pay the rent to landlords irrespective of the current price they receive in sales of the products at first-hand; In fact 'their land-leases, which are concluded for three, six or nine years, impose the payment of a fixed sum of money' (Sée, 1967, p. 26; see also Du Pont, 1767, p. 353).[39] Referring to cultivators, Quesnay speaks of 'the price of *fermage* they engage themselves to pay for the duration of their *baux*' (*Réponse au Mémoire de M.H.*, I.N.E.D., 1958, vol. II, p. 752). (*Bail* is an expression which indicates the landlease contract between the farmer and the landlord.) Rent is the result of a private contract by which the farmer acquires the right to exploit the soil for a certain number of years. These *baux* are 'free agreements established between these two classes', proprietors and cultivators (Le Trosne, 1777, p. 927, see also Mercier, 1767, p. 213).

Therefore the payment of rent implies a regular outflow of money, by the farmers, if they intend to carry on cultivation. But one must remember that the fundamental price of primary products has also to be defined both as the expenses of production and as that particular level of the current price at which farmers make neither losses nor profits. This price is given by the sum of the values of raw materials, wages, the interest on fixed capital and rent. From the point of view of society as a whole only the first three items are termed costs, and rent is a surplus element. Therefore the physical unit cost of production of agricultural commodities cannot now define their fundamental value, because it does not satisfy the second part of Quesnay's definition of this category.

Besides rent, which accrues to landowners, Quesnay makes some kinds of taxes part of the fundamental price of primary commodities (see *Hommes*, I.N.E.D., 1958, vol. II, p. 555).[40] The physiocrats include in the *prix fondamental* a particular tax, the *taille*, or 'territorial tax' (see Meek, 1962, pp. 140–1), which is a payment by farmers to the central administration of the country and constitutes the main source of revenue for the sovereign and the state. Quesnay and his disciples clearly regard rent and *taille* as net elements. More precisely, they are the shares of net product accruing to proprietors and the crown respectively, and hence cannot be taken as mere costs of production; nevertheless they are part of the fundamental price of corn.[41]

The physiocrats consider rent and *taille* as the shares of social surplus which are appropriated by the landlords and by the state; thus they are part of the net revenues of the country. But for Quesnay they are also part of the expenses of cultivators. He writes: 'the farmers, who are obliged during the term of their leases to pay constantly the same sums for rent, taxes and other fixed charges' (*Premier probléme économique*, Meek, 1962, p. 181, note 1; see also *Impôts*, I.N.E.D., 1958, vol. II, p. 616). Thus the actual amount of money paid by the cultivator to the proprietor was, at least at first, independent of the monetary value of the net product. The *baux* were normally renewed every nine years, and during this period changes in the value of the surplus did not affect the level of rent and *taille*. The amounts of rent, *taille* and other duties are fixed in terms of money, while their shares in the surplus obviously vary depending on the yearly variations in the value of the net product.

In the article *Fermiers* Quesnay looks at the expenses of a farmer for the cultivation of forty *arpents* of land using horses. Among other items we find: 'the rent of land . . . 640 *livres*, the *taille*, *gabelle* and other taxation . . . 320 *livres*' (Groenewegen, 1983, p. 15). A careful analysis of his figures shows that the total sum of money necessary for the cultivation of that piece of land is obtained by adding to rent and *taille*, whose sum is 960 *livres*, the physical and technical costs of production of corn, 2250 *livres*. The total expenses of cultivators are thus 3210 *livres*, which are 'the outlays of wheat for forty acres' (ibid., p. 16).[42] Quesnay then repeats the whole calculation in order to find the cost of production of buckwheat, instead of wheat, on the same area of land, and here too rent appears as a component of expenses of production (see ibid.).

From all of this, it is clear that Quesnay's term *frais*, the expenses of production of primary products, includes, together with rent and *taille*, the value of the physical costs of production. In his list of the expenses of cultivation he adopts the point of view of the farmers; he specifies all the items which entail a monetary outflow from cultivators in order to continue production. (Part of the *avances* are made up of primary commodities and do not need to be purchased by the farmers, who already possess them – see above Chapter 2, 2.6). Rent and *taille* are necessary payments made by cultivators. They therefore must be accounted for in the fundamental price of agricultural products, even if they are revenues from the point of view of the economy as a whole.

The interpretation which includes rent and *taille* in the concept of fundamental price is also supported by the figures and arguments Quesnay uses to describe the trading conditions of corn in France and England.[43] In the article *Hommes*, he calculates the fundamental price of wheat, starting from a figure, 74 *livres*, which, according to the heading of the last column of Table 1, is the sum of '*Prix, taille et fermage par arpent*'.[44] Seventy-four *livres* multiplied by five years give 370 *livres*, which are the cultivator's overall expenses for producing 25 *setiers* of wheat during the five years. Then Quesnay calculates the *prix commun fondamental* (remember that the term *commun* indicates that this is an average value): '370 *livres* of expenses divided by 25 *setiers* give 14 *liv*. 16 *d*. which is the average price that each *setier* costs the husbandman' (*Hommes*, I.N.E.D., 1958, vol. II, p. 532). Therefore the fundamental price of 14 *livres* and 16 *sous* (Quesnay erroneously writes *d*.) includes both rent and *taille*. This value of the *prix fondamental* is almost the same as the 14 *liv*. 15 *s*. 8 *d*. which constitutes the unit cost of production of corn in Table 2 (see *Grains*, ibid., p. 462), where it also explicitly includes *taille* and rent (see ibid., p. 463). It is the minimum selling price farmers would accept, at which they make neither losses nor gains.[45]

In an examination of Quesnay's notion of fundamental price one must not be deceived by the fact that he starts the calculation from a quantity, 74 *livres*, which is the sum of three items, *prix taille et fermage*, whose sizes are not yet specified; moreover one of these elements is rather vaguely called *prix* in Tables 1 and 3 (see *Hommes*, ibid., pp. 532–3). A joint examination of these two tables and those of *Grains* shows that Quesnay uses the term *prix* to indicate *only* the technical costs of production and that the fundamental price includes two net items; rent and *taille*. The tables in *Grains* (ibid., pp. 462, 474) have five columns instead of four; the last two columns have the headings '*Frais par arpent*' and '*Reste par arpent*' respectively (the fifth column of the table, which refers to England, has '*Reste*' only). The annual expenses for the cultivation of one *arpent* of land are given as 60 *livres*, and they are constant over the five years. The '*reste*', however, varies from year to year because it is given by the difference between the figures in column 3, i.e. the money received by the farmer for the sale of the output of an *arpent*, and the 60 *livres* of corresponding expenses. The total residual during the five years is 87 *livres*, and 17 *livres* and 8 *sous* is the average net product of cultivation on each *arpent* of land. This surplus is distributed between the *taille* for the government, the rent for the landlords, and a gain for the farmer (see *Grains*, I.N.E.D., 1958, vol. 11, p. 463).[46]

But there is an important difference between rent and taxes on one side, and the cultivator's gain on the other; only the first two items are part of the fundamental price. Quesnay writes: '60 *liv.* of expenses and 13 *liv.* 18 *s.* 6 *d.* for the landlords and for the tax, make 73 *liv.* 18 *s.* 6 *d.* for an *arpent* of wheat, which on average produces 5 *setiers*, thus each *setier* costs the farmer 14 15 8' (ibid.).[47] Therefore the sum of costs, *taille* and rent, for each *arpent*, divided by the average output of corn of an *arpent*, gives the cost of a *setier* of corn to the farmer; i.e. the fundamental price, which does not include the cultivator's gain. Notice that the sum of *frais*, *taille* and rent is 73 *liv.* 17 *s.* 1 *d.* and is almost equal to the 74 *liv.* of the last column of Table 1, which represents the sum of '*prix, taille et fermage*', where the word *prix* must be interpreted as including the expenses of cultivation, which are different from *taille* and rent.

To sum up: in the case of primary commodities the two elements of the notion of *prix fondamental* are satisfied by the overall expenses incurred by farmers in cultivating land. Some of these expenses are due to purely technical factors and are costs both for farmers and for the country as a whole. Other monetary outflows, rent and *taille*, arise for social, juridical and political reasons, and although they represent monetary expenses for cultivators, they also make up part of the surplus of the country. The fundamental price of one *setier* of corn is defined in the following way:

Fundamental price = costs + *taille* + rent

The technical expenses of production are:

costs = wages + raw materials + consumption of fixed capital

In Quesnay's terminology the costs are the annual *reprises*: the sum of the annual advances and the interest on the original advances (see *Analyse*, Meek, 1962, p. 154).

3.10 Rent as a cost and as a revenue

From what has been said above, the physiocratic category of *prix fondamental* looks very up-to-date for Quesnay's days, because it includes both costs and an item which is part of the surplus. One is immediately reminded of Smith's 'natural price' which is the sum of wages, rent and profits (see Smith, 1776, vol. 1, p. 62).[48] The originality of Smith's notion is unquestionable, but it may be interesting to analyse the reasons why Quesnay stressed the existence of a net element among the costs of the cultivator. The traditional views of the notion of fundamental price fail to highlight the very important role that this concept plays in physiocratic economics. It resolves the contradiction between rent as a cost and as a revenue. Rent can be considered as a cost for the farmer without losing its main characteristic of being a revenue for the country as a whole.

Quesnay sometimes underlines the revenue aspect of rent, and on other occasions he remarks on the fact that it is a cost. Like other notions, rent is used in different ways according to the particular economic aspect Quesnay wants to stress. Therefore rent is sometimes price-determining, as one of the costs of the cultivator (see, for instance, *Premier problème économique*, Meek, 1962, p. 181, note 1), while in other places it is price-determined, since its value depends on the market value of the products of land. In *Impôts* Quesnay writes that 'the revenues of a kingdom are in proportion to the prices of foodstuffs' (I.N.E.D., 1958 vol. II, p. 591, see also p. 594).[49] But if we place Quesnay's statements in the context of his political economy as a whole, some of the apparent discrepancies and inconsistencies vanish. In the case of rent the category of fundamental price provides the way out of the *impasse*, because it defines the overall expenses of production of primary commodities for farmers as including the net element, rent.

The *prix fondamental* is an analytical category which singles out the relationships of production in eighteenth-century France; it depicts the existence of the juridical right of proprietors to a share of the net product. The payment of rent to the proprietors of the soil is a basic feature of a socio-economic formation where the feudal mode of production is still dominant. Farmers are the true and only owners of the products, but they achieve this position only by subjecting themselves to the payment of *fermage* for using the soil. But in France in the middle of the eighteenth century this payment was not made in kind, by poor and miserable serfs, as in the early medieval age. The cultivators fulfilled their obligations towards landlords according to the rules of a market exchange economy; a system in which sales and purchases of commodities against money are the typical economic relationships among men (see Meek, 1962, p. 388). Therefore farmers used their monetary surplus, the part of receipts which exceeds the money necessary to pay wages to the workers and to replace the various kinds of capital, in order to fulfil their obligations towards the landlords.

In an age of transition, when serfs were being replaced by farmers, and when new social groups emerged to challenge the power of the *seigneurs*, monetary rent took the place of the *corvées*. The form of appropriation of part of the net product by the sovereign and the landlords obeyed the rules of market exchange. In order to describe the phenomenon of the appropriation of surplus in French society, rent had to be included in the fundamental price of agricultural products, otherwise it would have lost its characteristic feature of being a social relationship of production and become merely the difference between the current price of products and their physical cost of production. The share of the surplus accruing to the proprietor would fluctuate continuously, year after year, according to variations in the market value of goods in sales at first-hand. Given the methods of production of the primary sector, the amount of rent would depend only on market conditions and not on the social and political relationships between landlords and cultivators (see Chapter 6, 6.6). Moreover, if one does not distinguish the fundamental price from the technical unit cost of production, the farmer becomes a simple market agent who passes on to the landlords the effects of changes in the current prices of commodities. He loses any relevant role as independent cultivator with a direct interest in improving methods of production (see Chapter 5, 5.3).

3.11 The originality of Quesnay's theory of price and its legacies to Smith

Quesnay was not the first economist to put forward a notion of price based on the sum of costs and of items which are part of the social surplus of the country. Cantillon, who was known by the physiocrats, had already spoken of the famous 'three rents', which exhaust the social output of the country:

> The Farmers have generally two thirds of the Produce of the Land, one for their costs and the support of their Assistants, the other for

the Profit of their Undertaking (Cantillon, 1755, p. 43, see also pp. 121–3).[50]

The other 'third' accrues to the proprietors (ibid., pp. 43–5). And in his *Political Arithmetick* Petty divides the social product into wages, profits and rents (see Petty, 1676, p. 267). However, despite terminological similarities, Quesnay's fundamental price is quite different from the 'three rents' approach of Cantillon, because their different analyses of production entail specific differences in their theories of value and in the price notions they adopted. First of all, Cantillon does not link the 'three rents' theory with any precision to the notion of intrinsic value, which is ultimately explained by the amounts of land directly and indirectly used up in production. Therefore the phenomenon of value is not a bridge between the production and distribution of the social product and of surplus; these two features of the economy remain to some extent unrelated. By contrast, in physiocracy, not only does the notion of fundamental price underline the influence of production on the exchange values of commodities, but it also explicitly includes a social relation of production: rent. This notion plays the analytical role of transforming the part of the social surplus which accrues to direct producers (the farmers) into a revenue for the landlords, via the mechanisms and rules of market exchange.

The second major difference between Quesnay's fundamental price and the 'three rents' approach of Cantillon derives from their different views of the process of production. Cantillon stresses what can be regarded as a *linear* representation of production. The process can be described as employing only land and labour, which are the original, non-produced, means of production, purchased and organised by the entrepreneurs. This view of production complements the idea that the value of the social product is entirely accounted for by wages, profits and rent; that is to say, it is the sum of the incomes accruing to the participants in the productive process. Therefore for Cantillon the value of commodities and of national output is made up *only* of three different types of incomes. Two of them, rent and profits, are revenues, while the third item, wages, is the only type of cost left.

On the other hand, Quesnay stresses the circularity of the phenomenon of production and the crucial role of *produced means of production*, tools, equipment, instruments, etc. The fundamental value of national output is thus given by the sum of wages, the different types of revenues – *taille* and rent – *and* the value of the means of production consumed. There are three types of incomes, of which wages are costs and the other two are part of the surplus of the country. But there is also an item which *is not an income*, since it represents the value of those instruments and tools which are now called capital.

We can now try to evaluate Quesnay's contribution to the theory of value and his role as a precursor of Smith. Quesnay's analysis of price determination presents many important innovations with respect to those of his major predecessors, Petty and Cantillon, and of some contemporary authors, like Hutcheson and Steuart. Quesnay makes an important contribution to solving the dichotomy between price and value. First of all, he provides a detailed investigation of market phenomena, and in particular of the reasons for fluctuations in current and retail price. Moreover, he points out that for market prices it is possible to analyse a permanent and stable level, which Quesnay describes as the average price, *prix commun*. Therefore the existence of fluctuations does not make it impossible to single out regular market mechanisms. Even the notion of 'average price' makes it possible to organise the study of market forces and of the determination of current and retail price systematically. Thus the underlying relationships between social classes can emerge from investigation of the laws of markets.

There is still a mercantilist flavour in some parts of Quesnay's analysis of the contrasting interests of classes on the market. In fact the supremacy of merchants and the subordinate positions of farmers and consumers are explained by their roles in the process of market exchange. Professional traders can choose when to make their sales and purchases, while consumers must always buy goods in order to satisfy needs, and farmers must sell their products if they want to recover the expenses of production they have incurred (see Weulersse, 1910a, vol. I, pp. 519–20). Thus it is competition, or the fact that it cannot work appropriately, which explains the relative position of classes in the distribution of net product. But when we consider an economy where free trade rules, according to the natural laws of society, the difference between current and retail price is greatly reduced. Now the fundamental price comes to the fore, defining the permanent and stable price level in sales at first-hand. Market forces are no longer the only determinants of the appropriation of surplus, which also depends upon the socio-political structure of the country.

Quesnay's concept of *prix fondamental* represents his second, and perhaps most important, contribution to price theory. Market prices are linked, via the notion of fundamental price, to the process of production and to the problem of the organisation of labour, of natural resources and of means of production. With the fundamental price Quesnay provides a remarkable attempt to close the gap between market and production phenomena. He follows the lead of Petty and Cantillon, but the introduction of this original concept opens the way to the price theories of Turgot and Smith. In particular he makes a remarkable step forward in the direction of establishing the primacy of the sphere of production over that of circulation, in a market exchange economy. He abandons the old, commonsense, explanation of prices in terms of the difficulties of obtaining a commodity and of the generic desire for it. The cost of production of commodities becomes an extremely important element in the determination of their value, and its influence overshadows that of the market forces which go under the names of supply and demand.

However, Quesnay does not take the physical costs approach; and he does not investigate only the material features of production. The traditional view that he had a cost of production theory of value has obscured one of the most important innovative features of the physiocratic analysis of price determination. If one concentrates on an investigation of the analytical role of the different concepts of price, then it emerges that physiocracy provides the clearest example of the meaning and role of prices in an economy characterised by the reproduction of commodities. With the physical costs theory of Petty and Cantillon the costs incurred for the production of a commodity are necessarily the same for the individual entrepreneur and for society as a whole. Thus prices are strictly dependent on purely technical conditions, that is to say on the physical costs of production. But for Quesnay prices are not equal to the material expenses of production. They have become one of the major ways of representing and describing the relationships between the classes of society. The exchange values of commodities on the markets represent the social relationships which characterise the economic system, and in particular the way in which the social product is appropriated by each class. The distribution of output can no longer be regarded as a technical phenomenon, necessary only to guarantee the reconstitution of the means of production which have been used. The distribution of the social product, and of surplus in particular, is now a major social phenomenon which takes place in a market exchange economy, hence via prices.

Quesnay's analysis of prices shows that a purely cost-of-production theory of value is inadequate to describe a situation where the distribution of surplus among classes is increasingly regulated via the market. In physiocracy prices continue to be extremely sensitive to changes in the techniques of production, but the distribution of surplus also assumes an important role, and this second feature cannot be expressed by a theory of value limited to the idea of physical costs. For instance, variations in the shares of surplus of classes derive from changes in prices, when these are determined by forces outside the French economy, such as international competition. But a change in distribution due to the decision of a dominant social group, for example the introduction of new taxes which accrue to the government, must also be reflected in a change of some market value; for instance the fundamental price must increase to make room for the new tax beside rent and *taille*. In a surplus economy it would be better to use the term *price of production* instead of *cost of production*, which inevitably conveys the idea that prices are determined by purely technical conditions. The physiocratic notion of fundamental price makes it clear that prices of commodities are influenced by the methods of production, but also by the distribution of income.

The 'fundamental price' is Quesnay's most important analytical innovation in the study of the origin and distribution of surplus (see Chapters 4 and 5). In fact the inclusion of rent in the fundamental value of primary commodities provides the major analytical link between four important aspects of Quesnay's theory of production and distribution. First, the actual production of commodities occurs at the expense and risk of the agricultural entrepreneur who is in charge of the process of investment; secondly this activity takes place in a circular process of production; thirdly, only agriculture yields a surplus; fourthly, part of the surplus is appropriated by the proprietors.

We have seen that the new definition of the concept of *prix fondamental* shows that Quesnay's price theory presents extremely innovative features, which can in no way be reduced to the physical-costs view of prices. While the merits of Turgot and Smith in clarifying the role of the categories of natural and market prices in economic analysis is not to be questioned, there can be little doubt that Quesnay's notion of *prix fondamental* helps to explain the historical and analytical origin of these categories. First, it is the benchmark for all other concepts of price used by the physiocrats.[51] Secondly, the new interpretation of the concept of fundamental price makes it clear that this notion links three aspects of Quesnay's economic analyses: (a) the process of reproduction, (b) his description of the appropriation of the net product, (c) his view of the value of commodities and of the working of market mechanisms.

Therefore the notion of fundamental price appears as an intermediate step between the price theories of the seventeenth and eighteenth centuries and the analysis of price determination of Turgot and Smith; in particular it shows a strong similarity with the concept of natural price (see Smith, 1776, vol. I, p. 62). A detailed investigation of the similarities of these concepts is outside the scope of this book, but at least two remarkable differences between them must be pointed out. First of all, Quesnay does not believe that the fundamental price of a product fixes a level to which the market value of sales at first-hand will *necessarily* tend. He seems to think that the fundamental price is a sort of lower limit of the current one. In the tables in the articles *Grains* and *Hommes* the current price is always higher than the fundamental one and there is no indication of the existence of forces which should bring it down to this level. Secondly, and most importantly, Quesnay does not include the profits of the cultivator in the fundamental price of primary products, a fact which has important consequences in physiocratic economics (see Chapter 6).

Quesnay's theory of prices is important not only because it presents some original and innovative features; more than that, it throws an entirely new light on the physiocratic theories of production and distribution of wealth. Indeed, if we take prices into consideration, some rather neglected aspects of physiocracy come to light, thus opening the way to a general reinterpretation of Quesnay's role in the making of classical political economy. The next chapter deals with the problem of the role of prices in the physiocratic theory of the origin of surplus and wealth.

4 Capital, Competition and the Origin of Surplus

4.1 Traditional interpretations

The doctrine of the exclusive productivity of agriculture constitutes the physiocrats' reply to the question of the origin of surplus and wealth. This was their major concern and provides the necessary foundation for all their policy recommendations. The single tax on rent, a commercial policy in favour of the products of land, and the encouragement given to their consumption, are all measures deriving from the belief that only the primary sector yields a net product. This theory must be considered as a hypothesis in *some* works of the physiocrats, and above all in the different types of *Tableaux*, but it is *not* a postulate in the whole of physiocratic economics. Far from simply assuming the existence of a net output only in agriculture, Quesnay and his disciples want to explain this fact and try to convince their opponents. The physiocrats intend to put forward a theory of the origin of national wealth and of ways of increasing it.

We shall see that the concepts used by Quesnay to justify the exclusive, or at least the superior, productivity of agriculture, show that this theory is not founded on 'naturalistic' and 'material' preconceptions in favour of this sector. Traditional explanations of the physiocrats' distinction between sterile and productive activities fail to single out the arguments actually used by the physiocrats and their opponents in debating the idea that only the primary sector yields a revenue.

The most widespread and well known explanation of the doctrine of the exclusive productivity of agriculture ascribes to the physiocrats the opinion that surplus, in the form of rent, is due to the 'benevolence' of nature. Only the primary sector directly uses natural resources, hence it alone enjoys that surplus which is a 'gift of nature' (see Marx, 1963, vol. I, pp. 49–51; Weulersse, 1910a, vol. I, pp. 274–6). The physiocratic theory of the origin of surplus is thus a theory of the productive powers of nature (see Schicchi, 1978, p. 27). This interpretation describes the emergence of a physical surplus of corn over the corn input, and rests on the obvious fact that soil is fertile when properly exploited. 'The fertility of soil, which gives man the free gift of the net product, is after all a triumphant proof of the benevolence of nature' (Weulersse, 1910a, vol. II, pp. 112–3).

A second interpretation of the physiocratic view of the genesis of surplus considers agriculture as the only sector producing commodities which either directly or indirectly enter the production of themselves and of all other commodities; thus it can be regarded as a 'basic' sector.[1] The occupations which are directly associated with nature do not require the products of other activities for their own subsistence; the productive class 'can always exist by itself thanks to the outcome of its labour' (*Du Commerce*, I.N.E.D., 1958, vol. II, p. 820; see also Le Trosne, 1777, pp. 939, 943).

The primary sector, with its surplus, gives rise to and maintains all other economic activities of the country (see Oncken, 1888, pp. xvi–xvii, Ridolfi, 1973, p. xxviii, Giacomin, 1979, p. 34). The existence of a surplus in agriculture allows people to undertake other occupations, such as commercial activities, and the production of different types of commodities.[2] The development of the industrial and commercial sectors is thus both dependent on, and limited by, the size of the surplus in the primary sector (see Salvati, 1980, p. 55). It is agriculture which sets the pace for all economic activities (see *Impôts*, I.N.E.D., 1958, vol. II, pp. 585–6, 594). Thus the physiocratic theory of the exclusive productivity of agriculture seems to be 'demonstrated by the existence of non-agricultural classes' (Meek, 1962, p. 381).

More recently, the view that the physiocrats considered agricultural surplus as a historically given feature of the economy, and as such took it for granted, has gained popularity. It is true that Quesnay's 'insistence upon the exclusive producitivity of agriculture . . . expressed a historically reality' (Fox-Genovese, 1976, pp. 55–6; see also Dobb, 1973, p. 40). Thus this view 'can be said to have "fitted the facts" with a reasonable degree of accuracy' (Meek 1962, p. 379). Weulersse had already expressed the opinion that the physiocrats took the surplus as a datum because it 'can in no way be proved mathematically' (Weulersse, 1910a, vol. II, p. 125; see also Salvati, 1980, pp. 29, 48). These authors seem to believe that the physiocrats regarded the existence of seigneural rent as a proof of the exclusive productivity of agriculture (see Meek, 1962, p. 381). Note that McCulloch had already adopted this view in a footnote in his edition of the *Wealth of Nations* (see McCulloch, 1853, p. 305, note 1). Other interpreters of physiocracy believe that surplus, in the form of land rent, is one of the data on which the physiocrats built their analysis, and in particular their price theory (see Gilibert, 1977, pp. 80, 103;

Cartelier, 1976, pp. 51–3). By referring to the two-sector model which determines relative prices, Cartelier says: 'there it is clear that the theory of the net product is a *postulate* and not a *result* of the system' (Cartelier, 1976, p. 57, italics in the text).

All these interpretations of the physiocratic doctrine of the exclusive productivity of agriculture emphasise interesting aspects of physiocracy, but they fail to pick up Quesnay's actual efforts to justify his view of the origin of surplus. As a matter of fact none of the three aspects underlined by the above interpretations was really an issue between the physiocrats and their opponents. The fact that a fertile soil produces more output than has been employed in its cultivation is a fairly obvious and trivial observation. The idea that the primary sector maintains all other activities appears in some of Quesnay's works. In his early articles in particular he emphasises the obvious and unchallenged fact that the products of agriculture are more important for the satisfaction of men's needs than those of manufacture (see *Hommes*, Meek, 1962, p. 95). Here the distinction between productive and sterile activities seems to be based on the different use values of their products (see *Grains*, ibid., pp. 78–9). But even in these early works Quesnay does not rest his defence of the doctrine of the exclusive productivity of agriculture only on the specific qualities of its products. He sometimes emphasises the role of exchange value on the very same page. Hence surplus appears as a difference between value magnitudes; in agriculture the value of output exceeds the costs, while in manufacture the two coincide (see *Hommes* and *Grains*, ibid., pp. 96 and 72–3). The physical and value approaches co-exist in these early works and neither dominates the other.

As for a third interpretation, it is clear that nobody challenged the view that the landlord had the right to receive compensation from the cultivators who used their domains. The opinion that the exclusive productivity of agriculture is a historical postulate confuses the physiocrats' efforts to explain the emergence of a net product only in agricultural production, with the problem of its appropriation. For instance, Dobb writes that in France at the time of the physiocrats, 'rent of land appeared as the only natural form of surplus' (Dobb, 1963, p. 199). Thus, the particular socio-economic form which is assumed by the surplus when it is distributed is regarded as proof of the fact that net product *can be* originated only in the economic occupations which directly exploit soil and nature.

The confusion of surplus with rent is one which has overshadowed the actual debates which took place between the physiocrats and their opponents. Furthermore, the identification of the net product with the revenue of landlords has limited the analytical role of prices and of market forces in Quesnay's theory of the origin of surplus. In fact, in purely physical terms rent could be justified as 'a surplus of corn-output over corn-input' (Meek, 1962, p. 388). According to Meek the physiocrats' failure to explain the existence of rent in value terms has to be ascribed to the inadequacy of the value categories they employed. He believes that in physiocracy these notions were 'designed not to explain the exclusive value productivity of agriculture but merely to express it' (ibid., p. 389). Therefore, prices and value concepts would not play any relevant role in the physiocratic theory of the origin of surplus.[3]

4.2 The opposition to the doctrine of the exclusive productivity of agriculture

It is time to examine the arguments advanced by the opponents of physiocracy against the supremacy of agricultural production. The idea of the exclusive productivity of agriculture was strongly attacked by the classes whose interests would have been damaged by the implementation of physiocratic policy measures: the rising industrial bourgeoisie, the merchants and dealers, and all groups who were taking advantage of the contemporary fiscal system (see Weulersse, 1910a, vol. II, pp. 387ff. and pp. 626ff.).[4] The opponents of the physiocratic theory of surplus did not challenge the notions that people employed in industrial and commercial activities needed foodstuffs to carry on their work, or that seigneural rent had to be regarded as part of the surplus of the kingdom. They maintained that industry was not inherently sterile, and that it was even capable of yielding a larger surplus than agriculture, in proportion to the capital employed. The view that the productivity of manufacture was higher than that of the primary sector represented the real threat to the physiocratic theory of the origin of surplus.

The *Dialogues sur le commerce des bleds*, written by the *Abbé* Galiani and published in 1770 by Diderot,[5] form the best summary of all the arguments which were used against physiocracy, particularly in the second half of the 1760s. Galiani expressed doubts about the supremacy of agricultural production in two main arguments. First, according to him, the output of the primary sector cannot rise indefinitely, because the natural resources it employs are not unlimited. In the sixth dialogue, the *chevalier*, Galiani himself, tells the *marquis*, his opponent, that when the soil of a country 'is entirely cultivated . . . it is not susceptible of a larger product' (Galiani, 1770, pp. 149–50). Moreover, the rising population increases internal consumption and absorbs the whole of agricultural output, leaving none for export. A nation can grow rich mainly by selling manufactured commodities abroad because there are no limits to industrial production. Manufactures 'grow in proportion to men and can go, so to speak, to infinity' (ibid., p. 150, see also p. 153). Therefore, 'agriculture will give people their subsistence, but only manufacture will bring money and wealth to the State' (ibid.,). Thus, Galiani recognises that agriculture provides foodstuffs to those engaged in other activities, but this fact cannot prove its superior productivity. The importance of primary commodities for the satisfaction of the fundamental needs of people is undeniable. However, this cannot be regarded as proof that the wealth and opulence of the kingdom depend on agricultural production. Moreover, it does not constitute an explanation of the sterility of industry.[6]

Galiani's second argument is even more convincing; industrial production yields a more stable revenue to entrepreneurs and to the country because it is safer than agriculture; 'cultivation is exposed to the risk of seasons' (ibid., p. 115), while 'there are neither good nor bad years for the harvest in manufacture' (ibid., p. 41). Therefore manufactured commodities are characterised by stable market prices, as opposed to the huge variations which occur in the prices of foodstuffs (see ibid., pp. 41–2). Galiani's defence of the superiority of industry over agriculture, therefore, neither raises the issue of the different use values of their products, nor discusses the role of nature, but is founded on the different conditions of the production process in the two sectors.

4.3 The productiveness of capitalistic agriculture

The propositions of a 'gift of nature', of the existence of rent, or even the self-sustaining character of agriculture would not have been sufficient to refute objections like those of Galiani. First, it was the idea of a value surplus that was under attack, and value notions were needed to defend it. The study of market forces and prices was designed to explain and to justify the theory of the origin of the net product and not only to express it. (The next section will investigate the value concepts used by Quesnay to defend his theory.)

Secondly, Galiani linked the question of productivity to the different organisation of the process of production in the two sectors. This point leads to a very interesting aspect of the physiocratic theory of the origin of surplus, which should help to dismiss any particular emphasis on the role of nature as such. Quesnay strongly underlines the role of capital in securing the productivity of the primary sector. For him it is the amount and quality of the advances which determine the success of agriculture in exploiting natural resources. There is a direct relationship between the amount of means of production and the size of the surplus obtained. The capital invested by the farmer in agriculture is regarded as the most important cause of wealth and revenue: For instance, in *Hommes* Quesnay writes that '*the wealth of the farmers . . . produces the revenues*' (I.N.E.D., 1958, vol. II, p. 571, note 13, italics in the text; see also p. 566). Thus, the revenue of the nation depends on the advances employed in cultivation; it is neither a gift of nature, nor does it depend on the benevolence of God. Even more explicitly Quesnay states that the size of the net output produced by the annual advances depends on the amount and quality of the original ones. In the *Maximes Générales* he writes: 'if the original advances had been sufficient, cultivation would have easily been capable of yielding a *hundred* net product and even more per *hundred* annual advances' (Meek, 1962, pp. 242–3).[7]

Accumulation of capital in agriculture has two highly positive effects. First, more land can be cultivated, hence there are more goods available for domestic consumption and for export. Secondly, the improvement in methods of cultivation depends on the availability of large advances, because only rich farmers can undertake large-scale cultivation, which requires huge original advances and so higher initial financial investments. Therefore, the more capital is invested in the activities of the primary sector, the higher is the share of surplus in the gross output (see Weulersse, 1910a, vol. II, p. 266). The physiocrats seem to imply that the 'productive' quality is not inherent in soil. Lands need men to cultivate them, but land and labour alone do not justify the existence of a net product (see *Despotisme de la Chine*, I.N.E.D., 1958, vol. II, p. 926). Only with large financial means can cultivators make all the advances which allow the soil to be profitably exploited: 'man and wealth make agriculture prosperous' (Mirabeau, 1764, vol. II. pp. 352–3), writes Mirabeau in the *Philosophie Rurale* (see also Baudeau, 1767–70, vol. XI, pp. 137–38). But the physiocrats consider wealth rather than people to be the principal element of a productive agriculture and a wealthy nation. Quesnay writes: 'the wealth of the husbandman secures the revenue of the nation, the power of the sovereign and the prosperity of the State' (*Hommes*, I.N.E.D., 1958, vol. II, p. 566; see also Baudeau, 1767–70, vol. XI, p. 154; vol. XII, p. 150). For Quesnay and his disciples, therefore, the capital invested in agriculture is essential to secure the 'productivity' of the primary sector.

In order to be productive the exploitation of an estate needs the farmers' advances (see Weulersse, 1910a, vol. II, pp. 313–14). If farmers are poor and cannot make large advances, cultivation can be carried on only with old-fashioned techniques. Then agriculture is unable to maintain a large number of peasants, and lands are depopulated: 'if the countryside loses its inhabitants, it is because it lacks wealth; and these people are useless' (*Hommes*, I.N.E.D., 1958, vol. II, p. 568). Thus the lack of the appropriate advances makes the work of the peasants not simply sterile, but useless, because they cannot even satisfy their most essential needs (see ibid.). Without large means of production agriculture not only does not yield a surplus, but it does not even produce enough output to keep its scale of activity constant and to maintain the people it employs. Lack of capital causes the primary sector to shrink and produces backwardness and misery throughout the nation.

For the physiocrats productiveness is a quality of the labour of a particular sector of the economy, i.e. agriculture. But agricultural labour is productive only when it is assisted by the necessary amount of capital, and the more advances are made in the primary sector the higher is the productivity of the workers. Thus only large-scale farming is productive, while the small-scale techniques of production used by the poor *métayers* can hardly give a surplus (see *Fermiers*, Groenewegen, 1983, pp. 7, 18). But it is not simply a question of economies of scale; in fact rich farmers can introduce new techniques of cultivation (ibid., p. 18), capable of yielding a higher output per unit of land.[8] One of Quesnay's major economic contentions concerns the superiority of horses over oxen for the cultivation of soil (see ibid., pp. 1–4).[9] This is regarded as the main feature of the capitalistic organisation of agricultural production. But horses cost more than oxen, and above all they require more expenses for their use and maintenance (see ibid., p. 14–15). Therefore, only wealthy farmers can improve the methods of cultivation.

The existence and the size of agricultural surplus depend mainly on the techniques of production of agriculture. Quesnay always remarks that the share of surplus in the gross output of agriculture is particularly high in England, where wealthy cultivators can employ large original advances. His belief that productiveness is a quality of the labour of a particular sector, i.e. agriculture, when it is assisted by capital, anticipates one of the features of a capitalist economy. It is the presence of large means of production which ensure that agricultural labour is much more productive, not only than the work of artisans, but also than the work of poor peasants.

4.4 The different role of competition in agriculture and in manufacturing

However, Quesnay did not resort to the idea of the capitalistic organisation of cultivation to defend the exclusive, or at least superior, productivity of agriculture. In his last economic works, the articles which appeared in the *Journal de l'agriculture* and in the *Ephémérides du Citoyen* between 1765 and 1767, and which were particularly intended to defend his view of the origin of surplus and wealth, Quesnay approaches the problem of the exclusive productivity of agriculture directly in value terms, while physical and material considerations become less and less important in his arguments. He investigates the working of market forces in determining the prices of foodstuffs and manufactured goods. The notion of fundamental price includes the physiocratic proposition that only the primary sector earns a surplus (see Chapter 3, 3.11), while in manufacture this price is equal to the unit cost of production. But Quesnay and his followers do not want merely to assert the existence of rent in the fundamental price of primary commodities, they also wish to explain the emergence of a *value surplus as such*. They see the lower limit at which an excess value of the price of foodstuffs begins to exist as being their physical unit costs of production and not their *prix fondamental*. Thus, as far as the origin of surplus is concerned, one must compare the current price of commodities with their technical cost of production.

In the dialogue *Sur les travaux des artisans* Quesnay explains that the prices of primary products and manufactured commodities are determined by different forces:

> it is the labour which determines the price of the artisans' goods, and the competition of the latter sets limits to the expense of their

labour. It is not the same, I repeat, with the price of the products of the land, which is determined not only by the expenses of cultivation but also by many other causes (Meek, 1962, p. 228).

Quesnay justifies the sterility of industry and the productivity of agriculture by the fact that competition works in a different way in the case of agricultural products than in the case of manufactured commodities (see Spengler, 1958, p. 62; Woog, 1950, p. 27). Market conditions allow the emergence of a value surplus from sales at first-hand of the products of land, while the current value of manufactured commodities is consistently equal to their cost of production. Competition among the artisans brings the current price of their products down to their fundamental value, which coincides with the cost of production. However, this is not so in agriculture. The current prices of primary products are determined in such a way as to leave a surplus over the unit costs of production in the hands of farmers, even with freely competitive conditions in first-hand markets.

The physiocrats give a convincing explanation of the mechanisms through which the current prices of industrial products are ultimately determined by their cost of production. If some manufacturer makes a 'gain' other artisans enter that sector, and the output of the commodity increases up to the point where the excess value of the price over costs is wiped out and the producers have no gain. Competition prevents the emergence of a permanent surplus for producers on top of the expenses they have incurred (see *Répétition de la question proposée dans la 'Gazette du Commerce'*, I.N.E.D., 1958, vol. II, p. 779).[10] The destiny of French industry is regarded by the physiocrats as being as insecure as that of all small countries whose economies are based on the production of manufactured commodities. In fact the gains and the salaries of the people of these countries are always threatened by the competition of other countries. Thus the rivalry among the workers of these small countries force them to diminish their salaries and this fact favours the agricultural nations which import manufactured good (see ibid.).[11]

Thus, the arguments against the possibility of a surplus in industrial activities are reinforced by considering international trade. The physiocrats believe that the possibilities for French manufactures are highly insecure; with *laissez-faire* they have no hope of making any profit (see Woog, 1950, pp. 29–30). According to the physiocrats the exports of French manufactures are always threatened by competition from foreign industries.[12]

The physiocrats do not deny the possibility that some manufacturers may make a profit. But this happens mostly when they are protected by 'exclusive privileges', which give them the 'unjust right of selling their products above their natural value' (Du Pont, *Journal de l'Agriculture*, May 1766, pp. 109–10, note, quoted in Weulersse, 1910a vol. I, p. 303). Quesnay and his disciples propose the abolition of all these 'unnatural' regulations, because the gains of artisans and traders are made at the expense of any increase in the country's wealth (see for instance *Répétition de la question*, I.N.E.D., 1958, vol. II, p. 779). The administrators must implement measures which guarantee the existence of the highest degree of competition in French industry (ibid.). As soon as exclusive privileges are suppressed, the nation experiences 'the effects of free competition in the practice of commerce and industry; thanks to competition merchants and artisans are compelled by their rivalry . . . to reduce their remunerations' (*Suite de la répétition de la question des fabricants des bas de soie de Nimes sur le effets productifs de la classe prétendue stérile*, I.N.E.D., 1958, vol. II, p. 792). Thus the prices of manufactured commodities are continuously pushed down to their technical costs of production, which include payments for raw materials and wages (see Chapter 3, 3.9). For the physiocrats the existence of a profit in industrial activities is incompatible with the characteristics of a competitive system. In a *laissez-faire* economy where there is competition among manufacturers, the current prices of industrial products cannot regularly and consistently exceed their costs of production.[13]

However, competition does not have the same effect on the prices of primary commodities. Quesnay and his disciples are convinced that the existence of competitive market conditions for the products of land is compatible with a permanent and stable surplus value over costs (see Spengler, 1958, p. 60). Above all, the more competitive the system is, the greater is the difference between the current prices of products of the soil and their unit costs of production (see Chapter 3, 3.5, 3.6). But 'if competition causes manufacture to be sterile, why does it leave agriculture productive?' (Meek, 1962, p. 387). What are those 'many other causes, which are capable of maintaining the market value of the products, notwithstanding economies in the costs of cultivation', to which Quesnay refers in the dialogue *Sur les travaux des artisans*? (ibid., p. 228). According to the Physiocrats, competition should have the same features in markets for the products of land as in those for manufactured commodities. Hence, one is immediately tempted to think that the working of competition, in the case of primary products, must be hindered by the existence of some monopolistic situation. But this is not what Quesnay has in mind. Agricultural surplus is a normal and regular feature of agricultural production, which springs from the general laws of the natural order of society. Indeed monopoly is condemned because it goes against this natural order. Quesnay does not resort to a fact monopoly, whose existence is not only occasional but must be prevented, to explain another fact, the surplus of agriculture, which is regarded as being highly positive and which is part of the natural order of society.

Since monopolies cannot satisfactorily explain why the prices of foodstuffs are permanently higher than their cost of production, one must look for some other reason. We shall see that this part of Quesnay's economic theory is not very successful. Nevertheless, his arguments highlight some rather neglected aspects of physiocracy, namely the notion of aggregate effective demand and the physiocrats' true attitude towards free competition in international trade.

4.5 The effective demand for the products of land

Quesnay must explain why competition on first-hand markets for primary commodities permits the existence of a value surplus over costs. He says that the prices of agricultural products are regulated 'by the quantity and by the competition of purchasers, whose needs are always greater than the total amount of the reproduction' (*Sur les travaux des artisans*, Meek, 1962, p. 227). Quesnay seems to mean that for the products of land there is a permanent excess of demand over supply (Meek, 1962, p. 388; Johnson, 1937, pp. 232–3). Unfortunately he does not explain clearly why there is such an excess demand for the products of land, while the supply of manufactured commodities is always equal to their money demand. Hence one must try to reconstruct his opinions by grouping together several scattered comments and hints. In particular, all these passages must be set in the overall context of physiocratic analysis.

The physiocrats believe in the existence of a hierarchy in the wants of humanity (see Chapter 2, 2.2; Molinier, 1958a, pp. 49–51). Primary commodities are designed to satisfy the fundamental needs and desires of people, as they are the most important human necessaries. Thus the products of agriculture are always intensively sought after and their absolute demand is always high, because 'needs always exceed consumable stuffs' (*Du Commerce*, I.N.E.D., 1958, vol. II, p. 831). Certainly in the France of the physiocrats there was a chronic shortage of foodstuffs, but they did not limit the existence of a value surplus in agriculture to a specific historical period or a particular country.[14] The existence of a demand for food which is permanently higher than production seems to be a constant feature of the world economy. Even if agricultural output rises, this sooner or later provokes an increase in population, which reinforces the demand for primary commodities; 'agriculture, which produces goods, is, at the same time, the main centre for the multiplication of consumers' (Mirabeau, 1764, vol. III, pp. 83–4). Thus there will always be people eager to buy foodstuffs and other primary commodities; agriculture should never experience a crisis due to lack of potential consumers.[15]

However the physiocratic view of the importance of the products of land is not a revised version of the 'naturalistic' and physical explanations of the superiority of agriculture. In fact, Quesnay quite clearly distinguishes the two aspects of use and exchange value. These are two distinct features of the commodity, which are by no means regulated by the same laws (see Chapter 3, 3.1). Therefore the particular use value of primary commodities justifies their high *absolute demand*. But a large number of potential consumers does not necessarily imply a correspondingly large consumption of the products of land. Quesnay explains that in France there are plenty of people who would like to buy meat and wine, but who are compelled to consume black bread and water, because they are too poor even to afford firewood. He concludes: 'thus, there is no lack of consumers, but of consumption' (*Réponse au Mémoire de M.H.*, I.N.E.D., 1958, vol. II, p. 756). The huge numbers of poor, looking for necessaries but unable to pay for them, do not justify the permanent difference between the price and the cost of production of foodstuffs. Quesnay makes a sharp distinction between people's desires to possess commodities and the actions of consumers who are actually able to pay for products in the market (see Woog, 1950, p. 22).

When Quesnay emphasises the influence of consumption on prices he is referring to the actual market demand of consumers who can purchase the commodity at its current price. He does not mean the sum of the needs and desires of all individuals, irrespective of whether they are able to actually purchase the commodity. It is the demand which exists on the markets, among consumers who can pay the current prices of commodities. In *Hommes* Quesnay writes 'the very prices of the commodities are a sure indication that a money demand for them, proportionate to their current prices, actually exists' (Meek, 1962, p. 92; see also *Questions intéressantes*, I.N.E.D., 1958, vol. II, p. 629). Henceforth, this money demand not only influences the prices of primary products, but also gives them the very quality of being marketable commodities. In fact, the products of land have an exchange value on the market only if there are effective consumers rich enough to pay the required prices.

In order to indicate the quantity of a commodity which can be actually purchased, Quesnay uses the words '*recherchées pour de l'argent à la raison de leur prix actuel*' (*Hommes*, ibid., p. 528). Meek translates *recherchées pour de l'argent* as *money demand* (see Meek, 1962, p. 92). This term certainly captures the physiocrats' stress on the money which is necessary to purchase a commodity. But the physiocrats adopt several other words in order to indicate this kind of effective demand. *Les moyens de payer*, says Le Trosne (see Le Trosne, 1777, p. 963); Quesnay speaks also of *la faculté d'acheter* (*Du commerce*, I.N.E.D., 1958, vol. II, p. 831), and even more clearly of *consommation effective* (ibid., p. 824), thus justifying the use of the term *effective demand* for his view of the quantity of a commodity actually sold in the market.

We can now see the precise content of Quesnay's statement about the existence of an excess demand for products of the soil, which keeps their prices higher than the costs of production. Effective demand for first-hand sales of foodstuffs is always greater than the quantity produced and brought to the market. The physiocrats must explain why, at a price which corresponds to the physical unit cost of production, the quantity of each primary commodity demanded by those actually prepared to pay that price is *systematically* higher than output, irrespective of absolute demand. For Quesnay this is not a temporary situation in which the market price of a commodity depends on its demand; he is not referring to some kind of market disturbance. On the contrary, he believes that this a typical condition of markets for foodstuffs.

4.6 Aggregate demand in a reproduction economy

However, the physiocrats must not only justify the existence of a 'high' price for *each* agricultural product; since they maintain that there is a surplus only in agriculture they must also show why the *aggregate effective demand* for the products of land, by consumers able to pay remunerative prices, is always larger than total production. An analysis of the items which make up aggregate demand appears to be necessary to show why an overall effective demand higher than output is typical of markets for primary commodities. This characteristic justifies the existence of a surplus in this sector. Therefore the physiocratic theory of surplus is linked to an analysis of consumption and expenditure. Quesnay writes that 'it is by means of consumption that the products reproduce themselves, that they acquire a market value and become wealth' (*Questions intéressantes*, I.N.E.D., 1958, vol. II, p. 629). Consumption secures a high and stable effective demand for the products of French agriculture, which in turn sustains their prices.

In physiocracy, the analysis of demand and expenditure is an essential element of the theory of the origin of surplus and wealth; it is also part of a general study of the conditions of reproduction of the economy. As Mercier de la Rivière says in a famous phrase, which is worth quoting in French, '*la consommotion est la measure de la reproduction*' (Mercier, 1767, p. 254).

The physiocratic theory of the origin of surplus requires an examination of the component elements of aggregate demand, in order to see which of them can help to justify the permanence of excess demand over the quantity produced. According to Quesnay, the overall demand for foodstuffs is the sum of domestic and foreign consumption. In the article *Grains* he writes: 'one must encourage the sale [of the products of land] everywhere by means of exportation and internal consumption, which together with the sale abroad, sustain the prices of foodstuffs' (I.N.E.D., 1958 vol. II, p. 495; see also *Maxime Générales*, Meek, 1962, p. 259). The level of internal consumption depends on historical features of society and in particular on the number of inhabitants (see *Extrait*, Kuczynski and Meek, 1972, p. 16). But above all domestic demand for the products of agriculture is influenced by the wealth of the people of a country, and hence by the size of its revenue. In *Hommes* Quesnay says that 'consumption is proportionate to the wealth of consumers, and this wealth is proportionate to the nation's revenue' (Meek, 1962, p. 100). Unfortunately the majority of people in France are poor and can buy from agriculture only the necessaries of life. These poor consumers cannot contribute much to increasing the prices of foodstuffs (see Weulersse, 1910a, vol. I, pp. 486–8). The landlords, the king and the church are the wealthy consumers, because they are the main owners of the revenues of the kingdom. Their purchasing power and their expenditures are the only variable part of domestic demand, in the sense that they can be deflected from manufactured goods towards primary commodities. According to the physiocrats, proprietors must increase their purchases of the products of land, *luxe de subsistance*, instead of buying manufactured products, *luxe de décoration*,.[16]

However, the physiocrats are not resigned to accepting a situation with a small number of wealthy consumers. They confirm the importance of effective demand in securing wealth and surplus for the country in passages which seem to anticipate Keynes. Quesnay suggests to the rulers that it benefits the whole nation to introduce policy measures in favour of the poor and homeless.

For with their wages they can consume 'food, clothing and other expenditures', thus contributing 'to the sale of the foodstuffs of the farm', and they also sustain 'price and production' (*Questions intéressantes*, I.N.E.D., 1958, vol. II, p. 632). By helping poor people to establish themselves somewhere and to find a work the country will reap a double advantage. First, the expenditures of new and old producers stimulate the development of existing activities and the establishment of new ones; thus the overall output increases (see for instance *Hommes*, ibid., p. 541). Secondly, the revenue of the newly employed workers returns to the producers via consumption, since they are now able to pay for the necessaries of life and hence contribute to aggregate effective demand for the products of land. Therefore the government and the landlords must spend their money on employing poor people. In effect, besides producing more commodities, the successful employment of more workers 'brings about consumption and expenditures, which are in themselves another source of wealth' (ibid.).

For the physiocrats the overall level of domestic demand for foodstuffs depends directly on the expenditures of the state and of the landlords. The appropriate use of their revenues by these two classes is a major impulse to setting the pace for all the country's economic activities. The expenditure decisions of landlords determine the level of competition between buyers, and the amount of sales and purchases (see *Du Commerce*, I.N.E.D., 1958, vol. II, p. 850). This is a consequence of the fact that internal demand depends on people's actual consumption possibilities, that is to say, on their incomes. Thus, in a nation 'there can be buyers only in so far as they are themselves paid to be able to buy' (ibid.).[17]

Therefore the domestic demand of agricultural commodities can be divided in two parts; on the one hand there is the private consumption of landlords and wealthy people. On the other, there is the consumption of the poor, which depends on the productive use of revenues by the proprietors of land (who can employ more workers) and above all on public spending by the government. The sum of the exports of foodstuffs and of the two components of domestic demand gives the aggregate demand for the products of French agriculture.

We have seen that Quesnay analyses the question of the origin of surplus using the concepts of expenditure and consumption; moreover, he believes that the scale of activity is determined by the level of money demand for the products of land. This follows from the fact that he regards the economy as a circle, in which production, distribution and consumption of commodities are different parts of a single process of reproduction of the social and economic system. The revenues of the nation are the source of the purchasing power of people, and hence of their consumption. If these revenues are properly spent, they help to sustain the prices of the products of land, thus securing the re-creation of surplus value in agriculture. Therefore Quesnay regards the processes of production and of circulation of revenue as the main parts of the economic circuit. In *Hommes* he writes: 'everything a man spends, either from his gains, or from his incomes is a profit for other men, and it goes back to the source where it has been produced and which will reproduce it' (I.N.E.D., 1958, vol. II, p. 541). Quesnay links the notions of reproduction and surplus to those of consumption and effective demand.

4.7 *Laissez-faire* or neo-mercantilism?

The physiocratic views of the proper ways of spending the revenue are meant to secure the sale of the entire output of agriculture at remunerative prices. A high level of consumption of primary products gives rise to strong competition among buyers, which increases the price of foodstuffs (see Weulersse, 1910a, vol. II, p. 18; vol. I, p. 272; see also *Du Commerce*, I.N.E.D., 1958, vol. II, p. 825). High and stable prices for the products of land are seen as a basic feature of a prosperous nation (see Weulersse, 1910a, vol. I, pp. 474, 480). Unfortunately French agriculture is not in such a favourable situation. *Absolute* domestic demand for corn is always high enough to absorb the whole output; thus 'the sale is always secured by internal trade' (*Du Commerce*, I.N.E.D., 1958, vol. II, p. 831). Agricultural producers who want to sell their entire output will always find enough purchasers willing to acquire their products. But they must be prepared to lower the prices in line with the limited financial possibilities of the consumers, which hinder their effective consumption (see ibid., pp. 824, 831).

The physiocrats take a gloomy view of the purchasing power existing in France. Even if the landlords make their expenditure pattern conform to physiocratic recommendations, the internal money demand for the products of land is not sufficient to bring about a current price of corn which leaves a substantial revenue in the hands of farmers.[18] The measures taken by the government to relieve the miserable situation of the poor people, *le bas peuple*, and to raise their standard of living, do not seem by themselves to be sufficient to sustain the prices of foodstuffs. In France there is an endemic shortage of purchasing power; the 'inability' to pay of French consumers makes it impossible to establish high and stable prices for primary commodities, which would permanently cover the costs of production (see Du Pont, 1764, pp. 66).[19]

According to the physiocrats domestic demand is too uncertain; there are too many obstacles in the way of increasing French consumption of primary commodities. Thus, in order to raise demand from the low level which hinders the development of agriculture, it is necessary to resort to sales abroad; French primary products must be exported to foreign countries. The implementation of *laissez-faire* in international trade is a necessary step in order to broaden the market for French foodstuffs and to secure for them a high and stable level of effective demand. Foreign effective demand is added to that of French subjects (see Herlitz, 1961b, p. 139; Mirabeau, 1760b, pp. 239–41). As Mercier de la Rivière says: 'a country which does not have a number of consumers capable of securing a good price for her products . . . is compelled to look for other consumers abroad' (Mercier, 1767, pp. 265–6).

The government must take all the measures necessary to remove obstacles to foreign trade. In particular, exports of wheat must be encouraged; this is the only economic policy which can increase the demand for the products of French agriculture, thus securing their profitable sale. In April 1766, in the *Remarques sur l'opinion de l'auteur de l'esprit del lois*, Quesnay wrote: 'let us open our ports to the merchants of all countries' (I.N.E.D., 1958, vol. II, p. 789). The home merchants can now sell corn abroad and foreign traders can purchase primary commodities from French farmers. By removing all impediments to external trade 'we shall have many more buyers and a much more advantageous sale' (ibid.).[20] Favourable conditions on first-hand markets facilitate the sale of corn at a high and profitable current price which yields a surplus. Therefore an economic policy which encourages free foreign trade in primary commodities is the only way 'of preventing the fall of foodstuffs below their ordinary current price abroad' (*Impôts*, I.N.E.D., 1958, vol. II, p. 602; see also *Questions intéressantes*, ibid., p. 653). It is clear that the main purpose of the physiocrats' recommendation of free trading conditions is to sustain and increase the price of corn in sales at first-hand. The free exportation of corn can fulfill this aim by increasing the number of wealthy consumers, thus boosting the aggregate effective demand for foodstuffs on French markets (see Mercier, 1767, p. 264).

This new interpretation of the physiocrats' analysis of the exclusive productivity of agriculture brings to light the novelty and orginality of their use of the notion of aggregate effective demand and their analysis of its component items. Moreover it provides a new view of the physiocratic approach to the problem of complete freedom in international trade, which conflicts with traditional interpretations. Thus, Quesnay and his disciples are not fully committed supporters of complete *laissez-faire*.[21] On the contrary they regard it only as the most convenient and profitable way of selling the products of French agriculture and hence of increasing the value of its net product. Quesnay does not ask the government simply to step side and not to intervene on domestic and international markets. His faith that competitive market mechanisms would by themselves establish a profitable exchange value for French foodstuffs is not unlimited. Indeed the authorities must act positively in favour of exports of foodstuffs. The physiocrats advocate the active intervention of the government, which must protect foreign trade 'as much as it is possible' (*Impôts*, I.N.E.D., 1958, vol. II, p. 602). France can become rich and wealthy only if the state implements all the measures necessary to support trade in the products of agriculture, and not if it refrains from intervening in the economy. The physiocrats are in favour of *laissez-faire*, because this appears to be one of the few ways of stimulating the development of French agriculture, but they do not espouse economic liberalism. Their recommendations in favour of free trade concern only the possibility of exporting the products of French agriculture, so as to sustain and increase their prices in France.

This unusual view of the role of free trade in physiocracy is supported and supplemented by several facts. First, the physiocrats stress the importance of exports of primary commodities, but do not care about the possibility of exporting manufactures. France must achieve the highest possible sales of primary products and leave the production of manufactures to other countries. These trade relationships are most advantageous to the country 'because one obtains a much higher profit from the sale of foodstuffs' (Mirabeau, 1764, vol. II, p. 343). On a few occasions the physiocrats put forward the idea that the products of French industry should be freely sold abroad, but this is just a way of by-passing the difficulties of directly exporting raw materials and foodstuffs. 'Foreign trade of agricultural products which a country can carry on through a manufacturer, is a *necessary* commerce in all the cases in which domestic consumption will not be sufficient' (Mercier, 1767, p. 316, italics in the original). Foreign demand for the products of French industry is only another way of increasing the prices of agricultural products, which are necessary to make manufactured commodities. The *manufacturier* acts as a middleman, and his *entremise* facilitates the sales of raw materials, by transforming them into commodities which can be transported more easily and which are in greater demand.

A second consideration shows even more clearly how wrong is the traditional view of the physiocrats as being among the first convinced propagators of *laissez-faire*. Even free corn trade and exports of primary products are regarded as necessary, but unfortunate circumstances; 'foreign trade is a necessary and indispensable evil needed to sustain the value of the products' (*Du Commerce*, I.N.E.D., 1958, vol. II, p. 848). Free exportation is a *pis-aller*, a device by which the rulers increase the total consumption of foodstuffs when 'domestic trade is not sufficient for a profitable sale of the products' (ibid., p. 849; see also Mercier, 1767, pp. 265, 266; Bloomfield, 1938, p. 731).

However, if domestic consumption and expenditure are large enough to give rise to a level of effective demand, and of competition among French merchants, capable of increasing the price of corn, it is much better to abandon foreign markets and to sell the entire production in France. According to the physiocrats domestic trade has the advantage that it requires lower transport costs, which are detrimental to both consumers and producers. Therefore if it is possible to avoid sales abroad 'the country gains at least the savings on transportation costs' (*Répétition de la question proposée*, I.N.E.D., 1958, vol. II, p. 777, note 1).[22] Not only has free international trade no inherently positive features according to the physiocrats, but it is also regarded as a *mal*, which they would immediately abolish if only there were enough purchasing power in the country, so that the prices of foodstuffs could rise.

However, given the miserable conditions of the majority of the French people and, perhaps, a lack of confidence in the likelihood of proprietors abandoning *luxes de décoration* in order to buy more primary commodities, foreign demand appears to the physiocrats to be the only historically viable way of raising the prices of the products of French agriculture. The backwardness of the country can only be overcome by a major shock, which, by securing a surplus for agricultural producers, will prime the development of the economy and increase the wealth of the nation. This exogenous stimulus can be provided by an undesired but necessary freedom to export corn.

From all this emerges a second feature distinguishing physiocracy from the nineteenth-century doctrines of *laissez-faire*. For Quesnay, free trade is not designed to bring prosperity to all France's commercial partners; on the contrary the economic success of the country may be detrimental to them. The physiocrats believe that exporting corn is precisely the trading policy which will allow France to exploit her 'double advantage' with respect to other countries (see Le Trosne, 1777, p. 988). A free trade policy can be successful because it is based on two very simple considerations. First, French exports are made up of necessaries of life, thus they are certainly required for consumption by people in every country and their sales are certain (see Du Pont, 1764, pp. 40–1). Moreover, France has fertile land, which is particularly suitable for producing the goods necessary to satisfy people's basic needs (see ibid; see also Le Trosne, 1777, p. 988). Thus France takes advantage of the fact that while every country has to consume primary commodities, 'not all nations can produce a lot of foodstuffs' (see Weulersse, 1910a, vol. I, p. 251, note 7), and its land is the most fertile in Europe.

Secondly, free exports of primary commodities exploit the favourable geographic position of France, which is surrounded by countries whose primary sector cannot satisfy the needs of their citizens (see Le Trosne, 1777, p. 988).[23] Therefore, while competition may be lethal to French industry, agriculture enjoys all its advantages. In fact, France is a 'kingdom which has a large territory and which is favourably placed for the sale of its products' (*Impôts*, I.N.E.D., 1958, vol. II, p. 586, see also pp. 600–1). French agriculture has a sort of 'natural privilege in international competition' (Weulersse, 1910a, vol. I, p. 251); so, not only is *laissez-faire* compatible with a value surplus in agriculture (see Woog, 1950, p. 31), but it also tends to increase it. Thus the real problem for French policy in foreign trade consists in directing the enormous wealth and purchasing power of the whole of Europe towards the products of French agriculture. If the wealth of French citizens is not enough to secure high prices for foodstuffs, monetary demand from other European countries will certainly boost both effective consumption and prices.

Thus, the physiocrats envisage a type of international free trade which can make France economically, and perhaps politically, the most powerful country in the world, to the disadvantage of her trading partners. They do not care whether a free trading system is advantageous for all the participant countries. On the contrary, they stress that a free corn trade is profitable for France, which can become the granary of the world. The free exportation of the products of land guarantees the realisation of the value of their output by French farmers, and hence the welfare of the whole country. It is clear that with regard to international trade Quesnay and his followers were concerned with one simple thing: that France should become a net exporter of agricultural products. Indeed the physiocrats believe that, given the fertility of the soil, with the implementation of free trade France will become a net exporter (see Le Trosne, 1777, p. 988).

Despite their 'mercantilistic' flavour, these words fit well with Quesnay's theory of surplus and of the causes of national development. Free exportation of foodstuffs is a device to secure a positive balance of trade to the country. Thus his reasons for advocating free trade in corn have little in common with the point of view of the supporters of complete *laissez-faire* (see Sauvaire-Jourdan, 1903, p. 616).

4.8 Competition among producers

The physiocrats present a detailed investigation of both internal and foreign demand for the products of land. But this analysis is not sufficient, by itself, to justify the permanent difference between the current price and the unit cost of production, which constitutes surplus value. One must also examine what happens on the production side in the primary sector, when the cultivators obtain a surplus. Why does production not catch up with the level of effective demand? The search for gain by old and new cultivators should raise agricultural output until effective demand is wholly satisfied and current price falls towards the unit cost, thus eliminating the surplus. This is the traditional Smithian argument which explains that market prices of commodities tend towards their natural levels because of competition among producers, who increase output in the sectors with higher rates of profit (see Smith, 1776, vol. I, p. 62ff.). Quesnay's notion of market competition has some features in common with that of Smith;[24] there are many buyers and sellers, an efficient transport system, no monopolies or exclusive privileges (see Chapter 3, 3.5). Moreover, Quesnay explicitly uses the free entry argument to show that artisans can make no profit, because competition keeps the prices of their products equal to the costs of production (see 3.9).

However, according to the physiocrats, the existence of a competitive system permits a permanent surplus value in agriculture. Their analysis of competition among cultivators is the weakest and most unconvincing aspect of their theory of the origin of surplus. They fail to provide a full description of the relationship between output and price variations. Quesnay points out that production is abandoned when the price does not cover the costs of cultivation; 'when the value of a commodity does not equal the expenses one must abandon the work' (a letter to Mirabeau, in Bauer, 1895, pp. 20–1). The poor farmers, who cannot stock their products (see Chapter 3, 3.4) but are compelled to sell the entire output, either suffer continuous losses, or, more likely, give up cultivation (see *Fermiers*, Groenewegen, 1983, pp. 13–14).

Quesnay also examines the situation in which the higher consumption of a commodity brings about a rise in its current price; then 'the cultivators will so much multiply it [the good], that soon its price will not exceed those of other products' (*Réponse au Mémoire de M.H.*, I.N.E.D., 1958, vol. II, p. 754). Therefore the quantity of a good which is produced and brought to the market for sale increases, both because there are new farmers wishing to produce, and because existing cultivators are induced to raise their output. Competition among the producers, who must sell their entire output, should bring the current price of the commodity down to its cost of production in all sectors of the economy. However, according to Quesnay this mechanism does not rule out the existence of a permanent excess of demand over supply in one sector of the economy: agriculture.

Quesnay provides only rare and meagre hints about the reasons which prevent the output of primary products from adjusting to effective demand. The main reason concerns the organisation of the productive process in the primary sector. Agricultural output cannot be increased easily, because large financial means are required to start and to expand cultivation, and not many farmers can afford to invest so much money (see Weulersse, 1910a, vol. II, p. 313). Capitalist agriculture is productive when it can use modern methods of cultivation, which yield a larger surplus per unit of capital invested (see 4.3). But the original advances necessary to introduce large-scale cultivation are very expensive. Moreover, in order to become a farmer, the cultivator must pay a fixed rent to the proprietor for a number of years (see Chapter 3, 3.9). On top of all these expenses, at the beginning of each productive cycle the cultivator must meet the annual advances, that is to say wages and raw materials. Moreover, monetary returns only appear later in the productive cycle, and sometimes it is necessary to wait several years. But above all, these gains are highly uncertain, since they are threatened by many different factors; good and bad harvests, the power of merchants, etc. Thus, the need for huge financial means limits the possibility of increasing output through the entry of new producers, because not many people can become farmers. As Weulersse says: 'the number of producers entering competition is limited' (Weulersse 1910a, vol. I, p. 251; see also p. 272). This relative absence of competition among producers is not due to any regulation protecting the existing farmers; it is a straightforward lack of wealthy cultivators.[25]

4.9 Some weaknesses in the physiocratic theory of the origin of surplus

Quesnay's theory of surplus is much more refined than the simple idea of a 'gift of nature'. In particular he analyses two important features of the economy; the role of tools and equipment in production and the influence of effective demand on the exchange value of products. The physiocratic efforts to justify the exclusive productivity of agriculture oscillate between two poles: the sphere of production and that of the market. Some writings focus on the importance of means of production and technology, others stress the role of consumption and expenditures. However, there are remarkable differences in the ways the physiocrats deal with these two problems. They put forward a precise analysis of the working of market mechanisms and of the role of aggregate effective demand for commodities. The distinction made between use and exchange value, and the examination of free foreign trade, provide clear and convincing explanations of the high effective demand for French primary products. But on the production side, Quesnay and his disciples present a very poor investigation of competition among producers and fail to give a satisfactory description of the process of output and price variations.

As a result of this lack of balance in the analysis of market and production phenomena, physiocracy provides no convincing and conclusive explanation of the doctrine of the exclusive productivity of agriculture. This remains open to major and damaging criticisms, due to 'flaws' in the reasoning adopted to support it. A first cause for dissatisfaction derives from the fact that Quesnay does not explicitly relate the existence of surplus to the capitalistic organisation of agriculture. He saw important features of capitalistic production; for instance he stressed that different means of production give rise to different amounts of gross and net output (see Marx, 1963, vol. I, p. 44). Thus production is not a simple relationship between man and nature; nature is exploited and appropriated by people by means of tools and equipment. Capital, that is to say products used for further production, is a decisive factor in the success of the organisation of the productive process; the higher the advances, the higher the net product yielded by agriculture. Thus Quesnay recognised the importance of capital in securing a high and stable net product, but he failed to explicitly relate surplus to the division of labour (see ibid., p. 385) and to explain precisely why and how larger advances increase the productivity of the workers.[26]

Of course it is unreasonable to accuse Quesnay of not having singled out all the features of the capitalistic labour process, which had not yet displayed all its characteristics in 1760 France. But this fact has important consequences for his theory of surplus. Although Quesnay discerns several elements of capitalistic production, he does not use these features to distinguish between productive and unproductive activities. For instance, he points out that the surplus is particularly high in large-scale cultivation, which is the truly capitalistic sector of the economy. However, he never takes the step of ascribing the existence of surplus only to the labour which is assisted by capital. Thus, in analysing the production side of the economy, Quesnay is ultimately unable to relate surplus to the capitalistic division of labour. He resorts to the idea of a permanent excess demand for French foodstuffs in order to justify the net product of agriculture. The theory of the genesis of surplus is thus linked to the sphere of the market, and to its characteristics. The detailed analysis of market mechanisms has to explain the extraordinarily high effective demand for French primary commodities, which should justify the existence of a net product in *only one sector* of the economy.

But a second and most important weakness emerges here; Quesnay's theory suffers from a vicious circularity. The physiocratic argument runs as follows: landlords must spend their revenues on purchases of the products of agriculture and the government must encourage their exportation, *because* this is the only sector which yields a surplus to the country. But *only if* there is a large domestic and foreign consumption is there also a high effective demand for the products of French agriculture, thus securing the existence of a surplus over costs in this sector. The measures favouring the consumption of foodstuffs are justified by the doctrine of the exclusive productivity of agriculture, but this theory is based on the existence of a huge aggregate demand. To use Quesnay's own words, he puts '*la charrue avant les boeufs*' (see note 19).

Certainly the economic and social conditions of Europe in the eighteenth century help to explain the origin of Quesnay's idea of a permanent excess of demand over supply for primary commodities (see Meek, 1962, p. 362). These considerations are particularly important if one bears in mind that there is a lack of competition among French cultivators, and that French agriculture has enormous productive possibilities. These reasons certainly justify hopes for the potential economic performance of the French economy; but they do not necessarily provide a good explanation of a general theory of surplus and wealth. The particular historical conditions of a country cannot explain the doctrine of the productivity of agriculture and the sterility of manufacture, which are supposed to be *universal* features of economic systems. However, our interpretation of Quesnay's analysis of productive and sterile activities brings to light the analytical reasons for the inconsistencies of his theory of the origin of surplus. Quesnay and his disciples are facing an awkward task; they want to explain the existence of a value surplus in a *single* sector of a freely competitive market exchange economy.

Even with its flaws and contradictions, Quesnay's theory of surplus leaves some important legacies to classical political economy, and to Adam Smith in particular. First of all, in this type of economics the theory of the origin of surplus and wealth is of overwhelming and central importance, and certainly cannot be regarded as a datum. Secondly, in a market exchange economy the net product is conceived *also* as a value magnitude and not only as a physical quantity of products. Therefore the problem of production of surplus and wealth involves and requires an analysis of prices. Thirdly, the study of the capitalistic organisation of production emphasises the relationship between the quantity and quality of the means of production and the level of productivity in agriculture. Fourthly, the analysis of the laws of markets, that is to say the study of the working of competition introduces the peculiar concept of effective demand and an examination of its components, with particular attention to foreign trade.

Some commentators have seen important similarities between Quesnay's notion of demand and Smith's more famous *effectual demand* (see for instance Johnson, 1937, p. 219; Johnson, 1966, p. 621). This problem calls for some discussion. The only clear similarity between the two concepts is that they both indicate the amount of a commodity which can be exchanged against money; by which Quesnay and Smith intend to oppose a view of demand as the mere sum of the needs and desires of people (see Smith, 1776, vol. I p. 63). This distinction is not restricted to the physiocrats, but before Smith, apart from them only Sir James Steuart stressed the role of the actual purchasing possibilities of people in the determination of prices (see Steuart, 1767, vol. I, pp. 164–5, 169–70, 176).[27] Moreover, both Smith and Quesnay relate this actual demand to the price of the commodity; it is the quantity which is actually purchased at a certain price. Here, of course, there is an important difference; on the one hand there is Smith's well-known notion of natural price (see Smith, 1776, p. 62), and on the other we have the concept of *prix actuel*, which has been translated by Meek as 'current price'.[28] We have already looked at the differences between the fundamental price, which exerts a major influence on the current one, and Smith's natural price (see above Chapter 3, 3.11). From the point of view of the theory of surplus, it must be remarked that the fundamental price reflects Quesnay's view that only agriculture yields a net product. In fact, this price includes an element of surplus, rent, together with costs, only in the case of primary commodities. However, this particular distinction between the fundamental price of foodstuffs and of manufactured goods does not provide a convincing justification for the fact that surplus exists only in one sector of a freely competitive economy. Smith introduced a natural rate of profit on capital invested in his notion of natural price; and this concept is defined in the same way for all commodities, because there is no longer a need to ascribe the quality of productiveness only to agriculture (see Smith, 1776, vol. I pp. 54–5, 62, 67; Turgot, 1766, pp., 572–4; Tucker, 1960, pp. 46–8). Therefore Smith does not link his concept of natural price to a theory of the origin of surplus which must distinguish between the different sectors of the economy, as is the case in Quesnay's economics.

Finally, there is an important distinction between the concepts of demand used by Smith and by Quesnay. Smith's effectual demand emphasises the relationship between the price and the quantity brought to the market of a single product. The physiocratic notion of effective demand emphasises the macroeconomic aspect of demand, in the sense that it stresses the importance of securing a profitable sale of the whole output of a sector of the economy. Of course the physiocrats emphasise the macro-economic features of demand because they must explain the existence of a net product over costs in a single sector of the economy.

5 The Theory of Distribution

5.1 The appropriation of surplus: rent, *taille* and profits

Quesnay's analysis of prices and markets has important consequences for his theory of the distribution of surplus. It is usually believed that in physiocracy the surplus accrues entirely to the landowners, as rent (see for instance Marx, 1970, vol. I, p. 477; 1967, vol. II, p. 784). The net product also includes the *taille*, which makes up the sovereign's revenue, and the church's *dîme*. In the first part of this chapter it will be shown that rent is not the only form taken by the net product when it is distributed among the classes because the physiocrats also regard the profits of farmers as part of the social surplus. It emerges that this interpretation of the physiocratic theory of distribution is perfectly consistent with the price concepts put forward by Quesnay; in particular profits are shown to be given as the difference between the current and the fundamental price. Textual evidence will show that it is possible to give a precise definition of Quesnay's concept of profit, and of its role in physiocratic economics. As a result of this new approach, the notion of *bon prix* acquires a precise meaning and a definite analytical role. It includes the profits of cultivators, which are the normal and regular source of the accumulation of capital. In fact, apart from the philological evidence, it will emerge that the physiocrats regarded farmers' profits as part of the net product, because this is the only element of the annual surplus which can ensure an increase in the means of production in agriculture. For Quesnay only farmers, with their gains, can carry on the necessary process of accumulation, which is the seed of prosperity. According to the physiocratic scheme of reproduction, as depicted in the *Tableau Economique* where the social output includes its means of production and a surplus, the only logically consistent way in which accumulation can take place is through the reinvestment of part of the net product.

The second part of this chapter examines the reasons why, even in recent years, many commentators have believed that Quesnay did not consider profits a regular constituent of net product. This view seems to rest on the authoritative interpretation of the late Professor Meek, for whom Quesnay included profit in the surplus in his early articles because of the influence of Cantillon (see Meek, 1962, pp. 269, 301). But in later works, the gains of the farmers are just a '*temporary* share in the net product, which ultimately crystallized out into rent' (Meek, 1962, pp. 384–5, his italics). Rent and *taille* are the only true forms of surplus; the gains of the cultivators would be regarded by the physiocrats 'as an abnormal type of income' (ibid., p. 380, footnote). Since its appearance in 1959[1] this view has been accepted and adopted by many scholars,[2] and there is now a widespread belief that Quesnay considered profits as only a short-lived phenomenon.[3] It will be argued that this approach is based on an incorrect interpretation of passages in which Quesnay and his disciples maintain that competition among farmers encourages an increase in rents. However, contrary to Meek's opinion these passages do not represent the necessary logical development of physiocratic thought (see Meek, 1962, pp. 384–5). For the physiocrats, competition among cultivators is just a way to shift the tone of their writings in favour of the landlords, and to reassure the members of the first two estates that farmers do not represent an economic and political threat. Moreover, the analytical status of profits in physiocracy will be discussed with respect both to the problem of their permanence in time, and to that of their role as the source of new means of production. This analysis will provide further reasons for rejecting the opinion that in physiocracy the farmers' gains are only a temporary share of social surplus.

In a passage from *Questions intéressantes sur la population, l'agriculture et le commerce, etc.*, Quesnay quite clearly distinguishes 'the necessary expenses for the cultivation of corn' from the profits of the '*cultivateurs*' (I.N.E.D., 1958, vol. II, p. 651, note 10). Similar statements can also be found in the articles *Hommes* (ibid., p. 566) and *Grains* (Ibid., pp. 482–3, 505), which he wrote for the *Encyclopédie*. In *Grains* Quesnay says that in the cultivation of corn the net product

> must then be distributed approximately in the following way:
> | | |
> |---|---|
> | For the landlord | 3/5 |
> | For the *taille* | 1/5 |
> | For the farmer | 1/5' (ibid. p.463)[4, 5] |

This gain is not limited to the cultivation of corn, but arises in all the productive activities of the primary sector. For instance, in the production of wine the share of profits in the surplus is greater than that of rent: 'there are ten *livres* for the rent on each *arpent* [unit of land], 10 *livres* for the *taille*, 15 for the profit of the wine-dresser' (*Impôts*, ibid., p. 601).[6]

Other physiocrats also believe that part of the surplus accrues to the farmers as profit, particularly in large-scale cultivation. Du Pont de Nemours writes that the net product 'is divided between the proprietors and the workers' (Du Pont, 1764, p.78).[7] Le Trosne goes even further; he polemicises against Condillac, who maintains that 'the entire production belongs to the proprietors, who leave part of it to the farmers for their wages' (Le Trosne, 1777, p. 932). The physiocrat has a completely different opinion. First of all, the cultivator 'certainly is not a wage-earner' (ibid.). Therefore the income accruing to the cultivator is not a salary, even if a particularly high one; he must not be regarded as a wage-earner, but as an independent entrepreneur. Secondly, Le Trosne remarks that reproduction does not belong to the landlords; 'on the contrary the overall production belongs to the farmers' (ibid.). At the end of the production period the output belongs to the farmers, who are the only true owners of these products. The cultivators use the output of agriculture to continue the process of production; first they set aside the agricultural products which have to be employed in the next productive process. Then they can sell the remaining products on first-hand markets. At this stage in the process of circulation of money and commodities, the monetary returns from sales at first-hand belong entirely to them. Some of these yields must be used to purchase the manufactured goods which are part of the annual and original advances (see Chapter 2, 2.5). Then the farmer gives the landlord the share of net product they have agreed upon; this exchange takes place either in kind, or in money (see Le Trosne, 1777, p. 932).

These passages are not isolated or scattered examples taken from the writings of the physiocrats. On the contrary, Quesnay's notion of profit has a precise relationship with other parts of his work. In particular, it is linked to his analysis of the exchange value of commodities, and to the price notions he derives from it. As a matter of fact, the cultivators make a gain after they have met the technical expenses of production, rent and the *taille*. The sum of these three items is precisely the *prix fondamental* of a primary product: hence profits are given as the difference between the current and the fundamental price, as is clearly stated by Du Pont de Nemours:

the *prix commun de vendeur* must necessarily be slightly higher than the *prix commun fondamental*, because it is the husbandman who by the payment of his rent establishes the *prix fondamental*; he fixes this price according to the calculation of his expenses, and he must obviously leave a small margin for himself (Du Pont, 1764, p. 11, note 1, his italics).[8]

This interpretation of Quesnay's theory of profit is also confirmed by an analysis of the numerical examples in the tables in his articles *Hommes* and *Grains*, where he describes the conditions of the corn trade in France and England (see Chapter 3, 3.3). The gains of the farmers can easily be determined from these examples. Moreover, Quesnay's calculations are fully consistent with the price notions he derives from the same figures. In the last column of Table 2 Quesnay lists the '*reste par arpent*', which is the difference between the total revenue obtained by the farmer from the sale of the output and the expenses incurred, for each *arpent*. In year j the residual on each *arpent*, z_j, is $x_j \cdot y_j - K = z_j$, where K is the value of the annual expenses of the cultivator for each *arpent* (for the meaning of the symbols, see Chapter 3, 3.3).

The total revenue of the farmer depends on the changes in the current price of corn, y_j, which also determine the size of the *reste* and its variations, since expenses are fixed for each productive cycle. In order to calculate the part of this net product which constitutes the farmer's profits, we must examine his overall expenses, and the way in which the *reste* is shared. Both questions can be answered by jointly examining the headings and figures of Tables 1 and 2. The heading of the fourth column of Table 1 indicates that there are three components in the fundamental price of the products of land: expenses, *taille* and rent. (Note that the size of *taille* and rent are independent of variations in the current price itself.) According to Quesnay, the sum of these two items – say H – is 14 *livres*, i.e. the difference between the figures in the fourth column of Table 1 and those of the fourth column of Table 2. The technical expenses of production are 60 *livres* (fourth column of Table 2), while the farmer's overall costs are 74 *livres* (fourth column of Table 1). Hence the '*reste per arpent*' in the fifth column of Table 2 clearly includes rent, *taille* and farmers' profit. However, part of this residual has a fixed destination: 14 *livres* must be paid by farmers as rent and *taille*, irrespective of their annual yields.

The profits of the farmer can now easily be calculated as the difference between the figures in the third and fourth columns of Table 1, which are the value of gross output and of the farmer's expenses respectively. Each year j, the profit p_j is

$$(2) \quad (x_j \cdot y_j) - (K + H) = p_j.$$

The following relations link the magnitudes which appear in the two tables:

Gross revenue of the farmer	−
Expenses	−
(Rent + *Taille*)	=

Profit of the farmer

We can now add a fifth column to Table 1, showing the profits and losses of the cultivator for five years; the table will look as follows (all figures are per unit of land, an *arpent*):[9]

Table 5

x_j	y_j		$K + H$	p_j
Output	Price	Value of gross output	Costs + rent + taille	Profit
7	10	70		− 4
6	12	72		− 2
5	15	75	74	1
4	20	80		6
3	30	90		15

The average profit per unit of corn over the five years is given by the ratio between the overall profits, 17 *livres*, and the total output of five years, 25 *setiers*. In Quesnay's example this figure is 13 *sous*, 7 *déniers* and one-fifth of a *dénier*, which is precisely the difference between the average current price of corn and the average fundamental price as indicated by Quesnay in *Hommes* (see I.N.E.D., 1958, vol. II, p. 532). Dividing (2) by the annual production of each *arpent* we have the annual profit of the farmer per unit of output:

(3) $y_j - (K + H)/x_j$

In the above, y_i is the current price of corn and $(K + H)/x_j$ is its fundamental value. Therefore, according to Quesnay, in order to see whether the cultivator makes either a profit or a loss, one 'must examine the fundamental price of corn and the average price that the farmer obtains ' (*Hommes*, I.N.E.D., 1958, vol. II, p. 550; see also Du Pont, 1764, p. 11, note 1). A profit accrues to the farmer in so far as the price at which he sells the product exceeds the overall expenses incurred for the production of one unit of output.

5.2 Profit upon alienation

We must now examine the analytical features of Quesnay's concept of profit. The gain of the cultivator is regarded by Quesnay as a typical residual in the distribution of the net product. In fact, the technical costs of production, the rent and the *taille* are given and fixed, for different reasons, before the actual sale of the products. The sum of these three items is the fundamental price, which depends on three sets of data: (a) the methods of production, (b) the value of rent, (c) the value of taxation.[10] The fundamental price is known before the products are sold on the market and does not include profits because it is the price at which the cultivator makes neither losses nor gains (see Chapter 3, 3.9). Given the above three sets of data the size of the profit depends entirely on market conditions in the sales at first-hand. The physiocratic notion of profit has most of the features of a *profit on alienation* whose size is influenced by the selling price of a commodity (when it is higher than its fundamental value). There are a few passages in which Quesnay relates the size of profits to the expenses of production. For instance it seems that the ratio of profit to productive expenses increases in a direct proportion to the latter magnitude. In the cultivation of corn, 60 *livres*, per *arpent* yield a profit of 3 *livres* 9 *sous* and 6 *déniers*; that is to say a ratio approximately 6 per cent (see *Grains*, I.N.E.D., 1958, vol. II, p. 463). The production of wine requires 100 *livres per arpent* and has a ratio of profit to expenses of 15 per cent (see *Impôts*, ibid., p. 601).

In the *Analyse de la formule arithmétique du Tableau Economique*, Quesnay also speaks of the 'interests on the advances' of the productive class (Meek, 1962, p. 154), an expression he had already used in the 1756 article *Fermiers* (see Groenewegen, 1983, p. 15). These interests are given by Quesnay as 10 per cent of the original advances of the cultivator, yet they seem to be much more a sort of return for the depreciation of the means of production than a regular and normal rate of profit on the capital invested.[11]

Despite the fact that Quesnay sometimes links profits to the advances and expenses of farmers, his analysis of prices and markets clearly shows that he considers the gains of entrepreneurs much more as part of the social surplus than as a necessary cost of production, which obviously includes subsistence for himself and his family. As a matter of fact, this is a further example of the importance of the analysis of prices and markets in physiocracy. The notions of current and fundamental price explain why profits are highly variable, while the other elements of net product are much more stable. Actually, the economic mechanisms which allow the farmers a profit are very different from the ways in which the proprietors and the state obtain their shares of the surplus. Laws and historically accepted traditions explain why the sovereign and the proprietors of land are entitled to receive part of the surplus. The *taille* and the other taxes falling on the farmers must secure for the state a revenue which enables the rulers to meet the expenses necessary for the order and security of the country: defence, justice, administration, public works, etc. The existence of the landlords' right to a share of the net product in the form of rent is regarded by the physiocrats as a basic feature of the economic system. The actual sum paid by the cultivator to the proprietor disregards the monetary value of the net product, at least until the renewal of the land lease (see, for instance, *Premier problème économique*, Meek, 1962, p. 181, note 1; and Chapter 3, 3.9, 3.10).[12]

Thus in France during the *ancien régime*, rent and *taille* were essential and permanent components of the net product of society. The profits of the farmers were not a well-established economic fact; their size was volatile and highly unstable, and in some years farmers could even make a loss. Profits were a residual element of surplus; they absorbed the year-to-year variations in net product, which were borne by the farmers, leaving the king and the landlords with much more stable revenues.

Before Smith, the concept of profit on alienation was fairly widespread among authors (see Herlitz, 1961b, pp. 130–2). The physiocrats' investigation of the problem of farmers' gains certainly owe a debt to Cantillon's *Essay sur la nature du commerce en général*, with which they were well acquainted.[13] Cantillon states that the cultivator is a real enterpreneur, who organises the process of production (see

Cantillon, 1755, p. 61), takes all the risks, and whose gain is uncertain (ibid., p. 55), although he generally receives one-third of the output as the profit on his undertaking (ibid., p. 43).

But the physiocratic concept of profit is defined by the difference between two precise notions of price and is not the same as Cantillon's. The physiocrats reject much more decisively than Cantillon the possibility of the existence of a profit upon alienation due merely to the activity of 'buying cheap and selling dear'. In fact the current price varies from year to year depending on market conditions, but the second term of the difference, from which profit comes, is the fundamental price and not just any market price at which the commodity has been purchased.[14] The fundamental price has a precise relationship with the cost of production of commodities, both in its technical and in its political and social aspects. Therefore, even if Quesnay stresses the influence of a high current price on farmers' profits, they are also affected by technical changes in the process of production, by which the cultivator manages to reduce the expenses and hence the *prix fondamental*. The same is true of a reform in the fiscal system, which relieves the farmers of most of the duties falling on them. But their gains can also be affected by a process of political change, which modifies the power relationships between them and the landed aristocracy. All three situations imply a change in the fundamental price of the products of land, and hence in farmers' profits.

The physiocrats' notion of profit on alienation is much closer to that of Sir James Steuart than to that of their predecessor Cantillon. Steuart writes: 'in the price of goods, I consider two things as really existing, and quite different from one another; to wit; the real value of commodity and the profit upon alienation' (Steuart, 1767, vol. I, p. 159).[15] The 'real value' depends on three sets of data: the average time required to produce a good, 'the value of the workmen's subsistence and necessary expenses' (ibid., p. 160), and the value of raw materials. The price of commodities 'cannot be lower than the amount of the three'; Steuart continues: 'whatever is higher, is the manufacturer's profit' (ibid., pp. 160–1). As for Steuart, Quesnay's fundamental price is a threshold above which the farmer makes a profit, and whose size depends on the price in sales at first-hand (see Vaggi, 1983, pp. 11–12).

There is a further similarity between the theories of profit of Steuart and of physiocracy. Like Steuart (see Steuart, 1767, vol. I, pp.161–2) the physiocrats stress the importance of effective demand, and of the resulting degree of competition among buyers, in determining the gains of cultivators. Quesnay insists on the necessity of securing the most favourable conditions for the sale of the products of land, 'because there is no profit from cultivation without the sale of the products' (*Questions intéressantes*, I.N.E.D., 1958, vol. II, p. 623). On the contrary, when there is a high effective demand for the products of land in retail markets, there are also many competing merchants prepared to pay a profitable current price to the farmers, because they know that there are large numbers of final consumers wealthy enough to pay a high retail price. This is a further indication that in physiocracy there are close relationships between the theory of value and that of the production and distribution of surplus and wealth.

5.3 The *bon prix* and the incentive to investment

The above analysis of the physiocratic notion of profit also allows us to provide a satisfactory definition of *bon prix*; this is the best known notion of price in physiocratic theory, but its fame often seems to be equalled only by its semantic vagueness. The *bon prix* is the level of price on first-hand markets which is brought about by free international competition, and which leaves a gain for the producer (see *Grains*, I.N.E.D., 1958, vol. II, pp. 507–9). Thus this concept is defined with reference to the fundamental price, which is the sum of all the expenses incurred by the farmer. But this does not mean that any current price which leaves a gain over the fundamental price is a *bon prix*. The physiocrats regard the existence of a profit as a necessary, but not sufficient, condition to allow for a *bon prix*. That the existence of any kind of profit is not in itself enough to bestow the quality of *bon* on a current price can be seen in the tables of *Grains* and *Hommes*. From Table 1, which refers to the corn trade in France, Quesnay calculates that '*the prix commun du vendeur* is higher than the fundamental price by 13 *d*. 7 *d*.' (*Hommes*, I.N.E.D., 1958, vol. II, p. 532), which is the profit of the farmer on each *setier* of corn. But he does not regard the current price of 15 *liv*. 9 *s*. 7 *d*. one fifth of *dénier* as a *bon prix*, although it leaves some profit to the cultivator. For Quesnay the *bon prix* of corn must be in the range of 18 *livres* per *setier*, as in England, where free international trade brings about a current price of 17 *liv*. 12 *s*. per *setier* and the profit is 2 *liv*. 16 *s*. (see *Grains*, ibid., p. 475).

Therefore the existence of a profit is a necessary, but not a sufficient, condition for a *bon prix*. Profits must be high enough to stimulate farmers to reinvest them in production, thus increasing the advances. This essential feature of a *bon prix* cannot be quantified because it depends on the farmer's opinion concerning the amount of profit which is sufficient to justify new investments in agricultural production. Mercier writes that 'without a *bon prix* the cultivator will lack both the means and the *bonne volonté*' (Mercier, 1767, p. 288) to increase his advances. If farmers do not expect to make the reasonable profits guaranteed by a *bon prix*, they do not have the *good will* to invest their gains, and the process of increasing national wealth cannot commence. Therefore the physiocrats clearly ascribe two roles to the profits of cultivators; they are: (a) the fund for the accumulation of capital, (b) the incentive to investment.

The above interpretation of the *bon prix* is confirmed by the fact that the physiocrats always associate this concept with the process of development and growth in the economy. Quesnay writes that if commodities 'are sold at a price which is high enough to yield a gain sufficient to encourage people to maintain or increase their production, they are at their *bon prix*' (*Hommes*, Meek, 1962, p. 93; see also *Analyse*, ibid., p. 164, note 1). Thus the 'good price' of the products of land can increase the welfare and prosperity of the nation because 'profits multiply the products' (*Hommes*, I.N.E.D., 1958, vol. II, p. 535). Farmers use their gains to increase the original and annual advances, and thus raise both agricultural production and revenues: rent, *dîme* and taxes for the sovereign.[16] The path to prosperity and plenty depends on the process of accumulation of capital which results from the reinvestment of cultivators' profits, when they sell their products at the *bon prix* (see Spengler, 1945, pp. 209ff; Landry,

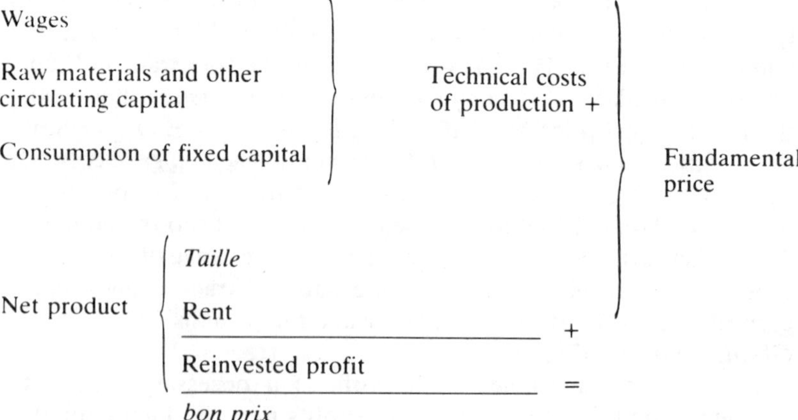

1958, p. 44). Therefore a current price can be regarded as a *bon prix* if the profit that it leaves to the farmer not only exists, but is high enough to stimulate the cultivator to invest and risk his gain in increasing the advances of production (see Herlitz, 1961b, p. 140; see also an anonymous writer in the *Observateur* of 1759, quoted in Weulersse, 1910a, vol. I, p. 482, note 4). The scheme presented in this section summarises the relationship between profit and prices in physiocracy.

5.4 The expenditure of surplus; farmers and investments

The notion of *bon prix* draws attention to the fact that for the physiocrats there are important differences between profits and other constituents of the net product. On one hand, the proprietors and the sovereign do whatever they like with their shares of the net product. Naturally the physiocrats offer advice about the proper ways of employing these revenues. The landlords' income should sustain the effective demand for the products of land (see *Extrait*, Kuczynski and Meek, 1972, p.11); taxes should be in proportion to the revenue of land, and should be used to fulfil the collective needs of the country. But these are mere suggestions; economic behaviour and policy measures rely totally on the good will and wisdom of landlords and administrators. The landlords' usual pattern of expenditure was very different from that advocated by the physiocrats; the nobles purchased large amounts of manufactured commodities, *luxe de décoration*, and of foreign-made products. The way in which public revenue was levied and spent was even worse; many different duties oppressed the cultivators, and instead of employing the revenue to build canals and roads, which would have lowered transport costs, the state undertook high and continuous military expenditures.

On the other hand, the profits of the cultivators are almost inevitably associated with an increase in the advances of agriculture, and farmers are always described as reinvesting their gains in the productive process (see, for instance, *Premier problème économique*, Meek, 1962, p. 180). The profits of farmers are the fundamental source of the accumulation of capital. Of course the cultivators are not obliged to reinvest their gains in production; the very concept of *bon prix* makes it clear that it is up to them to decide whether profits are high enough to justify their reinvestment. But certainly the physiocrats seem to believe that if farmers decide to spend their incomes they can purchase only tools, equipment, horses, carts, and other means of production for agriculture. Their final use is restricted to increasing the existing amount of advances. Quesnay never mentions the possibility that cultivators may purchase manufactured commodities for their own consumption, or the need for them to adapt their expenses to a particular pattern. Provided that there is a good current price, the mode of expenditure of profits seems to be unambiguously determined.

Although farmers' profits are a share of the net product, they are not regarded by the physiocrats as being 'disposable' in the sense that rent and *taille* are. These two parts of the net product can be spent in the purchase of almost any type of good or service; profits can either be invested or not. We can divide the components of social surplus into two elements; profits on one hand, and the revenues: rent, *taille* and tithes, on the other (see Woog, 1950, p. 22).[17]

For the physiocrats there is a second major difference between the two parts of net product, profits and revenues – that is to say rent and *taille* – in terms their expenditure. The landlords purchase goods and services for their own consumption, while the profits of farmers are reinvested in production. Thus the revenues of proprietors make up the most important item of domestic consumption, but there is hardly any mention of the possibility that nobles might invest their incomes in the advances of large-scale cultivation (see Baudeau, 1767; vol. XII, pp.150–2). They should leave to wealthy farmers the task of providing the tools, equipment and financial means necessary to maintain the workers and to buy raw materials (see ibid., pp. 152–3).[18]

The different ways in which farmers and landlords spend their share of surplus reflect the physiocrats' opinion that the features and roles of the two classes are clearly separated in the process of economic development (see Fox-Genovese, 1976, p. 28). The farmers invest their gains 'in the works and undertaking of cultivation . . . at the same time that the Proprietors by increasing their expenditures . . . will multiply the jobs, and will facilitate the subsistence of workers who live in cities ' (Du Pont, 1764, p. 79). Both classes have the positive task of securing the prosperity of the country. On the one hand, all that the proprietors have to do is to consume the products of French agriculture in order to sustain the demand for primary commodities (see *Questions Intéressantes*, I.N.E.D., 1958, vol. II, pp. 623, 631). On the other hand, it is to the farmers that the physiocrats assign the crucial and essential role of procuring new capital and improving the methods of cultivation.

Despite their instability, the profits of farmers perform an extremely important task in physiocracy, that of securing the accumulation of capital in agriculture and of increasing agricultural productivity. Thus, not only does a well-defined concept of profit exist, but it also has the crucial and unique role of starting the growth process of national wealth.

The notions of profit and of *bon prix* therefore help to clarify the physiocrats' view of the economic role of the cultivators. In the France of 1760 the capitalist entrepreneur was still the exception rather than the rule. Nevertheless, the physiocrats assign to the farmer most of the roles and functions of a capitalist; the cultivator is regarded as a modern independent entrepreneur, who deliberately employs and risks his money in the process of production (see Fox-Genovese, 1976, p. 111; Woog, 1950, p. 19). *In Grains* Quesnay wrote:

> here we do not consider the wealthy farmer as a labourer, who himself works on land; he is an entrepreneur who rules his undertaking and makes it valuable by means of his skill and of his wealth (I.N.E.D., 1958, vol. II, p. 483; see also a letter by Quesnay to the *Intendant* of Soissons, quoted in Weulersse, 1910, vol. I, p. 360).

Farmers bring together all the necessary means of production, but they are not mere supervisors of this process, because they own the tools and equipment, the *avances annuelles* and *primitives* (see ibid.). Moreover, the cultivator pays rent to the landlord and hires workers to whom he must pay wages during the period of production (see Du Pont, 1772, p.374). Once the farmers have met their obligations towards the landlords, they are free to decide the quality and quantity of the products to be produced and the methods of production to be employed. They are the owners of the output and they take the risks and reap the benefits of cultivation. Thus, Baudeau's comment that the cultivator is 'the true Headmaster and Entrepreneur of cultivation' (Baudeau, 1767–70, vol. XII, p. 142) seems justified.

However, we have already seen that the most important activity, which is assigned by the physiocrats exclusively to farmers is that of reinvesting in agriculture their share of the surplus.[19] The cultivators are the social group which controls the process of accumulation of capital. In some passages Quesnay invites the proprietors to become entrepreneurs on their own lands (see for instance, *Hommes*, I.N.E.D., 1958, vol. II, p. 559). The physiocrats would like to see the nobles abandon their luxurious city existence and to go back to the frugal and useful activities of country life. But these are only memories of the 'golden age' of agriculture, as it was during Sully's ministry at the beginning of the seventeenth century (see Weulersse, 1910a, vol. I, p. 1). For the physiocrats, the well being of French agriculture in the second half of the eighteenth century requires a different organisation of production. Many more advances are required and much more attention, knowledge and perseverance are needed from entrepreneurs. The French aristocracy does not seem to have any of these characteristics, so the necessarily arduous process of investment cannot result from its activity.[20] In order to carry on a system based on large-scale cultivation, France requires a specific figure, quite different from the landlords, such as the entrepreneur farmer.[21]

The fact that in physiocracy there is a close link between profits and investments does not mean that Quesnay regarded farmers as mere agents of accumulation, who transform part of the net product into new means of production. The cultivators are in no way obliged, whether by law, by custom, or by nature, to use their income to increase the stock of capital. Like everybody else, cultivators act in pursuance of their own gains and interests (see Mirabeau, 1760b, p. 199). We have seen that the very notion of a good price means that profits are the source of accumulation, but if the farmers do not see the possibility of making a gain from the sale of output they will not reinvest them. Indeed Quesnay points out that: 'it is impossible to reconcile such a small profit with the increase of cultivation' (*Hommes*, I.N.E.D., 1958, vol. II, p.549).[22]

To summarise: in physiocracy the proprietors and cultivators play quite different roles in the process of economic growth which should bring welfare and prosperity to the nation. The cultivators must reinvest their gains and supervise the growth of production, while the landlords must sustain the level of activity by spending their incomes appropriately. All the proprietors can do for the welfare of the country is to consume the products of the soil. The functions of the farmers are certainly much more important; they actually coordinate the process of capital accumulation, which is considered as *the* decisive feature of the process of development and growth in the country.

5.5 The process of development

In a passage in the *Analyse* Quesnay describes the various steps which characterise the process of development in the French economy. He says:

the more that products constantly sell at high prices, the more assured are the annual returns of the farmers, the more cultivation is extended and the more revenue the land brings, as much through the proper price of the products as through the increase in the annual reproduction (Meek, 1962, p. 164, note 1).

The previous sections of this chapter provide all the elements necessary for a precise description of the economic mechanisms outlined by Quesnay in this excerpt, which should lead France to prosperity and wealth. Let us assume that some of the economic policy measures and recommendations advocated by physiocracy have already been implemented (see above Chapter 1, 1.10):

(a) Landlords spend most of their incomes in the purchase of the products of land;
(b) there are no taxes on agricultural production except the *taille*, which is in proportion to the net product (we leave out tithes and other types of duties);
(c) the power of the merchants has been strictly limited, their gains are irrelevant and can be assumed to be at zero;
(d) there is a good transportation system both inside France and with foreign countries, transport costs are very low and can be neglected.

Given the above hypotheses, which serve to simplify the argument, the process of development is characterised by the following relations:

1. Free foreign trade	*causes*	high and stable current prices for primary goods, which implies the existence of a *bon prix* and a profit for the farmers;
2. Profits	*cause*	accumulation of capital in agriculture;
3. Accumulation of capital	*causes*	increases in output, in net product and in revenues.

Each stage represents the physiocratic view of the causal relationship linking two aspects of an economic system which is working according to the laws of the natural order.[23] The following is a brief explanation of these relationships.

1. Free foreign trade implies the possibility of exporting the products of French agriculture, and hence provides a decisive support for effective demand, which then provokes a remarkable degree of competition among the merchants in purchases on first-hand markets. This fact causes a rise in the prices of sales at first-hand.

Moreover, thanks to free foreign trade, international competition stabilises the current price of foodstuffs (see Du Pont, 1764, p. 45). The farmers no longer suffer from huge and detrimental variations in these prices, and the difference between the current and the retail price is minimised, leaving a negligible gain for the merchants (see Weulersse, 1910a, vol. I, p. 520). The increase in the current price of the products of land up to a value which is regarded as a *bon prix*, leaves more profits for farmers.

Thus it is clear that for the physiocrats the attainment of a good price for the products of land is the starting point of economic development; Le Trosne writes that 'it is by reestablishing the value which must start the circle of prosperity' (Le Trosne, 1777, p. 899; see also Conan, 1958, p. 56). Mirabeau is even more explicit; in a passage which appeared in the *Ephémérides* of 1769 he says: 'only the increase of the exchange value of foodstuffs in the sales at first-hand, can lead to . . . an increase of Cultivator's profit and of the revenues, subsistence and wealth of Society' (Mirabeau, 1769, pp. 47–8). Therefore the achievement of a *bon prix* for the products of land should be a major preoccupation of French administrators. But the physiocrats do not regard the *bon prix* as a purely normative concept; on the contrary they are convinced that a good level of the current price follows inevitably from the implementation of free trade.

Moreover, *laissez-faire* in foreign trade is the only way in which international competition will raise the current prices of French primary commodities to a *bon prix* level.[24] For Quesnay, a nation wishing to increase the prices of its products 'can obtain this *bon prix* only by means of free competition in its foreign trade' (*Du Commerce*, I.N.E.D., 1958, vol. II, p. 832).

2. Sections 5.3 and 5.4 above have clearly shown that for the physiocrats profits are the source of capital accumulation. And as the price increase precedes the profits of farmers, these gains must exist before the increase in the means of production. If prices are too low 'the cultivator will not make the advances, because he can only make them thanks to the profits he will obtain from the present harvest; these profits must precede the increase of the products' (Mirabeau,

1760c, p. 72). Profits are a fundamental condition for the accumulation of capital in agriculture, and for the growth of national output (see Deane, 1978, p. 31). But 'this increase in wealth cannot continue when the individuals incurring these expenses do not draw any profit from them' (*Fermiers*, Groenewegen, 1983, p. 17).

Thus farmers must be induced to make new investments by the possibility of making stable and regular gains in their activity. 'The certainty of the sale, the relative stability of the prices, by reassuring the farmers, encourage them to increase their advances and to improve cultivation' (Weulersse, 1910a, vol. I, pp. 518–19). If these conditions exist farmers can become wealthy and will keep on investing their profits in agriculture, so that the original and annual advances increase.

3. The increase in the advances of the primary sector makes possible drainage schemes and the cultivation of new lands and hence an increase in quantity of the country's primary products. Moreover, larger stocks of means of production raise the revenue of the nation. In fact, high original advances characterise capital-intensive agriculture (where large-scale cultivation is the dominant method of production), which alone enhances the productivity of the primary sector (see Chapter 4, 4.3). Mirabeau wrote: 'in order to sustain the opulence, the population and the power of a Nation, it is necessary that the advances of the Farmers should be sufficient to guarantee that the land will produce a higher net product' (Mirabeau, 1760b, p. 143). The existence of wealthy farmers is necessary for improving the methods of cultivation, and for achieving a one-to-one ratio between the net product and the annual advances. Therefore the increased stock of advances brings about more products and revenues and makes France rich and powerful, as is assumed in the *Tableau* (see Chapter 1, 1.10).

B PROFITS AS A TEMPORARY SHARE OF THE SURPLUS

5.6 Competition among farmers

In the light of the results of the first main section of this chapter, it might appear strange that it is still widely believed that Quesnay did not regard the profits of cultivators as part of the net product of the country. This interpretation deserves close examination, because it has the merit of pinpointing some real ambiguities, and even contradictions, in the physiocratic analysis of profits. The most authoritative view of the problem was put forward by Professor Meek, in his 1959 article *The Physiocratic Concept of Profit*, and three years later in the essay *The Interpretation of Physiocracy* (both works are in Meek, 1962).

Professor Meek apparently based his interpretation on two main pillars. On the one hand he says that Quesnay does not include farmers' profits in the country's surplus in his later writings, mainly for reasons of logical coherence. He must reconcile three political aims: to spare farmers from taxation, to reaffirm the principle that only the net product has to be taxed, and to encourage the introduction of the single tax on rent. Thus according, to Meek, only by taking profits out of the social surplus could Quesnay achieve his three main purposes in a logically coherent way. In particular, he could continue to maintain that only the net product must be taxed, and that, at the same time, the profits of farmers must be exempted from taxation. To use Mirabeau's words 'the cultivator is absolutely necessary to production', therefore 'one cannot ask him to undertake any other duty, any other service, than the activity with which he is associated' (Mirabeau, 1766, vol. I, p. 37; see also Mirabeau, 1760b, p.185). Profits are the part of surplus which has to be reinvested; hence the physiocrats are reluctant to regard them as being completely disposable for taxation, as a net product should be.

> Had the Physiocrats admitted that the farmers regularly and normally received a part of 'disposable surplus' in the form of profit, therefore, they would have been hard put to it to defend their proposal that the farmers should be completely exempted from taxation (Meek, 1962, p. 384; see also Herlitz, 1961b, pp. 143–4).

As well as a logical motivation for leaving profits outside the net product, Meek singles out some passages in Quesnay's writings which support his view. These are about the role of competition among cultivators, at the time of renewal of their land leases. Farmers compete one against the other in order to obtain land to cultivate, thus offering higher and higher rents to landlords. 'The entrepreneurs might be able to earn net profits during the course of their leases but these extra gains were assumed to crystallize out into rents when the leases came up from renewal' (Meek, 1962, pp. 279–80; see also pp. 303–4). Competition among farmers eventually brings all the surplus to the proprietors; ultimately, rent is the only disposable surplus and profits are nothing but a temporary share of net output (ibid., p. 268). The proposal of a single tax on rent is in full agreement with the general principle that taxes must only be levied on the net product.

According to this interpretation, there are both philological arguments (farmers' competition) and analytical reasons (tax exemption) to believe that in his mature economic thought Quesnay considered *all* the net product as ultimately accruing to the landlords.[25]

This view picks out a very interesting aspect of physiocracy and finds some textual support in the physiocrats' writings. However, it can lead to a misleading picture of physiocratic economics; in particular, it does not give an acceptable account of the process of the accumulation of capital, which is the crucial element of the physiocratic route to wealth and prosperity. This approach has to be rejected for three main reasons. Two of them concern the logical and philological foundations of the interpretation. First of all, no modification of Quesnay's view of profits as part of the surplus was needed in order to exempt farmers from taxation. Secondly, the above view does not place the change in the physiocrats' attitude towards profits in the correct economic and social context. Therefore it misinterprets the reasons which lead Quesnay to propose the argument of farmers' competition. These do not derive simply from the internal logical evolution of his thought, but reflect the physiocrats' preoccupation with the political situation of the country (see 5.7–5.9). The third reason for opposing the idea that cultivators' profits are not part of the net product derives from the fact that this interpretation confuses the physiocratic definition of surplus, which is the difference between the value of the social product and that of its means of production, with the problem of the permanence in time of its component elements (see 5.10).

On the first question one must notice that if tax exemption for farmers were Quesnay's only concern, he would *not* need to modify his original view about their profits. In fact, as early as the 1757 article *Impôts*, he clearly separates profits from the other elements of surplus. He wrote: 'the profits of the farmers . . . ought to be distinguished from the revenue . . . for the proprietors' (*Impôts*, Meek 1962 p. 106). And a line later: 'it is the costs and the profits of the husbandmen which assure cultivation and the revenue'. Profits are neither a cost nor a revenue to be taxed, but a peculiar part of the social surplus. The profits of cultivators are not included in the costs of cultivation, hence they are part of net output, even though they are different from the revenues of proprietors.

As we have seen in section 5.4 the elements of surplus are distinguished according to the way in which they are spent. This difference in the use of the two shares of net output has a very specific and limited aim: to establish that, although profits are part of the surplus, they *are not disposable* in the same sense as rent. Taxes must be levied on the part of net product which constitutes the revenues of landlords, because this is the only share which might be spent in the purchase of consumption goods, and is not reinvested in cultivation. However, the exemption of profits from taxation does not mean that they are not part of the surplus, but simply that they are a particular share in it; in fact, they are the source of and the stimulus for new capital and technical progress. Thus profits ensure that cultivation will continue and improve (see 5.3).

5.7 Wealthy cultivators and noble proprietors: the seeds of revolution?

The second reason for dissatisfaction with the idea that profits are not part of the social surplus concerns the problem of the role of competition among cultivators in the physiocratic theory of distribution. If we examine the philological evidence and set the physiocrats' statements about farmers' competition in their proper textual and historical context, we see that they do not reflect a concern about exempting profits from taxation. Their major preoccupation was to reassure the proprietors, and more generally the nobles, the Church and the sovereign, that agricultural entrepreneurs would not become too rich and powerful. Thus there are mainly historical and political reasons behind the physiocratic argument that farmers' competition limits their profits. Indeed Quesnay and his disciples were worried about the unfavourable reception by the dominant classes of some of their economic advice, such as the single tax on rent and the need for long land-leases.[26] These considerations suggest that one should be cautious about concluding that the passages about farmers' competition show that Quesnay ceased to consider profits as part of the net product. We have seen that in their attempt to encourage the introduction of capital-intensive methods of cultivations, the physiocrats ventured into long and enthusiastic commendations of cultivators.[27] At the very beginning of the article *Fermiers*, Quesnay uses the following words of praise defining cultivators: 'farmers are those who by farming give value to the wealth of the countryside and who obtain the most essential riches and resources for the upkeep of the state' (Groenewegen, 1983, p. 1).

Wealthy farmers bring about the welfare of the whole country because they play the most important and delicate role in the process of development (see Chapter 4, 4.3). Yet the physiocrats go even further in associating the prosperity of the country with the existence of rich farmers. On the one hand, 'the more wealthy the husbandmen the more the proceeds of the land and the strength of the nation are increased by their resources'. On the other hand, 'a poor farmer can only cultivate to the detriment of the state' (*Fermiers*, Groenewegen, 1983, p. 13).[28] England provides the admirable example of a country which protects and favours wealthy cultivators. 'In England the occupation of farmer is most opulent and highly valued and an occupation singularly favoured by the government' (ibid.). In England cultivators are not oppressed by arbitrary taxation, which deprives them of their gains and wealth. Le Trosne pushes his commendations of the agricultural entrepreneur even further. He says that indirect taxation and trade restrictions 'make the condition of the farmer uncertain' (Le Trosne, 1777, p. 901); they diminish the 'number of rich farmers', who are replaced by 'poor sharecroppers, who cannot make the appropriate advances' (ibid.). Thus, a wrong economic policy can cause the disappearance of wealthy farmers; for Le Trosne this means that 'there is almost no net product left' (ibid.).

Statements of this kind were not likely to gain the sympathy of the French aristocracy . While proprietors must pay taxes, farmers should be exempted; the cultivator is described as the master and the hero of the process of development, while all landlords have to do is to spend their revenues in the purchase of primary commodities (see Baudeau, 1767, vol. I, p. 190, vol. II, p.104). They cannot decide anything about the way in which their lands are to be exploited. The first and second estates certainly did not like the description of the economic conditions of the English farmers which appeared in an article of the *Journal Economique* in April 1770: 'The English cultivator is rich and abundantly enjoys all the comforts of life . . . They are wealthy enough to have taste of ownership and have enough free time to satisfy it' (in Weulersse, 1910a, vol. I, p. 361). The text continues by describing the luxurious life of farmers' families.

The English cultivator looked much richer than most French nobles.[29] But the physiocrats held even more specific and provocative opinions; they gave cultivators the characteristics of owners. Quesnay wrote that 'in agriculture the possessor of the land and the possessor of the advances necessary for cultivation are both equally proprietors, and that on this account there is equal dignity on each side' (*Maximes Générales*, Meek, 1962, pp. 255). Also Mirabeau believes that the 'farmer, by means of the wealth he employs in cultivation, is *co-propriétaire* with the owner of land' (Mirabeau, 1764, vol. I, p. 26, italics added; see also Pattullo, 1758, p. 280). It follows that 'in the economic order, the farmer is equal to the proprietor of the farm' (ibid.). The physiocrats put much stress on the idea of joint ownership between the landlord and the cultivator; an idea which was unacceptable to the French nobility since it obviously included the ideological seeds of a possible change in the economic, juridical and political class relationships of the *ancien régime*. The aristocrats might be able to accept not being the owners of the product, but they would certainly be hostile to any statement that cast doubt on their rights to ownership of the soil.

With remarkable coherence, and less political caution, the physiocrats advocated policy measures and regulations in line with the above opinions. Beside the exemption of farmers from taxation there is another less famous, but equally important, change they wanted to introduce: the lengthening of the period of land leases.

The *baux* normally lasted three, six or nine years (see Sée, 1967, p. 26) and it was illegal to make a lease for more than nine years (see Weulersse, 1910a, vol. I, p. 405). In his *Essai sur l'amélioration des terres* (1758)Pattullo stresses the benefits of having lifetime *baux*, or even hereditary ones, as in England (see Pattullo, 1758, pp. 278–9). Two years later Mirabeau writes that 'the cultivator must be made attached to the land by means of ownership, or by a similar measure, like permanence on the same farm'; therefore, he concludes, 'it will be extremely important to facilitate the lengthening of *baux*, so that the farmer can consider the field as his own' (Mirabeau, 1760d, p.99; see also *Hommes*, I.N.E.D., 1958, vol. II, p. 560).

The debate about the lengthening of leases aroused the obvious interest of the *Sociétés d'agriculture*, which took the opportunity of suggesting that the cultivator should be the owner of the land he exploits. In November 1761 the *Société* of Britanny writes that it would be a good thing 'to encourage the farmer with the spirit of the property' which would follow the lengthening of leases to at least eighteen or twenty years (in Weulersse, 1910a, vol. I, p. 404). The French aristocracy was hardly likely to accept giving up its tax exemptions, and it would certainly have reacted strongly against the idea of being deprived of its landed estates in favour of the farmers.

5.8 The physiocrats and the need to reassure the dominant classes

By praising farmers the Physiocrats wounded the susceptibility of the proprietors, and by showing how powerful and rich the cultivators could become they gave the first and second estates cause for concern. Instead of creating harmony and co-operation, their writings aroused the suspicions of the dominant classes towards the cultivators. But it was not just a question of envy on the part of landlords; most physiocratic proposals directly affected their interests. In particular, the effect of lengthening land leases would be just the opposite of securing to landlords the whole of the surplus brought about either by the introduction of new techniques, or by a higher current price. Farmers would have more time to enjoy their profits, to become wealthy and to regard themselves as the true owners of rented lands (see this Chapter, Appendix B).

The discussion of the length of *baux* reached a peak between 1758 and the beginning of the sixties (see Weulersse, 1910a, vol. II, pp. 403–8), when the first period in the development of physiocracy ended. But the new decade saw increasing suspicion and hostility from the aristocracy and the government towards the new doctrine. The opposition of landlords and administrators to physiocracy became particularly strong after the publication of Mirabeau's *Théorie de l'Impôt* in December 1760. Louis XV was extremely angry with the Marquis, who was imprisoned for a week and then banished to his countryside estate at Bignon for two months.[30] These events made the Physiocrats more cautious and they did not publish any major work for two-and-a-half years.[31] When their writings began to appear again, Quesnay and his followers were careful not to irritate the landlords and the government. In particular, they were much more cautious in emphasising the profits of the cultivator as a regular element of surplus. Certainly it is no coincidence that the first passage stating that all the surplus will ultimately accrue to landlords is to be found in the *Philosophie Rurale*, published in Amsterdam in November 1763. This work marks the beginning of the period of the later writings, during which, according to Meek, Quesnay no longer regarded profits as part of the net product.

Quesnay and his disciples realised that the nobility had to be reassured that physiocratic economic policies would not damage their interests and represented no threat to its power and the political order of France. To this end they used four different arguments. First, in November 1760 Quesnay promptly took a position on the question of the lengthening of *baux* with a letter to the *Intendant* of Soissons. He diluted Mirabeau's and Pattulo's enthusiasm for long leases by postponing their implementation for the future, when 'agriculture will be in its perfect state' (in Weulersse, 1910a, vol. I, p. 406). Thus contracts between proprietors and cultivators must not be too long because France had not yet reached a position where agriculture was prosperous and highly productive. The landlords could be sure that, at least for the time being, there was no need to change the old rules and customs.

A second factor which should disarm the landlords had already been used by Quesnay in the article *Impôts*, where he stated that 'none of the farmers's profit at all would be taken out of the proprietor's fund' (Meek, 1962, p. 107); if the cultivator makes a gain, this derives from his productive advances and not from those of the landlord.

However there is also a third reason why the dominant classes need not fear the wealth of the cultivators. Even if they should retain part of the net product which accrues to them in sales at first-hand, this would in fact be to the advantage of the proprietors. In fact, the accumulation of capital in agriculture and the improvement of the methods of cultivation which follows the reinvestment of profits, will eventually bring more revenue to the landlords and to state (see Baudeau, 1767–70 vol. XII, p. 152). If cultivators make gains they will reinvest them. Therefore the ruling classes must not oppress the farmers because, as Quesnay says: 'we shall not cease repeating that one cannot be too much afraid of *killing the goose that lays the golden eggs*' (*Premier problème économique*, Meek, 1962 p. 181, note 3, italics in the text). The landlords and the crown have no cause for concern; rich farmers are no threat to them, as they are in fact a *poule aux oeufs d'or*.

However, none of these considerations appeared sufficient to convince the aristocracy that it would not be harmed by physiocratic economic policy. The physiocrats had to show that there were in-built economic forces which would prevent farmers from retaining the whole net output of cultivation, and thus becoming too rich and powerful. The fourth decisive economic feature in which proprietors could trust was competition among farmers at the renewal of the *baux*, which would guarantee proprietors most of the agricultural surplus.[32] Of course this last argument required the physiocrats to reduce the emphasis on the fact that normally cultivator permanently retained part of the net product as profit on his entrepreneurship.

But the existence of competition among farmers cannot be regarded as a proof that *no surplus at all* is left to the agricultural entrepreneur. In fact, there is only one passage in the whole of Quesnay's writings in which he maintains that competition among cultivators wipes out the *entire* profits and leaves rent as the only item in the social surplus. In the *Premier problème économique* he writes:

'the farmers of landed property profit up to the renewal of their leases from the constant increase in the prices of products which occurs during the terms of these leases' (Meek, 1962, p. 180).[33] A few lines later he continues 'these profits increase the number of *wealthy* farmers, promote at the time of renewal of the leases a greater degree of competition between them, which then assure to the proprietors and the sovereign the full return of the net product' (Meek, 1962, pp. 180–1, my italics). In other important physiocratic works there are only few passages which maintain that no gains at all are left to the agricultural entrepreneurs because of competition among them. They are found in Du Pont's *De l'Exportation et de l'Inportation des Grains* (see Du Pont, 1764, pp. 20–1), in Le Trosne's *De l'intérêt social* (see Le Trosne, 1777, p. 900) and in Mirabeau's *Phylosphie Rurale* (see Mirabeau, 1764, vol. I pp. 37-8, 359 ff.).

5.9 The appropriate shares of profit and rent; with a dialogue between Mirabeau and Quesnay

From the analysis of the previous section it emerges that the importance of the few places where the physiocrats state that rent absorbs the whole net product must not be overestimated. It would be misleading to use them to affirm that Quesnay denies profits the status of an item of the surplus. Moreover, in these passages there are major ambiguities and remarkable contradictions which testify to the physiocrats' embarrassment on the subject of the appropriation of surplus. For instance, in the *Premier problème économique*, Quesnay says that the surplus will eventually accrue entirely to rent and *taille*, while four lines earlier, he asserts that the profits 'multiply the *wealthy* farmers' (Meek, 1962, p. 180). How can the cultivators become rich, if they can retain their gains only for a few years?

Such inconsistencies are particularly evident in the *Philosophie Rurale* and in *De l'Exportation et de l'Inportation des Grains*, which appeared a few months apart in 1763 and 1764.[34] Here Mirabeau and Du Pont produced two *tableaux* to show that the whole surplus accrues to the proprietors. Du Pont, talking about the difference between the *prix commun du vendeur* and the *prix commun fondamental*, says that the farmers' margin is given by the 'difference between these two prices' (Du Pont, 1764, p. 11, note 1). He then feels the need to reassure the proprietors that the gains of farmers will be limited by competition (see ibid.). Here it seems that Du Pont does not intend to wipe out the entire profits, but simply to prevent farmers from retaining the whole surplus, instead of passing part of it on to the proprietors. However, something more than just a statement might be needed to satisfy the dominant classes. Thus, a few pages later, he uses a numerical example to show that the proprietors and the sovereign will eventually receive the entire net product of agriculture (see ibid., pp. 20–1).

The contradictions in Chapter II of the *Philosophie Rurale* are more striking. In the space of four pages Mirabeau argues twice that landlords should obtain most of the surplus (Mirabeau, 1764, vol. I pp. 37–8, 39), and says three times that the profits of the cultivator are the part of net product which is accumulated (see ibid., pp. 37, 40, 41). Such is the schizophrenia in his reasoning that it is hard to resist the temptation to present these passages in the dialogue form, which was so popular in Paris during the eighteenth century, and which was also frequently used by Quesnay himself.

Thus, let us imagine being present at a conversation between the two physiocrats, in Quesnay's *entresol* at Versailles during the winter 1762, when the friends are working on the new *summa* of physiocracy: the *Philosophie Rurale*. They are talking about the relationships between proprietors and cultivators, particularly the problem of the distribution of the net output of cultivation. Mirabeau plays the role of the courageous supporter of farmers, while the more prudent *docteur* emphasises all the factors which should be used to reassure the landed aristocracy.

Mirabeau:

I am utterly convinced that 'the cultivator is absolutely necessary to production' (Mirabeau, 1764, vol. I, p. 37). Therefore, he must be exempted from paying taxes, because he owns and employs the *richesses d'exploitation*, which give value to the soil (see ibid.).

Quesnay:

You are certainly right, but the point that we must stress is that the farmer 'gives to the proprietor *everything*, that, with his labour, he adds to production, which is *excédent*, on top of what is necessary to his own consumption' (ibid., pp. 37–8, italics added).

Mirabeau:

Then we should conclude that no surplus remains in the hands of the cultivator; but 'this last point seems to be in opposition to the previous one' (ibid., p. 38). Indeed you have agreed that the existence of wealthy farmers is necessary to increase the advances of agriculture.

Quesnay: My dear Marquis I accept this point, but we must show the landlords that they will always retain control of the process of production of commodities, at least as regards the possibility of obtaining the surplus. For instance, 'it is not impossible for the Landlord to compel the Cultivator, as long as the latter has a natural fear of expatriation' (ibid.). The landlords must not fear losing their privileged position in the economic system, since they will always maintain their political and juridical power.

Mirabeau: Nevertheless, let us 'assume that he [the farmer] can keep a large part of his profits, which he conceals from the landowner' (ibid., p. 39). After all, the cultivator might be able to circumvent the power of the proprietor by cheating him. But what will eventually be the only activity of the farmer who has managed to enrich himself? Surely he works for the welfare of the whole kingdom. He 'improves the soil by means of the expenses he can now make, in order to have a higher output, and he switches from a smaller undertaking to a larger one. Besides, a wealthy farmer can obtain more profits from his undertaking than another, who is less well off" (ibid., pp. 40–1).

Quesnay: *Mon ami*, I can see that your literary vein springs directly from your heart. All you are saying is true, but can't you see that the words you are using could displease both the proprietors and the king himself? They must be convinced that the cultivator can gain from his activity, 'without increasing his wealth at the expenses of the revenue of the landlords. On the contrary everything is a gain for them' (ibid., p. 41). I insist on this point; farmers must not appear to take their profits out of those parts of net product which constitute the revenues of the proprietors and the sovereign.

Mirabeau: I don't think there is a real difference between us. We both agree that the interests of the proprietors and of the state are not in opposition to those of the cultivators. In fact, the landlords 'go against their interests either by envying or taking away farmers' profits' (ibid.). The kingdom will be ruined if we 'envy the cultivator because of his *superflu*' (ibid., italics added). Don't you think we are rapidly closing the gap between our opinions?

Quesnay: *Non, mon ami*, I really don't see how you can claim to reconcile your view that the farmer retains *part of the net output* of cultivation, with my initial remarks. There I stressed that the proprietor receives *all the surplus* above the subsistence salary of the cultivator. Indeed, your arguments don't seem to be very useful for reducing the worries and suspicions of the landlords.

We can end the dialogue with a purely imaginary answer from the wise Quesnay, which perhaps gives a good description of the feelings of the reader of Mirabeau's pages. Indeed, after all his arguments and comments, Mirabeau ends up with a position in which the farmer has a surplus – *superflu* – which can hardly be reconciled with the statement three pages earlier, where he says that the farmer gives the landlord *all* the surplus beyond (*excédent*) his necessary consumption.

These considerations suggest some caution in interpreting the few cases where the physiocrats say that rent absorbs the whole surplus. Indeed it seems that they use competition among farmers to reassure the landowners that economic forces do exist to guarantee that the net product of cultivation will be *appropriately shared* between them and the farmers. Quesnay does not deny profits the status of an item of surplus, he simply believes that the farmers cannot keep the *entire* net product over costs which they receive by selling their products. In the *Premier problème économique* he uses the grounds of competition to argue that farmers will be compelled to 'bring the rent in conformity with its *true* rate' (Meek, 1962, p. 185 italics added. The French term is *veritable prix*, see I.N.E.D., 1958, vol. II, p. 876). 'Then it would come about', continues Quesnay,

> that the revenue [of the cultivator] imperceptibly settles down at the *just* level, in conformity with the products and expenses involved in cultivation; and *order* would also be established in the same way between taxes and the *portion* of the revenue which belongs to the proprietors (ibid., italics added).

Quesnay seems to think that there is a just, natural and appropriate division of the surplus between the proprietors, the sovereign and the cultivators.

The idea of competition among farmers appears as early as 1757 in the article *Impôts*, where he writes that 'the renewal of the leases always brings the proprietor's revenue *into proportion* with the product of his property' (Meek, 1962, p. 107, italics added).[35] Here rent is a given share of output, and in the *Premier problème économique* we have just seen that profits too are 'in conformity with the products' (ibid., p. 185). Therefore the higher the output of agriculture the higher the rent; the profits of farmers must also follow the increase of production, and thus the two incomes constitute constant percentage shares of output. Competition is the mechanism which, in a market exchange economy, prevents farmers from keeping the entire increase in the value of the surplus and compels them to '*share* this benefit with the Proprietors' (Du Pont, 1764, p. 79, italics added).[36] Thus when the *baux* are renewed profits do not disappear, for the competition among cultivators simply re-establishes a fair and just distribution of the net product.

That competition among cultivators is not designed to wipe out all their profits is also confirmed by the fact that the physiocrats believe that excessive competition can be damaging for the whole nation, because it prevents farmers from becoming wealthy enough to increase advances and introduce new techniques (see *Hommes*, I.N.E.D., 1958, vol. II, p. 560). Quesnay praises the *maisons religieuses* which are considerate of their farmers, since they refuse to take advantage of the 'abusive competition' of other cultivators, who come and offer 'inconsiderate' increases in rent (ibid.). Thus, the wise landlord must not deprive the cultivator of the whole surplus, even when the leasing situation on the market allows for an enormous increase in his rent. The proprietor should even help the farmer who has economic difficulties. Monasteries are a good example, because 'they make it easier for the farmers to have gains, by granting them favourable delays for their payments' (ibid.). All great landowners should concede 'delays in the payment of rent' (ibid., pp. 559–60). The physiocrats are seeking harmony between the proprietors and their farmers, and competition among the latter is a way of ensuring that neither class can deprive the other of its share of the net product.

Finally, it must be remarked that the physiocrats often mention the necessity of having large farms, directed by wealthy farmers, in order to secure the prosperity of the country. For instance, one of the *Maximes Générales* reads as follows: 'that the lands employed in the cultivation of wheat should be brought together, as much as possible, into large farms worked by rich husbandmen' (Meek, 1962, p. 235; see also, Mirabeau, 1764, vol. II, p. 349). In fact, only large-scale cultivation can guarantee a high surplus in agriculture. But certainly *la réunion des fermes* would not increase the degree of competition among producers, since only the wealthier cultivators would be able to pay the rents on very large farms.

5.10 Short and long run and the concept of surplus

We must now present the third reason for disagreeing with an interpretation of physiocracy which does not consider profits as part of surplus. This opinion is founded on the idea that farmers' profits cannot be considered a normal and regular part of the net product, because they are just a *temporary* share in it (see Meek, 1962, pp. 268, 306); 'in the *long run* these profits must either disappear or crystallize out into rents' (ibid., p. 301, italics added). Rent, because it is always there, is the only true constituent of surplus. Thus the characteristic of being a normal component of the net product depends only on *duration in time*, adopting a straightforward chronological view of the long run. This could be any period of nine years or more, as this was the usual length of land leases in France at the time of the physiocrats.

The problem of the long-run permanence of an income as part of surplus is an important aspect of physiocratic economics. However duration in time is not the criterion used by the physiocrats to decide whether a particular economic magnitude is a systematic part of the net product of the country. Quesnay defines the surplus of a nation as that part of its social product which is left in the hands of the entrepreneurs after they have set aside all the items making up the necessary advances of production, including wages at subsistence level. In physiocracy, the notion of national surplus emerges because Quesnay believes that it is possible, and indeed important, to define the difference between the value of the gross output and the value of the means of production required to obtain it. This definition of net product has nothing whatsoever to do with a particular time span, except that in which the surplus itself has been produced. Therefore the physiocrats consider cultivators' profits as part of the net product of agriculture, because these profits *are not* included in the value of the means of production of the primary sector. And from this point of view it does not matter whether or not they will be entirely absorbed by rent at the time of the renewal of land leases.

The criterion of duration thus does not provide an appropriate definition of net product, and cannot be usefully employed to identify its normal component elements. In addition, there are two other good reasons in physiocratic economics for regarding the profits of the cultivator as part of the country's surplus. The first concerns the origin of farmers' profits. Even if for the physiocrats these are profits on alienation, their size is neither erratic, nor fortuitous, and they must not be regarded as a pure windfall. Profits are influenced by variations in the current price of products; but these exchange values are not determined by mere chance, rather they depend on the laws of the markets, including commercial customs and administrative regulations (see Chapter 3). Thus the gains of the cultivator can be influenced by the trade policy of the government. But above all the farmer himself can increase his profits by using technical progress and a better organisation of labour to reduce the cost of production.

Moreover, in some years the cultivator may suffer losses, but on average the farmer does make a profit, and this is a constant feature of the economic system. Profits would disappear only if the farmer stopped being an independent entrepreneur who risks his advances in cultivation, and became a salaried worker, or even a serf (see 5.11). As a matter of fact, in physiocracy profits would continue to be part of the net product, even if they lasted only few years, because competition among farmers would eventually transfer them to the landlords. The cultivator obtains at least part of the surplus before the *bail* is renewed. Even if after nine years he loses all his gains, once the contract has been renewed the pattern will repeat itself; during the nine years of the following lease he will again retain the entire net product over the technical expenses of production. Thus, even in this case, the farmer's gain is no windfall, since it regularly exists as an average over the nine years.[37]

There is a second factor which shows the inadequacy of the criterion of *chronological long-run* permanence for deciding whether Quesnay considered profits as a regular part of the surplus. In spite of competition among farmers, which limits the size of these gains over time, profits are *the* decisive magnitude for the long-run development of France. Of course, here the term *long run* does not simply indicate a number of years, but covers the process of transition from a backward to an advanced economy.

We have already seen that Quesnay distinguishes revenue from profits, because these two shares of the surplus are employed in different ways when they are spent (see 5.4). Revenues are free to be spent on the purchase of any sort of consumption goods, while profits are almost inevitably invested in future production. But, in order to judge whether or not profits are part of the surplus, it is immaterial that they seem to be considered *less* disposable than proprietors' rents, because landlords have many different ways of spending their revenue, while farmers have the choice of either investing their gains or not. The quality of surplus does not derive from a judgement about the *greater or lesser* disposability of an income. Net product is disposable by definition, because it is not part of the means of production necessary to reproduce the system on the same scale. The cultivators are stimulated to reinvest their gains, according to the physiocrats, only if they think they will get a reasonable return from such investment. But if profits are not reinvested and cultivators dispose of them in a different way, the economic system will still reproduce itself with the same level of output.

5.11 Profits between comparative statics and dynamics

In the previous sections I hope to have raised some doubts about the possibility of using the frail and contradictory passages, in which Quesnay discusses the role of farmers' competition, to maintain that he did not consider profits as an element of social surplus. In fact it is clear that the physiocrats resorted to this issue mainly to reassure the aristocrats that there were economic forces preventing cultivators from becoming too rich and powerful. In some of his later works, Quesnay tries to reduce the emphasis on the importance of having wealthy farmers, even though this produces ambiguities and contradictions. However, the attempt to restore the logical coherence of physiocratic analysis by leaving profits outside the surplus and sparing them from taxation creates more problems than it solves, particularly for the theory of capital accumulation. In fact, the view that competition among cultivators wipes out the *entire* profits (instead of simply redistributing them in the appropriate proportions between proprietors and landlords) leads to conclusions which contradict not only one or two sentences, but some major arguments of physiocracy. The process of investment which should lead the country towards wealth and prosperity fades away; it loses all the features linking it with the historical conditions of France.

First, the farmers – those in control of investment and production – can hardly sustain a continuous and vigorous process of capital accumulation, since their profits survive only until their leases are renewed, and decrease rapidly during this period. Therefore the potential source of new advances, which relies on an increase in the current prices of the products of land, is greatly limited. It is hard to believe that the physiocrats regarded such a meagre and unstable income as the source of the large funds needed to spread the methods of large-scale cultivation throughout France.

Secondly, and more important, farmers become the most incredible and a-historical figures: mere agents of capital growth, with no personal motive or economic interest in it, since they are always bound to pass all the benefits on to the landlords. But for Quesnay profits are not simply the source of new advances, but also the main motive for cultivators risking their wealth in production, as the concept of *bon prix* makes very clear. These considerations do not seem to be compatible with a situation in which farmers know, from previous experience, that in nine years' time they will be deprived of all their profits.

Thirdly, accumulation of capital is accompanied by continuous technical innovation, and both processes are carried out by wealthy cultivators who can make large advances. Mirabeau wrote:

> the more wealth is used in the cultivation of wheat, the fewer men it employs, the more it is prosperous, and the more it yields a *net profit*. Such is the case of large-scale cultivation by *wealthy Farmers*, in comparison to the small-scale one of poor Sharecroppers (Mirabeau, 1760b, pp. 184–5, italics added).

If all gains eventually accrue to landlords why should cultivators bother about introducing new methods of production? How can the farmer become rich, and distinguish himself from the poor sharecropper, who periodically loses all his gains?

The interpretation which identifies surplus with rent fails to give an acceptable account of a process of investment which will procure prosperity and welfare for the whole country. Thus I prefer to accept the physiocrats' statements as they stand. Profits are an element of surplus and at the same time they are non-disposable and non-taxable, and must be reinvested in the productive process.

I hope to have shown that there are both good philological reasons, and evidence from the social and political *milieu* of the France of Louis XV for believing that Quesnay regarded cultivators' profits as part of the net product, throughout his work. However, it must be remarked that the choice between the two interpretations does not depend only on textual analysis. As a matter of fact the two ways of considering farmers' profits seem to derive from partially different approaches to physiocracy, which focus their attention on different aspects of its economic analysis.

The authors who deny profits the status of a surplus item seem to emphasise the point of view of comparative statics. In fact, they consider economic conditions at particular moments in time, i.e. after the renewal of leases. Thus a comparison is made between the state of affairs every nine years, if this is the usual length of the *baux*. These moments should be regarded as long-run equilibrium positions, because all the short-run forces of competition between buyers and sellers have already produced their effects, at least on the land-leasing market. Since one of these forces, namely competition among farmers eager to rent a piece of land, can reduce and even wipe out profits, such gains do not exist in these 'equilibria', and are therefore not considered as a true and systematic part of the surplus.

The choice of this approach implies that all the relevant economic aspects of physiocracy can be grasped by comparing the economy at different moments in time while what happens between them can be ignored.

We believe on the contrary that an analysis of the process of economic transformation and development not only constitutes Quesnay's most important aim, but is *the* essential feature of physiocratic economics. Therefore, we prefer to emphasise its dynamic aspect. Here, the share of the surplus which accrues to cultivators becomes the most important analytical concept for explaining the laws of motion of the economy. For Quesnay this dynamic process is not due to a mere passing of time, but is linked to the transformation of the French economy, whose evolution is associated with structural changes which will make underdeveloped France a developing country. Profits are the only source of new advances, hence they are logically essential to explain both capital accumulation and technical progress in agriculture; two elements which constitute the bridge between a poor and a prosperous economy.

The notion of a rate of profit on capital invested only appears with Turgot and Smith;[38] yet in physiocracy there is already a precise concept of profit. This still has some features of a profit upon alienation, which was the traditional view during the first half of the eighteenth century. Certainly, Quesnay provides a link between this older notion and the analysis of capitalist entrepreneurial profit by Turgot, Smith and Ricardo. In particular, he introduces a typical feature of classical political economy: the accumulation of capital depends on the share of surplus which is the profit of the entrepreneur. Thus this share becomes the link between the surplus of the previous period and the new means of production. Finally, the physiocratic analysis of profits and investment illuminates the close relationship which exists between the theory of distribution of output, especially surplus, and that of its expenditure, which are two pillars of the overall dynamic analysis of the transformation process of the economy.

APPENDIX A: **TWO *TABLEAUX***

The two *tableaux* appear in Mirabeau's *Philosophie Rurale* (see Mirabeau, 1764, vol. II, pp. 366–7) and in Du Pont de Nemour's *De l'Exportation et de l'Inportation des grains* (see Du Pont, 1764, pp. 20–1). These two pieces are among the physiocrats' major efforts to convince landlords that they will ultimately benefit from an initial increase in the profits of cultivators. However, in both cases the figures and calculations present contradictions and inconsistencies, which testify to the authors' embarrassment at playing down the gains of the farmer when describing the process by which the revenue and wealth of the country increase.

The *tableau* in the *Philosophie Rurale* (p. 156) describes the effects of a once-and-for-all increase in the price of corn (see Mirabeau, 1764 vol. II, pp. 355–6), which gives rise to a new net product of 672 million *livres* (ibid., p. 359).[39] The following symbols are used to represent Mirabeau's magnitudes: PN, net product; ΔAP, annual increase in the *avances primitives*; ΔAA, annual increase of the *avances annuelles*; ΔY, increase in the revenue of the landlords; ΔIP, the share of the new net product accruing to farmers as profits, which must be reinvested in production. Mirabeau assumes that agriculture adopts the methods of production typical of large-scale cultivation, where the annual increase in net output is 100 per cent of annual advances; therefore we have $\Delta AA = \Delta PN$. (Here Mirabeau refers to the increase in surplus which is due to the existence of larger means of production in agriculture, and not to an occasional rise of the net product following a price increase.)

The data of the problem are: the initial increase in the net product, $\overline{PN}_1$, due to the price rise; and the proportions in which PN is divided between ΔAP, ΔAA, ΔIP and ΔY. The magnitudes are linked by the following relationships (all figures are millions of *livres*; Mirabeau's miscalculations do not undermine the structure of the relationships);

1) $\Delta AP_t = 4/5\ PN_t$
2) $\Delta AA_t = 1/5\ PN_t + \Delta AA_{t-1}$

The annual increase of AA is one-fifth of the increase in net product of the same year, plus the increases of AA in previous year. (The subscripts refer to the years; 1761 is 1.) Since in the first year, 1761, there is no previous increase of AA, we have : $\overline{PN}_1 = \Delta AP_1 + \Delta AA_1$.

3) $\Delta IP_t = 6/7\ \Delta AA_{t-1}$

The newly invested profits are equal to six-sevenths of the increase in annual advances of the previous year.

4) $PN_t = \dfrac{t-1}{9}\ \overline{PN}_1 + \Delta IP_t.$

ANNEES.	PREMIER FONDS de bénéfice qui augmente chaque année par l'addition successive du surcroît de produit net.	ACCROÎT des avances primitives qui est formé chaque année des quatre cinquiemes du fonds du bénéfice annuel, & de son accroît successif.	ACCROÎT des avances annuelles qui augmentent chaque année par l'addition de celles de la précédente.	SURCROÎT de produit net, dont la dime enleve un septième, reste aux Fermiers six septièmes.	ANNEES.	ACCROÎT du produit net qui se reúnit successivement au revenu des Propriétaires, du Souvetain & des Décimateurs, & qui s'augmente chaque année du nouveau surcroît des avances annuelles & d'un neuvième des 672 millions de premier fonds de benéfice.
1761.....	672.........	537........	135 .			
1762.....	598 115 } .713....	572.......	143 135 } 278	115	1762.....	75 135 } 210
1763.....	524 237 } .761....	608.......	152 278 } 430	237	1763.....	75 277 } 352
1764.....	450 368 } .818....	655.......	163 429 } 592	368	1764....	75 429 } 504
1765.....	375 507 } .882....	706.......	166 592 } 768	507	1765.....	75 592 } 667
1766.....	300 658 } .958....	767.......	191 768 } 959	658	1766.....	75 768 } 843
1767.....	225 822 } 1047....	838.......	209 959 } 1168	822	1767.....	75 } 1034
1768.....	150 1001 } 1151....	921.......	230 1168 } 1398	1001	1768.....	75 1168 } 1243
1769.....	75 1199 } 1274....	1019.......	255 1398 } 1653	1199	1769.....	75 1398 } 1473
1770.....		6 milliards 623 millions.		1417	1770.....	75 1653 } 1728 ou 1481, dîme prélevee

Each year's net product derives partly from the original increase in net output, and partly from the new net product of the same year.

Coming to the revenue of the landlords one sees that it is equal to one-ninth of the first increase in net product, plus the entire increase in the surplus of the previous year, which, according to Mirabeau's hypothesis about technology, is equal to the increase in annual advances;

$$5)\ \Delta Y = 1/9\ \overline{PN}_1 + \Delta AA_{t-1}$$

Therefore, as Meek notices (Meek, 1962, p. 143), there is double counting. In fact, given the increase in net product, $\Delta PN_t = \Delta AA_t$, six-sevenths, of it must, in the following year, go to the farmers in order to be invested (column 4, equation 3). But the same new surplus should go entirely to the landlords (column 5, equation 5). Mirabeau wants to assign the whole surplus to the proprietors, without however losing the possibility of capital accumulation which derives from the investment of farmers' profits!

Du Pont's *tableau* (see pp. 158–9) describes the effects of a *continuous* increase in the price of corn over six years and explicitly shows that this is the cause of the rise in the country's surplus. The table has two sections; the first eight columns describe the process which give rise to the net output, while the last five represent its distribution. The circularity of the overall process of reproduction is clearly shown by the fact that annual and original advances appear in both parts of the table. The data are: the price of a *setier* of corn, p, the overall output, X, the initial amounts of annual and original advances AA_0 and AP_0.

The figures at time 0 are easily explained. There are 3000 *livres* of *reprises*, means of production invested in agriculture (1000 *livres* are interests on the original advances). Thus the net product is 600 *livres*; that is to say the difference between the value of output, X, 3600 *livres*, and that of the inputs:

$$6)\ X_0 - (1/10\ AP_0 + AA_0) = PN_0$$

$X/p = 266.67$ gives the output in *setiers* of corn for time 0. If we divide the *reprises*, R, by this figure it is possible to obtain the unit cost of cultivation: 11 *liv*. 5 *s*.

In year 1, the increase in the current price of corn raises net output, and in all subsequent periods the increase in surplus is defined according to the formula:

$$7)\ \Delta PN_t = PN_t - PN_0$$

However, starting from the first period, problems and inconsistencies arise in Du Pont's figures. For instance the cost of production per *setier* $R/(X/p)$ varies even if both the overall physical output, X/p, and the *reprises* do not change! From the second year the figures in the second column can no longer be reconciled with the other magnitudes.

Moving to the right-hand side of the table one sees that the increase in surplus PN is divided between landlords and capital accumulation. Each year the proprietors receive one-ninth more of this increase:

TABLEAU

De l'éffet de la liberté du Commerce extérieur des Grains, par rapport à l'accroissement de l'Agriculture & du Revenu, pendant le tems nécéssaire pour renouveller tous les Baux; en supposant que la liberté ne produise dans l'abord qu'environ la moitié du bien que l'on en espére, & qu'il faille six ans pour établir en France ce Commerce dans tous ses avantages, & encore en supposant que la Culture aye toujours à supporter le contre-coup des charges indirectes qui retombent au double sur le Revenu.

	Prix du Septeir		Reprises du Laboureur fur chaque Septier			Reproduction totale	Produit Net	Avances Primitives	Avances Annuelles	Rapport du Produit Net aux Avances annuelles
								Qui augmentent chaque jour par l'accroit des riches ses productives, mentionné en l'autre part		
	liv.	sol.	liv.	sol.	den.		liv.	liv.	liv.	
Etat actuel.	13	10	11	5		3,600	600	10,000	2,000	30 p. $\frac{0}{0}$.
1re. Année de liberté	15	14	11	12	4	4,054	1,054	10,000	2,000	52 $\frac{28}{40}$ p. $\frac{0}{0}$.
2e. Année	16	15	11	15	10	4,402	1,281	10,323	2,081	63 $\frac{3}{40}$ p. $\frac{0}{0}$.
3e. Année	17	5	11	17	6	4,961	1,484	10,706	2,187	67 $\frac{34}{40}$ p. $\frac{0}{0}$.
4e. Année	17	9	11	18	2	5,265	1,608	11,217	2,304	69 $\frac{32}{40}$ p. $\frac{0}{0}$.
5e. Année	17	11	11	18	6	5,532	1,708	11,665	2,416	70 $\frac{30}{40}$ p. $\frac{0}{0}$.
6e. Année	17	12	11	18	8	5,763	1,791	12,059	2,515	71 $\frac{8}{40}$ p. $\frac{0}{0}$.
7e. Année	*Idem.*		*Idem.*			5,938	1,847	12,377	2,594	*Idem.*
8e. Année	*Idem.*		*Idem.*			6,061	1,887	12,599	2,650	*Idem.*
9e. Année	*Idem.*		*Idem.*			6,124	1,907	12,713	2,678	*Idem.*
	p		*R*			*X*	*PN*	*AP*	*AA*	

… qui se partage entre	L'accroit du Revenu des Propriétaires, du Roi & des Décimateurs		L'accroit des Avances primitives		Et L'accroit des Avances annuelles		Produit Net Nouveau causé Par L'accroit des avances Productives, selon le rapport où la Culture est dans l'année.		Revenu a Partager entre les Propriétaires, le Roi & les Décimateurs	
liv	liv.	sol.	liv.	sol.	liv.	sol.	liv.	sol.	liv.	sol.
.	……………		……………		……		…………		600	0
454	50	8	322	18	80	14	……………		650	8
581	151	6	423	12	106	2	19	7	751	6
384	294	13	471	8	117	19	126	15	894	13
008	448	0	448	0	112	0	212	14	1,048	0
108	615	10	394	0	98	10	293	17	1,215	10
191	794	0	317	12	79	8	366	9	1,394	0
247	969	17	221	12	55	11	423	10	1,569	17
287	1,144	0	114	8	28	12	463	1	1,744	0
307	1,307	0	0	0	0	0	483	8	1,907	0
PN	ΔY		ΔAP		ΔAA		*PNN*		*Y*	

8) $\Delta Y_t = t/9 \cdot \Delta PN_t$, and $Y_t = \Delta Y_t + \bar{Y}_0$.

The rest of the surplus goes to farmers, who use it to raise the original and annual advances:

9) $\Delta AP_t = (1 - t/9) \Delta PN_t$ and $\Delta AA_t = 1/4 \cdot \Delta AP_t$.

But the major problems arise from the second year onwards; once more it is clear how dangerous and misleading it would be to base an interpretation of the physiocratic notion of profit on these calculations. First, the agricultural output X_2/P_2 diminishes to 262.81 *setiers*, even if, according to Du Pont, the productivity of agriculture increases, as is shown by the change in the annual ratio between the net product and annual advances in the eighth column, whose figures go up to $PN_2/AA_2 = 63.3/40^{40}$. Moreover, in the second year the net product is lower, by 8 *livres*, than the difference between the value of output and that of the *reprises*. But this is not a simple miscalculation; in fact from the third to the ninth year the surplus is defined according to the following new formula:

10) $PN_t = X_t - AA_t - (1/10) (AP_t + AA_t)$.

Du Pont now subtracts from the value of agricultural output an additional 10 per cent on the *avances annuelles*. But in other physiocratic writings there is no mention of this deduction to obtain the value of the annual surplus; the 10 per cent interest only affects the original advances (see *Analyse*, Meek, 1962, pp. 154–5).

This interest on annual advances can obviously only accrue to cultivators, and is another clear example of the physiocrats' dilemma between the need to show the ruling classes that they receive the whole surplus, and the need to leave part of it to the farmers' future investments. On the right-hand side of the table Du Pont states that the entire surplus, according to a new definition, accrues to landlords, but on the left-hand side he changes the definition of net product and 'invents' an interest for cultivators on their annual advances.

The right-hand side of the table demonstrates two more inconsistencies. First, the fourth column in this part of the table gives the new net product brought about by the increase in advances:

6) $PNN_t = \sum_{1j}^{t-1} AA_j \cdot (PN_t/AA_t)$.

(The correct value for the figure in year 1 is 51 *liv.* and not 80 *liv.* 14 *s.*) There is no indication whatever of how this new net output is distributed, but it is clear that it does not accrue to landlords, at least during the nine years considered in the *tableau*. This surplus, 2389 *liv.* and 3 *s.* for the whole period, must accrue to the cultivators, who thus benefit from the entire net product which follows the increase in the means of production. (In the table in the *Philosophie Rurale* the new net product was the point of disagreement;

it had to be appropriated both 100 per cent by the landlords and six-sevenths by the farmers.) Note that Du Pont does not mention that this new surplus must necessarily be invested by the cultivators.

The second contradiction is in the column which concerns the annual increase in landlords' revenue, Y (equation 8). Here Du Pont exaggerates his arguments in favour of the proprietors, for from year 2 onwards these figures are higher than they should actually be. As a matter of fact, each year the same number of lease contracts are renewed; Du Pont writes: 'these leases are stipulated for nine years: and almost the same number expires and is renewed every year' (Du Pont 1764, p. 20). Thus he believes that the proprietors' revenue increases each year by one-ninth of the size of surplus (ibid.).

Du Pont's figures would be correct if he had assumed a *once and for all* price rise, as Mirabeau does in the previous table. But if the corn price rises gradually over six years, the farmers who have renewed their *baux* at the end of the first year will not contract with the landlords again until the tenth year. Therefore these cultivators, one-ninth of the total, retain the net product which is due to price increases from the second to the sixth year, because the landlords cannot claim it until the end of the *baux*. Hence in year 2 the proprietors receive one-ninth of the net product of *that year*, PN_2, from the one-ninth of farmers who must renew their contracts in that period; *i.e.* 75 *liv.* 7 *s.* instead of 151 *liv.* 6 *s.*. Equation 8) should be:

$$8b) \quad \Delta Y_t = (1/9)\Delta PN_t.$$

Of course the net product which does not accrue to landlords should be invested in advances by the farmers. Du Pont himself remarks that proprietors will receive the entire net product only at the end of the fifteenth year, that is to say nine years after the price has ceased to rise (see note 1 to the *tableau* in Du Pont 1764, pp. 20–1). However, he does not notice that this implies that each year only one-ninth of the surplus of that year goes to the landlords, and not two-ninths, three-ninths, and so on.

APPENDIX B: PROFITS AND THE LENGTHENING OF *BAUX*

Farmers take advantage of the increase in the 'first-hand price' of products during the years which elapse between renewals of a land-lease. Let us now try to determine the precise nature and size of these gains. Suppose there are f farmers and that the initial period of lease is n years; each year f/n *baux* are renewed.[41] Take a first case in which there is a *once-and-for-all* increase, S, in the surplus of each cultivator. The situations of the renewals can be represented by the following table.

baux renewed each year	f/n	f/n	f/n	. . . .	f/n
years					
1	$S/2$	S	S	. . . .	S
2		$S/2$	S	. . . .	S
3			$S/2$	. . . .	.
.				. . . .	.
.				. . . .	.
.				. . . .	.
n				.	$S/2$

Each of the f/n farmers belonging to the last group makes a gain of $S/2 + (n - 1)S$, farmers in group $n - 1$ make a profit of $S/2 + (n - 2)S$, and so on, until the farmer in the first group who makes only $S/2$. Thus, since each group includes f/n cultivators, the value of overall profits accruing to farmers during the first year is $(f/n)[(n - 1)S + S/2]$, for the second year it is $f/n[(n - 2)S + S/2]$, and so on. Therefore, the overall profits which accrue to all farmers during the n years are:

$$12)\ P_1 = \frac{f}{n}\left(n \cdot \frac{S}{2} + \sum_{0}^{n-1}{}_t\, t \cdot S\right) = \frac{fS}{n}\left(\frac{n}{2} + \sum_{0}^{n-1}{}_t\, t\right).$$

If the duration of *baux* is now extended to $m > n$ years, the profits of cultivators become:

$$13)\ P_2 = \frac{f}{m}\left(m \cdot \frac{S}{2} + \sum_{0}^{m-1}{}_t\, t \cdot S\right) = \frac{fS}{m}\left(\frac{m}{2} + \sum_{0}^{m-1}{}_t\, t\right).$$

Since $\dfrac{n}{2} + \displaystyle\sum_{0}^{n-1}{}_t\, t = \dfrac{n^2}{2}$ and $\dfrac{m}{2} + \displaystyle\sum_{0}^{m-1}{}_t\, t = \dfrac{m^2}{2}$ it is:[42]

$$P_1 = \frac{fSn}{2} \quad \text{and} \quad P_2 = \frac{fSm}{2}, \quad \text{that is to say,} \quad \frac{P_2}{P_1} = \frac{m}{n}.$$

The overall profits of cultivators rise in proportion to the increase in the period of the *baux*. But

$$\frac{P_2}{m} = \frac{P_1}{n};$$

even if overall profits are higher, annual profits are the same in the two cases. Of course the average profit accruing to each farmer in each year is also the same, because farmers are still f.

Now take a case in which the net product increases not once, but *twice*; first in year 1, and then in period $n + 1$, each time by the amount S. If the

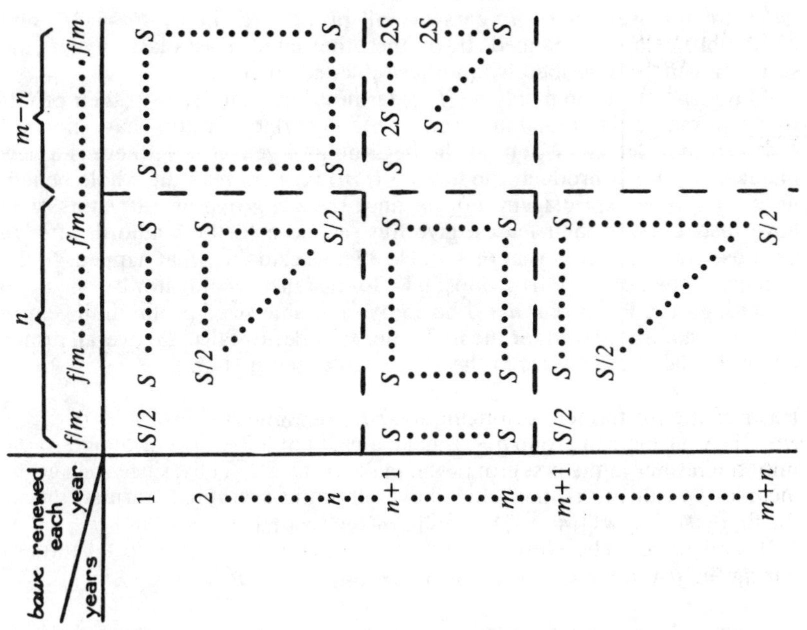

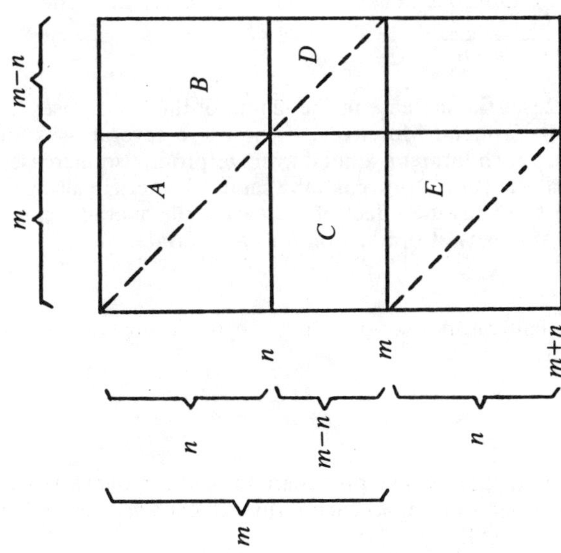

baux are renewed every n years overall profits are simply $P_3 = 2P_1$ and annual profits are unchanged. If, on the other hand, leases last m years the situation can be described by another table, see p. 163.

At the end of period n only $n \cdot (f/m)$ farmers have handed over their profits to proprietors; the remaining $(m - n) \cdot (f/m)$ cultivators have not yet renewed their leases. When, at the beginning of year $n + 1$, there is a new increase, S, in net product, the first $n \cdot (f/m)$ farmers reap the whole benefit until their *baux* expire again. For instance the nth group of cultivators, who have just renewed their leases, give this second S to the landlords after m periods, that is to say in year $m + n$. Now let us examine what happens to the farmers in the last $(m - n)$ groups; take for instance a cultivator belonging to the mth group. From year $n + 1$ he enjoys a double-sized profit, until year m when his *bail* is renewed for the first time. In order to calculate overall profits one can relabel the spaces in the above table, see p. 163.

It is easy to see that $P_2 = A + B + 1/2\ D$; moreover:

$$B = C = \frac{f}{m}\ [(m - n) \cdot n] \cdot S \text{ and}$$

$$A = E\frac{f}{m} \cdot (\frac{n}{2} + \sum_{0}^{n-1}{}_t\ t) \cdot S. \text{ Therefore one has:}$$

$$P_2 = E + C + 1/2\ D; \text{ the overall profit is now } P_4 = 2P_2.$$

However, the *profit per year* is now higher than before, because twice as many profits now accrue to farmers in a period of $m + n$ years, which by definition is shorter than $2m$.

$$\frac{P_4}{m+n} > \frac{P_2}{m} = \frac{P_1}{n} = \frac{P_3}{n}$$

To sum up: in both cases the increase in the length of the lease raises the total profits accruing to farmers. Moreover, if there are several price increases rather than one, each farmer's annual average profit also increases. And if one assumes that the cultivators make the same advances in all cases, the lengthening of the *baux* has the effect of increasing the average annual rate of profit per unit of means of production for each farmers.

6 Physiocracy and the Origin of Political Economy

6.1 New elements in physiocratic economics

In the previous chapters we have seen that an analysis of the role of markets and prices in Quesnay's economics brings to the fore many new elements, which call for a reassessment of its place in the history of economic thought. Most of the traditional reasons for praising Quesnay are confirmed by examining his value theory; but it appears that he has unfairly been held responsible for such failures as the lack of an analysis of prices and markets. However, a reinterpretation of physiocracy cannot be limited to a vindication of Quesnay, and it would be equally useless simply to single out the bits of economic theory which he first put forward.

An evaluation of Quesnay's contribution to economics requires a further examination of the real flaws and contradictions, some of which could even be called 'mistakes', which exist in physiocracy. It is necessary to analyse these 'black spots' in physiocratic economics in order to understand its legacy to the classical economists. This can be properly ascertained only by investigating the reasons for inconsistencies in Quesnay's economic theory, and by establishing their importance, which may have a 'positive' as well as a 'negative' value.

In Chapters 3, 4, and 5 Quesnay's contribution on specific economic questions was compared both with the state of economic knowledge in his day, and with the analysis of later economists, Smith in particular. Here I will attempt a more general evaluation of Quesnay's place in the making of economics as a science. In physiocracy it is possible to find anticipations of many aspects of more recent economic theories, from general equilibrium to input–output analysis (see Chapter 1, 1.2). However, Quesnay's contribution to economics must be evaluated first with respect to the origin and development of the approach to economic events known as classical political economy. However important Quesnay's role may be in the general development of economic science, his major merit is that he contributed to the foundation of the theories of surplus. The previous chapters have shown that Quesnay can rightly be regarded as the first economist who explicitly adopted the notions of surplus and reproduction in analysing the economic system (see in particular Chapter 3, 3.9–3.11; Chapter 5, 5.4, 5.5, and 5.10, 5.11). In order to properly evaluate Quesnay's place in economics it is necessary to set his work in the historical and economic context of his times, and to study the relations between his theory and those of the other classical economists and of Marx. This is the purpose of the present chapter.

First, it may be useful to recall briefly the major results deriving from our analysis of physiocracy, which have been examined in the previous chapters. It has been shown that the passages in which Quesnay and his followers describe wealth and revenue as being value magnitudes are not scattered or unimportant aspects of physiocratic economics. On the contrary, they are the manifestation of an attempt to provide a systematic explanation of the working of a system of reproduction in a market economy. The physiocrats devoted much of their attention to the analysis of market phenomena and to the problem of price formation. Quesnay put forward several concepts of price which are linked together by precise logical relationships. In particular, the categories of current and retail price are essential to describe the process of circulation of commodities, and give analytical support to the physiocrats' opposition to the activities of merchants and professional traders (see Chapter 3, 3.3). Thus the notion of 'first-hand price' clarifies the physiocratic distinction between activities which produce wealth and the 'sterile' occupations of 'resale trade', which simply exchange commodities whose values have already been determined (see Chapter 2). But the most important feature of Quesnay's investigation of price determination is the fact that his analysis is combined with a view of the economy as a circular process of production. This feature of the economic thought of the physiocrats emerges clearly from their definition of *prix fondamental*. Traditional interpretations have in fact been contradicted, in showing that this category also includes a net element, rent, together with the technical expenses of production (see Chapter 3, 3.7–3.9). Two important results derive from this view. First, Quesnay's *prix fondamental* is the analytical category which relates market phenomena to reproduction. Secondly, this notion is clearly a bridge linking pre-physiocratic price theories and Smith's concept of 'natural price'.

In Chapters 4 and 5 we have seen that Quesnay's analysis of markets and prices leads to a new interpretation of the physiocratic theories of production and distribution. For instance, the physiocrats use the concept of market competition to support their view that only agriculture normally yields a surplus. Free exports of French foodstuffs are adopted by the physiocrats to justify the existence of a permanent excess demand for them, and hence their high current price, exceeding the unit cost of production. Price notions also inform a new interpretation of the physiocratic theory of distribution; the difference between the *bon prix* and the fundamental price of agricultural commodities leaves a profit for farmers (see Chapter 5, part A). The physiocrats regard these profits as the primary source of new advances, and hence as the crucial feature of the process of economic development. However, in order to reassure the dominant classes that their economic and political power would not be challenged by the wealthy cultivators, the physiocrats had to play down the importance of farmers' profits as a share of the surplus. The argument that farmers' competition wipes out the whole profit was thus inserted for political, rather than for analytical, reasons, and cannot be advanced to show that in physiocracy farmers do not receive part of the surplus (see Chapter 5, part B).

However, the present examination of physiocracy is not limited to studying the analytical role of price concepts. In order to have a complete view of Quesnay's economics it is necessary to analyse his methodology, the problem he wanted to study and the way in which he presented his results. The *Tableau Economique* cannot be regarded as a synthesis of physiocratic economics, as it is traditionally believed. Many interpreters have been concerned with translating the *Tableau* and Quesnay's view of prices into mathematical models. But we have seen that these approaches are unable to represent many important features of physiocratic thought (see Chapter 1, part A).

These are the main points which can lead to a reassessment of Quesnay's impact on economics. But in a general interpretation of physiocracy it is necessary to bring together all these aspects, according to some overall guidelines. These guidelines must provide an explanation of the achievements and failures of Quesnay's economics, with particular attention being paid to their effects on the theories of Smith, Ricardo and Marx. This interpretation of physiocracy tries to understand and to explain the successes and weaknesses of Quesnay's analysis in the light of the fact that he investigated the features of an economic system which was experiencing major changes. Quesnay described and studied the contrasting mechanisms and forces of two different modes of production. He lived in an epoch which saw the transition from feudal society to industrial capitalism;

he and his disciples picked up and described the features of the two modes of production which co-existed in eighteenth-century France.[1] Their attention and interest move continuously between new economic aspects and old, well-established facts which can hardly be described by a single formal scheme. Professor Meek provided a first attempt at distinguishing between the phenomena that were regarded as *typical* by the physiocrats, and those that were *becoming typical* (see Meek, 1962, pp. 377–9).

However, Meek's most valuable contribution to our understanding of physiocracy is limited by his underestimation of the role and importance of price concepts, and of the physiocrats' analysis of the laws of markets and the working of competition. Therefore he fails to provide a view of the full extent to which the physiocrats oscillated between old and new facts. Value and price concepts bring out the way in which Quesnay and his disciples detect some aspects of the rising capitalist mode of production, while conserving most of the social, political and economic features of the *ancien régime*. An interpretation of physiocratic economics which takes into account the examination of values and markets clarifies the analytical categories employed. Thus it depicts their contribution to classical economics, that is, the way in which they set the stage for the development of economic analysis in the nineteenth century.

An analysis of the material presented in the previous chapters according to the above guidelines permits some conclusions about the role of physiocracy in the history of economic thought. From this it emerges that the physiocrats clearly saw that in the contemporary French economy features of both the feudal and the capitalist mode of production co-existed. The conflicting interests of the old dominant classes and the rising social group of agricultural entrepreneurs were emerging strongly. These opposing forces could be seen at work in the process of production and distribution of the net product (see Sections 6.1 and 6.2). The physiocrats tried to resolve the analytical difficulties deriving from the existence of these conflicts by resorting to a peculiar use of the notion of market competition; but their efforts were not successful. Their theories both of production and of distribution of the net product suffer from 'flaws' and 'contradiction' (see Sections 6.3–6.5).

However, an attempt to use concepts which are familiar in economics nowadays to amend Quesnay's 'errors' and to 'rationalise' his economic theory, may produce a misleading representation of the physiocrats' thought and of their vision of society (see 6.6). In contrast, a study of the historical and analytical reasons for these 'inconsistencies' gives a precise picture of the legacy of physiocracy in the making of classical political economy (see 6.7, 6.8).

6.2 The economic functions of classes and the analysis of the labour process

Physiocracy embodies the first serious attempt to base a definition of social classes on their different economic functions. The physiocrats believe that if civil laws are made to conform to natural ones all the inhabitants of the country will be better off, but in the natural order itself societies are made up of different parts, and each is characterised by its particular economic relations with the others. Thus the physiocrats separate social groups according to their role in the process of production and circulation of commodities. Quesnay speaks of 'the idea of *production*, or of *regeneration*, which here forms the basis of the differentiation between the general classes of citizens' (*Sur les travaux des artisans*, Meek, 1962, p. 204, Quesnay's italics). The proprietors and the sovereign spend their revenues on the products of agriculture and manufacture. The merchants contribute to the circulation of commodities between different countries and provinces. But Quesnay concentrates his attention on the farmer, who, provided he is wealthy enough to adopt large-scale cultivation, is regarded as a true capitalist entrepreneur (see Marx, 1970, vol. III, p. 604). He owns the means of production, in the form of original and annual advances, employs the workers to whom he pays a wage, organises the process of production, decides what to produce and what techniques of cultivation to employ, and eventually is the only owner of the output.

A part of the Physiocrats' analysis which merits particular attention is their treatment of the workers, who live on the wages they receive from entrepreneurs. In fact the physiocrats' examination of the labour process is an aspect of their work in which the features of the old and the new mode of production are particularly closely interlaced. We have seen that Quesnay analyses very carefully the role of capital in production, and in particular in agriculture (see Chapter 4, 4.3). He succeeded in singling out some of the most important features of capitalist production.

Besides studying the problem of accumulation of capital in itself, Quesnay relates this issue to that of the employment of workers in the primary sector. Thus he examines the role of machinery and of technical progress with regard to the question of unemployment. In fact, the increase in the available means of production enables farmers to reduce the expenses of agricultural cultivation; the unit cost of production diminishes and, with a given rent,[2] the *prix fondamental* decreases in proportion. Hence, the difference between this price and the *bon prix*, established on domestic markets by international competition, increases and more profits can be invested in agriculture (see Chapter 5, 5.2, 5.3). Quesnay believes that the introduction of machinery in cultivation may reduce the cost of production and the wage bill (see *Questions intéressantes*, I.N.E.D., 1958, vol. II, pp. 630–1; Baudeau, 1767–70, vol. I, pp. 141–2). In particular, he wants to reduce the expenses necessary to maintain the workers; the means of production must replace the peasants in cultivating the soil: 'it is necessary to increase production and to diminish the expenses, as much as possible, by means of livestock, machines, and all the other means which can replace the expenses of *main-d'oeuvre*' (*Question intéressantes*, I.N.E.D., 1958, vol. II, p. 631, italics added).

Quesnay is aware that increasing the original advances of agriculture and changing the methods of cultivation can imply labour redundancies in some activities, but he is convinced that the introduction of tools and machines does not generally create unemployment (see Weulersse, 1910a, vol. II, pp. 552–3). Even if some workers lose their jobs, this must not prevent the introduction of machinery which can reduce the cost of production of commodities, since reducing the expenses has the effect of favouring the profitable sale of commodities; 'all machines which can contribute to reduce the costs of men's labour, and all canals or rivers which avoid the costs which are paid to carriers, bring about a price which is favourable to the proper value of produce or commodities' (*Hommes*, Meek 1962, p. 100). The substitution of machines for workers can entail labour redundancies, but this fact does not worry Quesnay. He does not mention the compensating possibility that workers who become redundant in agriculture may be employed in the construction of the new machines. Quesnay suggests that if a problem of misery and unemployment arises in the countryside, the government must introduce subsidies for people who are out of work; a kind of poor law. In *Hommes* he always writes:

> people were worried about what would happen to the men employed in this work who had no other trade to earn their living by.

But they would have done better to support these workers for the rest of their lives than to suppress the machine and keep them on (ibid., p. 101 note, 1).

Two major preoccupations guide Quesnay's analysis of the labour process. First, he wants to secure the introduction of new machinery and new techniques in agriculture. These are the two main requirements for a rise in productivity, and all other aspects and elements of cultivation must therefore be subordinated to them. Secondly, the expenses of cultivation must be reduced, to make it possible to reduce the selling price of products, without a reduction either in farmers' profits, or in the revenues of the landlords and of the crown. In fact, with lower retail prices more people may consume the products of French agriculture, which, most importantly, become more competitive on international markets. Therefore, overall effective demand for French foodstuffs increases (see Chapter 4, 4.5, 4.6). Among the inputs of agriculture, labour appears to Quesnay to be the one which can most easily be used to achieve both purposes. Workers can be replaced by new machines and equipment, and this substitution makes it possible to reduce the general cost of production. It is therefore fair to say that Quesnay realised, at least intuitively, that labour is the most flexible element of production, and so can be moulded according to the requirements of what is regarded as the superior good of the country. The use of labour is a kind of dependent variable, which is subordinated to the size and technical characteristics of the capital employed.

6.3 Market competition and the origin of surplus

Despite Quesnay's study of the role of labour and capital in the production process, it is difficult to endorse Marx's praise of physiocracy as 'the first system which analyses capitalistic production' (Marx, 1963, vol. I, p. 49; see also Marx, 1967, vol. II, p. 360). Most of Quesnay's comments refer to the need to save labour expenses by introducing new capital equipment. But this fact is not sufficient to demonstrate that he fully appreciated the capitalist relationship of production between salaried workers and agricultural entrepreneurs. Quesnay failed to identify all the characteristics of the capitalist mode of production which was then becoming typical, and which a few decades later would be used to define the economic system itself. Of course it is pointless to criticise Quesnay for being unable to see the accelerating pace of capitalist production, but his failure leaves deep marks on physiocratic economics.

We have seen that Quesnay cannot relate the existence of surplus to wage labour (see Chapter 4, 4.3, 4.4), even though he does not believe that it derives simply from the bounty of nature. The physiocratic analysis of the origin of the net product is a clear example of the limitations of Quesnay's perception of the features of the rising capitalist mode of production. The physiocrats stress that the origin of surplus and wealth must be sought in the process of production of commodities, but they seem to be inclined to regard capital, rather than labour, as the decisive element of wealth.[3] Quesnay knows that production cannot take place without workers, even with modern methods of cultivation. But he is so anxious to secure the modernisation of the primary sector that labour appears as a residual element of production. Admittedly the introduction of new techniques of cultivation is possible only in so far as the necessary capital is available, but this preoccupation leads Quesnay to a general underestimation of the role of labour in production.

Quesnay's underevaluation of the workers' contribution to the production of surplus is linked to his belief in the sterility of industry. It is hard to say which of the two elements is the cause, and which the effect. Either Quesnay believed that manufacture does not yield a surplus, *because* he did not appreciate all the features of capitalist production; or he underestimated the role of wage labour, *in order to* emphasise the peculiarities and the superiority of modern agriculture (in which, as well as labour and land, a large amount of capital is needed in the process of production). In any case, the belief in the superior productivity of large-scale farming could be more easily defended if it were based on the idea that the net product derives from the employment of labour assisted by capital. The superiority of agriculture over manufacture could be justified *at least* in terms of the historical conditions of the two sectors in eighteenth-century France. However, an historically determined situation is not a sufficient foundation for a universal theory of the distinction between productive and sterile activities. Even if Quesnay had ascribed the existence of surplus to wage labour and capital, it would still have been difficult *always* to restrict the characteristic of 'productive' to agricultural activities; industry would have been sterile *only* because of the lack of capital.

Quesnay used a different argument to explain and defend the doctrine of the exclusive productivity of agriculture. This choice was certainly influenced by the fact that his analysis of production suffered from the absence of important features of capitalistic relations of production. Quesnay had a particularly clear view of the division of labour in society, where each individual has a role to play (see *Le droit naturel*, Meek, 1962, p. 51). However, he does not use the idea of division of labour to analyse the labour process, either on the land, or in factories. Thus, in order to explain his theory of the origin of surplus, Quesnay must introduce an analysis of market forces and competition. One certainly regrets that such a convinced supporter of the primacy of the sphere of production over that of circulation had to resort to the notion of market competition. However, Quesnay's attempt produces some remarkable aspects of his economic theory. They are: the study of demand and of free trade; and the analysis of market mechanisms and price determination.

The physiocrats also justify the existence of surplus in agriculture by arguing that with free competition in foreign trade, wealthy foreign merchants ensure a high effective demand for the products of land, which causes a high level of competition among buyers and therefore raises current prices (see Chapter 4, 4.7). The existence of permanent excess demand justifies and guarantees the existence of a net product. However, competition must also explain the fact that *only one* sector of the economy produces a surplus; hence the physiocrats describe the high degree of competition among artisans, which prevents them from securing a permanent gain over costs. The output of manufactured goods always adapts itself to demand and the current price coincides with the fundamental one. However, competition among cultivators is not strong enough to wipe out the net product of agriculture. The physiocrats try to defend the view that agriculture is productive and industry is sterile by invoking the *appropriate* working of competition on first-hand markets on one hand, and among producers on the other.

Therefore, despite their attacks on mercantilism, Quesnay and his disciples end up by welcoming a positive balance of trade for France, even though the net balance must be composed of the products of land. Advantageous foreign trade is still a condition for the physiocratic process of development and growth. Quesnay's analysis of the origin of surplus lacks the notion of capitalistic exploitation of labour and he does not fully appreciate all the implications of the division of labour in the process of production. He therefore has to resort to a sort of mercantilistic attitude, which is synthesized in the idea of a permanent excess demand for the products of French agriculture, in order to justify the exclusive productivity of agriculture, and, more generally, his view of the genesis of surplus.

We have already shown that the physiocratic arguments in support of the doctrine of the exclusive productivity of the primary sector are logically inconsistent (see Chapter 4, 4.9). The study of market competition does not seem to provide a sound basis for the physiocratic theory of the origin of surplus. In fact, Quesnay expects the notion of competition to solve major analytical problems in his economic theory, by fulfilling a number of *ad hoc* roles. However, the concept is unable to provide satisfactory explanations of some physiocratic contentions, which are thus left with flaws and inconsistencies. As far as the theory of the origin of surplus is concerned, it is hard to reconcile a generally free competitive system with the existence of surplus in only one sector of the economy. Too many 'appropriate' conditions for the working of competitive markets are needed to support the doctrine of the exclusive productivity of agriculture, and it becomes more and more difficult to limit the existence of a gain over cost for artisans and manufacturers to conditions in which they have exclusive privileges (see Weulersse, 1910a, vol. I, pp. 297–9). The main argument on which the existence of an agricultural surplus rests is the different working of competition among manufacturers on one hand and cultivators on the other. This is certainly a convincing consideration from a historical point of view, but it is a very weak argument on which to found a *general* view of productive and unproductive activities. Thus Quesnay ends up in the same sort of 'blind alley' as he would have reached if he had used the idea that agriculture was more productive than manufacture because it employed more capital. In their analysis of market forces, the physiocrats describe very well the economic conditions of contemporary France, and in particular of the primary sector, but this effort is insufficient to prove that manufacture is not productive. Indeed, the main undesirable effect of the failure to reconcile general competition with the existence of a surplus in one sector, is that there is no longer a valid explanation for the intrinsic sterility of industry (see Herlitz, 1961a, pp. 4–6, 18–20; Routh, 1975, p. 72).[4] And if manufacture is not sterile, all physiocratic economic policies in favour of agriculture lose most of their strength, and may be jeopardised.

6.4 The theory of distribution

Competition, prices and markets play a major role in the physiocratic analysis of the distribution of the social product between social classes. Here too, the results do not fulfil the physiocrats' hopes. In section 6.2 it was seen that the physiocrats did not bring to light all the features of the capitalist mode of production. This implies that their notion of wage can hardly be compared with the price of labour power, which in a capitalistic economy arises from the contrasting activities of workers and entrepreneurs. Quesnay and his disciples accept a subsistence theory of wages. The workers receive enough to buy the necessaries of life for themselves and their families. There are so many poor people willing to become workers that wages cannot rise above mere subsistence (see Spengler, 1942, pp. 200, 207; Weulersse, 1910a, vol. II, pp. 284, 324, 327). Money wages mostly depend on the prices of the necessaries consumed by workers.

> The wages of the workers who are employed either in cultivation or in activities similar to cultivation, are fixed in relation to the current price of the products they consume; it is on this current price [sic] that competition regulates their salaries (Mercier, 1767, p. 214).

Therefore wages are influenced by the prices of primary commodities, which are the most important goods in workers' consumption. Du Pont says that 'there must be a necessary relation between the value of foodstuffs and the price of a working day, which must secure to the worker the means necessary to satisfy his needs' (Du Pont, 1764, p. 28).

For the physiocrats, therefore, the economic interests of the working class depend on the prices of foodstuffs, because these regulate money wages. But since money wages should follow changes in the prices of primary commodities, real wages should remain constant. Each worker receives a fixed amount of goods, irrespective of price changes. In physiocracy, the idea that real wages are determined by the level of workers' subsistence helps to hide, or at least to play down, the significance of the opposition between workers and entrepreneurs. This is a feature of the new mode of production which sometimes appears in Quesnay's works, but which disappears on other occasions. Sometimes he recognises that workers and farmers have opposite economic interests, but this fact does not have a central position in the physiocratic theory of distribution. On most occasions the relationships between these two classes are overshadowed by other class conflicts; those between the merchant and the cultivator, and between the latter and the proprietor.

The physiocrats are aware that the division of French society into classes entails the existence of contrasting interests among them. Most of their efforts are dedicated to showing that the interests of merchants are opposed to those of all other classes.[5] Here too, the task of illuminating the particular aspects of this conflict is assigned to competition and to the notions of current and retail price (see Chapter 3, 3.3–3.4). In the sphere of circulation of commodities, the interests of professional traders are opposed to those of farmers because their activities depress the average current price. But they also conflict with those of consumers, since the retail price is higher than it would be without the merchants' gain. Landlords and the sovereign are damaged twice by traders: as consumers they must pay a higher retail price, and as revenue receivers they cannot demand high rents and taxes from farmers, who are harmed by fluctuations in the current price. The gains of professional traders reduce the revenue and the' wealth of the country, because they represent an additional burden on the unit cost of production of commodities. Therefore the introduction of measures against the monopolistic power of merchants benefits all social classes; as in England, landlords, consumers and farmers are all better off.

In the physiocratic theory of distribution the reduction of traders' gain, which is implicit in the reduction of the difference between current and retail prices and which follows the implementation of free competition in foreign trade, is like a safety-valve, preventing confrontation between workers, landlords and farmers.

Thus competition shows how the different economic interests of classes clash, but it also guarantees that there will be an appropriate division of the net product between farmers and landlords. According to the physiocrats, the interests of the cultivators coincide with those of the country as a whole, because they always act to obtain a higher net product; therefore they are sometimes called 'co-owners' of the state (see Chapter 5, 5.7). Farmers are the first possessors of the country's surplus, but competition among them guarantees that the appropriate share of net product accrues to landlords. The notion of fundamental price defines the problem of distribution of surplus between proprietors and cultivators by ensuring that the former receive part of the net output.

Competition should secure harmony between consumers and producers on commodity markets, and between farmers and landlords on the market for land. Workers, too, will not be harmed by the increase in the current price of wheat, since this is matched by a lowering of prices on retail markets. Thanks to the reduction in the power of merchants and in their share of national product, the workers are no worse off, and all other classes are better off.

6.5 The contrasting interests of classes

Competition and price concepts do not provide a satisfactory justification for the physiocratic theory of distribution of surplus, but they bring to light dangerous contradictions in the physiocrats' view of the distribution of the social product, and of surplus in particular. Rather than reconciling the interests of different classes, the physiocrats' analysis of markets and prices shows how they actually clash. It is interesting to investigate why physiocratic economics can lead to this embarrassing result. Free competition is designed to eliminate, or at least to reduce, the gains of professional traders, which are interposed between the current and retail price. But when the role and profits of merchants become almost irrelevant in the determination of prices, then the exchange values of commodities in the two markets rapidly approach each other (see Chapter 3, 3.5, 3.6). Thus there is a negligible difference between current and retail prices; they can be regarded as a single exchange value, which is no longer influenced by the market forces of supply and demand.

Now the value of products is regulated by their fundamental price, which is the lower limit of the current price (Chapter 3, 3.7), and which is also influenced by the technical cost of cultivation, as well as by rent and *taille*, which are part of the social surplus. Thus, a reduction of the merchants' gains brings to light the existence of a conflict between landlords and farmers over the distribution of surplus. The shares of the two classes in the net output depend on changes in the current and fundamental price. In particular, given the level of productive expenses and of the current price, which is influenced by international competition, the size of the net product which can be shared between farmers and landlords is fixed. The level of the fundamental price divides the difference between the current price and the cost of production into two parts, and therefore specifies the distribution of surplus between rent and profits. In physiocracy, neither the concept of competition nor that of fundamental price can convincingly demonstrate that there is perfect harmony between classes, and that adapting French economic policy to natural laws should bring prosperity and welfare to all the inhabitants and classes of the country.

(a) *The price of corn and the standard of living of people*

There are many places in the works of the physiocrats where it is clear that the classes of French society have opposite economic interests, even leaving aside the case of merchants. A first example is given by the relationship between the price of corn and the standard of living of people, in particular manufacturing workers. For Quesnay the free exportation of French foodstuffs is designed to raise their domestic prices. He wants a shift of the terms of trade in favour of agricultural France and against her trading neighbours, which mainly produce manufactured goods (see Chapter 2, 2.8 and Chapter 3, 3.6).[6] But this trade relationship will eventually produce a modification of domestic relative prices in favour of the products of land and against those of manufacture. This is a first reason for concern among French workers.

The change in relative prices in favour of agriculture, which results from the implementation of free trade for corn, damages the whole industrial sector. Independent artisans and manufacturers who own small workshops must pay more for their necessaries and the raw materials used up in production. Moreover, their selling prices cannot follow the rise in the prices of primary goods, so that the gains of manufacturers inevitably disappear, and by trying to increase the prices of their goods they can only hope to avoid losses. Even if France were to become richer at the expense of foreign countries, both French industrial workers and entrepreneurs would face a reduction in their incomes because of the shift in relative prices (see Weulersse, 1910a, vol. II, pp. 413–14).

The rise in the price of corn is also likely to adversely affect the well-being of *all* French workers, not only the artisans. (The physiocrats use the term 'workers' mainly to indicate the poor people of the towns.) The physiocrats maintain that money wages follow the variations in the price of corn; hence the standard of living of workers should be unaffected by an increase in this price. But this simple proposition does not seem to correspond with actual historical events in France. Most critics accused physiocracy of provoking a reduction in the real wages of the workers, and in the standard of life of the *peuple* generally (see ibid., pp. 568–9). Ultimately the increase in the price of corn benefited only landlords and wealthy farmers, since it implied a redistribution of income towards them, but was against the interests of all other classes, and of workers in particular.

Quesnay and his disciples were aware of the miserable living conditions of the people (see ibid., p. 570), and of the severe challenge to their theory presented by the accusation of contributing to their further impoverishment.[7] Du Pont tries to refute these criticisms with two rather weak arguments. First, he maintains that although the price of corn, and hence of bread, is higher, free trade reduces the fluctuation of this value and brings about a uniform price throughout the country (see Du Pont, 1764, p. 28). A meagre consolation for the people, but it seems that even this equalisation of prices between provinces did not actually occur (see Weulersse, 1910a, vol. II, p. 230).

Du Pont's second argument is even more feeble; he admits that the direct beneficiaries of increased corn prices are proprietors and farmers, but 'the wealthier is the Nation, the more the King and the Proprietors will be able to spend to the profit of everybody' (Du Pont, 1764, p. 33). Thus the workers are supposed to take advantage of the higher expenses and purchases made by landlords and the government out of their increased incomes. According to Du Pont, the workers benefit from the price rise, because 'their salaries . . . depend upon the *expenditure of revenue* by the Clergy, the Government's Employees and the Proprietors' (ibid., Du Pont's italics). Thus the workers must not fear increases in the prices of foodstuffs; Du Pont says that a rise of one-sixth in the price of corn trebles private and public wealth. Thus he concludes that 'this increase, which frightens people, becomes a remarkable relative reduction, which produces for them the same effect as if bread had actually been decreased by two-thirds' (ibid.). But Du Pont's optimistic calculations are not very convincing. As a matter of fact, it is easy to see that if more people are employed, either as workers on the farms or as servants by the landlords, overall wages increase, but there is no reason why wages per employee should also rise. Because of strong competition among them, workers cannot raise their wages above the level of subsistence. The rise in the wheat price might perhaps produce more jobs in the future, but in the meantime all the workers can hope for is simply to avoid a reduction in their real wages.

(b) *Farmers versus landlords*

Quesnay's major concern is not about people's living conditions, but about the fact that in physiocratic economics the interests of farmers and landlords cannot easily be reconciled. In fact, physiocracy shows that there are explicit points of conflict between the two groups, despite Quesnay's intentions and desires (see Meek, 1962, pp. 390, 298). The physiocrats always claim that the interests of both farmers and proprietors (including the sovereign and the church) coincide with that of the country, but their descriptions of the roles and functions of the two groups are not exactly alike. Cultivators are consistently praised, since they are the major agents of economic development: they increase the advances and improve the methods of cultivation. Farmers' interests and actions cannot be in conflict with the prosperity of the country; their gains are not a deduction from anybody else's income; on the contrary they are advantageous for the nation: 'a husbandman can have a gain from his undertaking in cultivation only by working for the profit of the State' (*Hommes*, I.N.E.D., 1958, vol. II, p. 565).

On the other hand, landlords must be instructed and guided according to the natural order, since their behaviour *might* be in conflict with the national interest. While farmers seem to be led inevitably to invest their profits (see Chapter 5, 5.4), proprietors are absolutely free to decide how to spend their revenues; a decision which influences the whole process of circulation of commodities (see Routh, 1975, pp. 73–4). For example, they can buy foreign manufactures, and this behaviour damages the wellbeing of the whole nation. Moreover the physiocrats more or less explicitly reproach the landlords because they do not take adequate care of their *domaines*. The idleness and indifference of proprietors, who live in big cities and spend their money on luxuries, is seen as a major cause of the disastrous condition of French agriculture (see Weulersse, 1910a, vol. II, p. 311).[8]

The conflict of interests between landlords and farmers is particularly clear in the distribution of the net product (see Weulersse, 1910a, vol. II. pp. 303–6; Molinier, 1958a, pp. 12–13, 43) when the *baux* have to be renewed. The 'fair proportion', by which competition should divide the surplus between the two groups, cannot hide the existence of opposing interests. The net product accrues directly to the cultivators, who can also affect its size by changing the methods of production. Moreover, all physiocratic policy measures have the immediate effect of increasing the farmers' net product, either by raising the current price, or by relieving the cultivators of duties and taxes (see Weulersse, 1910a, vol, II, pp. 176–86). But even if the cultivators were masters of the production process, political and juridical power remained firmly in the hands of the aristocracy. State and administrative control secured to the first and second estates part of the surplus of the country. A complex system of seigneural rights guaranteed the appropriation by the dominant classes of a share of the net product, even if their economic role was only that of deciding how to spend the revenue. The socio-historically established fact of land rent is still a type of *droit seigneural*, even if it also embodies the features of a private contract between two free individuals: the proprietor and the farmer. For the Physiocrats this political aspect at once justified and explained the existence of rent; the renewal of the *baux* was not the simple recontracting of a previous agreement, but an expression of the dominance of the class of proprietors over that of cultivators. The feudal mode of production was still dominant in the era of transition that France was then experiencing.[9]

Both chronologically and logically rent appears after the surplus has reached the cultivators, but according to the social and political order of the kingdom it is the first share in the net product. Land rent represents the fundamental relationship of production at the time, therefore, the process of circulation of commodities must guarantee that the proprietors receive their leases (see Chapter 3, 3.10); hence rent is a stable and permanent part of the surplus. The profits of cultivators are a residual share in the net product and are highly unstable; they even disappear in some periods and in small-scale farming their size is almost negligible. On one hand, the physiocrats must ensure the primacy of rent and *taille* in the distribution of the net product. On the other hand, Quesnay remarks that profits are the only source of capital accumulation in agriculture, and are the most important economic factor in the development of the country; these gains must therefore be protected by appropriate economic policy measures. The analysis of market forces does not help Quesnay to reconcile the interests of landlords and agricultural entrepreneurs; the categories of competition and fundamental price cannot conceal the conflict between rent and profits.

The existence of undesired reasons for confrontation between the social classes of landlords, farmers and workers, in the logical structure of physiocratic economics, can be judged in different ways. On one hand, the physiocrats miss their purpose; they fail to present the dominant classes with a model of society in which all groups can be wealthy and prosperous, with the exception of merchants. On the other hand, Quesnay has the merit of putting forward, despite his intention, an economic analysis in which some of the class conflicts typical of the capitalist mode of production are already emerging. Some of these class relationships are analysed in greater detail, such as those of farmers and landlords, while others, like the opposition of workers to entrepreneurs, remain in the shade. However, even though he was not always successful, Quesnay took very useful steps in linking the analysis of prices and distribution of income to the class structure of society.

6.6 The scarcity of land and the attempt to solve the physiocratic contradictions

It may be useful to examine the views of commentators who have tried to remove the inconsistencies in physiocratic theories of production and distribution in order to present physiocracy as a logically coherent model. A simple and straightforward way of solving these inconsistencies is that of ascribing to the physiocrats the view that lands are always scarce, with respect to aggregate effective demand for primary products.[10] If cultivable soil is scarce it is easy to justify the exclusive productivity of agriculture, which is the only sector using the limited natural resources directly; agricultural production cannot rise to meet effective demand. The current prices of primary products remain above their technical costs of production, and there is thus a surplus in agriculture, the only sector which employs a scarce resource. If land is scarce with respect to the required amount of output, the confrontation between farmers and landlords in the appropriation of surplus is also easily solved in favour of the latter group. Competition among farmers is fully justified by the scarcity of land; rent is now the price of the only non-produced means of production (leaving aside labour, which receives a subsistence wage).

This approach tries to 'rationalise' Quesnay's economics by applying to it analytical schemes only fully developed by his successors. In particular, the above interpretation ascribes to physiocracy a theory of 'absolute rent' in a single sector of the economy,[11] which is quite similar to that outlined by Smith a few years later; 'there are some parts of the produce of land for which the demand must always be such as to afford a greater price than what is sufficient to bring them to market' (Smith, 1776, vol. I, p. 163). These products 'always afford a rent to the landlords'. The amount of rent depends on the difference between the market price of the products and their natural price;

> It is because its price is high or low; a great deal more, or very little more, or no more, than what is sufficient to pay those wages and profit, that it affords a high rent, or a low rent, or no rent at all (ibid.).

However, the idea of scarcity of land certainly does not correspond with the physiocrats' view of the French economy in the middle of the eighteenth century. They explicitly deny that land can be regarded as scarce (see, for instance, *Questions intéressantes*, I.N.E.D., 1958, vol. II, p. 642). Of course, geographically the country has definite boundaries, but the amount of soil which is actually cultivated is only a tiny fraction of the whole (see Sée, 1967, p. 33). Most French lands were either idle or badly cultivated by *métayers* and one of the physiocrats' main prescriptions concerned the need for drainage so that new lands could be exploited. The government had to encourage the implementation of any measures which could increase the amount of French soil cultivated. The physiocrats regarded the fact that France had been endowed with a large and fertile territory as one of its most positive features. A theory of economic development based on a scarce resource would hardly have been considered as an argument in favour of physiocracy. In fact, the idea that lands were limited was used by the adversaries of the physiocrats to show that this limitation would prevent output from increasing (see Galiani, 1770, p. 142). The scarcity of foodstuffs was explained, according to the physiocrats, by the fact that too few lands were exploited using the most advanced methods of cultivation, which required huge means of production. The physiocrats underline the fact that in France *capital and not land* is lacking in the exploitation of soil (see Weulersse, 1910a, vol. I, pp. 323–4). Large advances are necessary to extend cultivation and to improve the methods of production (see Chapter 4, 4.3).

The idea that there is a scarcity of land in physiocracy might perhaps be applied to its description of the 'state of bliss', in which all physiocratic recommendations have already been implemented (see Chapter 1, 1.10). For instance, the *Analyse* depicts a country where all lands are fully cultivated using the best possible methods (see Meek, 1962, p. 151). By this expression

> Quesnay meant not only that all the kingdom's territory has been brought under cultivation, but also that large-scale capitalist agriculture, using the most productive methods then available, has been widely introduced (ibid., p. 273).

According to the authors who support the view that lands are scarce in physiocracy, the state of prosperity is achieved by reinvesting the profits of farmers during the years between two renewals of their *baux* (see Eltis 1975b, p. 341; Meek 1962, p. 304). Capital accumulation causes a generalised situation of large-scale cultivation throughout the country, with a high and stable surplus. But once the 'state of bliss' has been achieved and the process of development is completed, profits are eliminated by competition among farmers and rent appears as the only form of the net product (see Eltis, 1975b, pp. 343–4; Meek, 1962, pp. 303–4).

The fact that the idea of scarcity of land can only possibly be applied to the physiocrats' view of the state of prosperity, is the major reason for the misleading character of this interpretation of physiocracy. Quesnay would never have accepted the above view, which implies the existence of a major *discontinuity* between the actual French economy and the 'state of bliss' resulting from the adaptation of economic policy to the laws of the natural order. In fact these laws *would not be* the same in the two situations; and this conclusion would destroy the whole of physiocratic economics, which is consistently based on the need first to study, and then to follow, the laws of the natural order of societies. The physiocrats regard the natural order as describing an ideal situation, but the same forces are also at work in present-day economies. The *Tableau Economique* is not only designed to describe the features of the ideal economy, as does the *Analyse*. Most of the time Quesnay uses it to investigate the effects of specific economic policies in the actual French economy.[12]

As far as the production of surplus is concerned, the scarcity of land argument attempts to explain its existence in the 'state of bliss' in a way which would not satisfactorily account for it in the French economy in the eighteenth century. Had the physiocrats accepted this view, there would have been no justification for the existence of a surplus in agriculture in France in 1760, when there was plenty of uncultivated land. But Quesnay cannot wait to have a net product in the age of prosperity; the surplus must exist now, because it has to be reinvested in agricultural production in order to set in motion the process of development leading to the ideal society. The lack of a net product in France in 1760 would have prevented it from reaching the stage of welfare and prosperity.

It is difficult to accept the opinion that Quesnay used the scarcity of land argument to justify the exclusive productivity of agriculture; it is, however, even more unlikely that the physiocrats adopted this view in their theory of the distribution of surplus. Indeed this idea raises serious problems in physiocratic economics. A first reason for rejecting the opinion that Quesnay and his disciples took this approach concerns their analysis of the role of farmers in economic development. In fact, for the physiocrats agricultural entrepreneurs are masters of the process of production of wealth, they decide what to produce and how to produce it, moreover they accumulate advances by risking their own financial resources. Mirabeau depicts the cultivators as the 'great artists of the annual reproduction of the wealth of the Nation' (Mirabeau, 1760a, p. 97). The French economy can grow and reach the 'state of bliss' *only* if farmers themselves become rich and wealthy. Even commentators who espouse the idea of the scarcity of land recognise that the existence of rich farmers is the major feature of the physiocratic process of development. However, according to this interpretation of physiocracy, once the state of prosperity has been attained they cease to be one of the classes which appropriate part of the surplus. Notwithstanding their growing economic power, the farmers are systematically deprived of their gains when leases are renewed. Moreover, once all land is farmed on a large scale, under the leadership of wealthy and powerful cultivators, this class has no further economic role to play. The scarcity of land view implies the *non-existence* in a prosperous economy of the very agricultural bourgeoisie which plays such a decisive and unique role in the process of economic growth. It is hard to believe that the physiocrats solved the landlord–farmer confrontation by a complete victory for the former class. Again, there would be a major hiatus between the laws of the natural order in the actual economy and the same laws in the ideal society; farmers have no normal profit accruing to them, even if in reality they act and invest in pursuit of gain.

There is a second reason for considering the 'absolute rent approach' as an implausible interpretation of physiocracy. With scarcity of land, rent is justified on the basis of purely market mechanisms; landowners receive the entire net output *only* because cultivable soil is scarce. If, on the contrary, there is more than enough land to satisfy the whole demand for primary products no rent should be paid to proprietors, since they are now competing to obtain even a very small rent by leasing their lands. Therefore, land rent loses its characteristic of being a social relationship of production in the appropriation of surplus and becomes only the outcome of a private contract between farmers and landlords. The private ownership of land by the dominant political classes is not sufficient to explain the existence of a compulsory obligation, the payment of rent, in order to carry on production. Cultivators pay a rent to the first and second estates *only if* the total amount of French soil is scarce with respect to output, and the size of rent depends entirely on market conditions. The scarcity of land approach does highlight some aspects of physiocratic economics, by extending some of its analyses and contentions to an extreme case. But it certainly is not a faithful representation of the physiocrats' vision of society and of economic systems. On the contrary, these authors are attempting to 'rationalise' physiocracy, rather than to understand its merits and its limitations. This attempt to translate Quesnay's work into a logically coherent model is founded on two main ideas. First, the *Analyse* is regarded as a synthesis of the whole of physiocratic economics; therefore if Quesnay says that all the soil is cultivated, it means that he used this idea throughout his work. Secondly, these interpreters claim to explain physiocracy by applying to it concepts and categories which are typical of the English classical economists, and which were designed to investigate economic systems in which the capitalist mode of production was already dominant. This interpretation leaves behind the France of the *ancien régime* in order to move to Adam Smith's England, or perhaps even to the times when Ricardo and Malthus were debating the determination of rent and the rate of profit.

By trying to apply to physiocracy notions derived from the analysis of a fully developed capitalist economy, the interpretation of physiocratic economics on the basis of the theory of absolute rent presents a grotesque picture of Quesnay's vision of French society. It suggests that the aristocracy had already lost state power, and the farmers had already got rid of land-rent, of the other seigneural rights, and of all feudal obligations. The political structure no longer allowed landlords to compel cultivators to pay rent, by means of juridical and administrative power. However, although the first and second estates had lost political power, they maintained their supremacy in the division of the net product thanks to the newly established mechanisms of the capitalist mode of production, and in particular because of market competition among capitalist cultivators.

Thus we have a paradoxical situation, where the agricultural bourgeoisie is the new dominant class, but at the same time the cultivators do not succeed in keeping for themselves even a small part of the net product of agriculture. The surplus passes through their hands, but it eventually flows to the landlords. Farmers are deprived of their profits by the very same capitalist economic relationship which has just replaced the feudal features of the process of production of commodities. The new facts, which are becoming typical, work in favour of the proprietors and not of the cultivators. This attempt to build up a fully coherent model of physiocracy therefore leads to an 'anti-historical' and grotesque presentation of the physiocrats' description of 1760 France.

6.7 Physiocracy and the modification of French society

One of the most awkward tasks facing Quesnay was that of reconciling the new economic facts, which represented the growing power of the agricultural bourgeoisie, with the social and political structure of the *ancien régime*. The dynamic and progressive economic mechanisms and forces which are represented by the agricultural entrepreneur are confronted by old rules, constraints and laws which hinder economic development. The social structure of the country and the old property relationships do not encourage, but even obstruct, the process of investment (see Fox-Genovese, 1976, pp. 238–42).

The fact that physiocratic analysis stresses opposing class interests and the contrasting aspects of economic and political structures must be regarded as one of its major merits. But to the physiocrats this was a source of embarrassment. Their theory failed to convince the rulers and the public that welfare could increase overall and that no social group would be damaged by physiocratic economic policy. The idea of farmers' competition is their attempt to solve the farmer-landlord opposition in the economic sphere. Similarly, they try to deal with the problem of the co-existence of a centuries-old political and social structure with newly rising economic mechanisms and forces, by resorting to the idea of 'legal despotism'.

Moreover, the physiocrats maintain that the new economic features and the rising social classes do not need to challenge the political organisation of France. The enlightened sovereign, instructed in the laws of the natural order, guarantees the proper administration of the existing political system in such a way that the process of economic development can take place inside the traditional social structure.[13] Physiocracy seems to require only minor changes, affecting administrative aspects rather than the whole social organisation of France. However, *despotisme légal* and the 'new' version of the *ancien régime* are as unconvincing as the idea that farmers' competition brings *all* the surplus to the landlords. Inside the old property relationships and laws the aristocrats and the church should co-exist peacefully with the wealthy capitalist cultivators, who control the processes of production of primary commodities. *Despotisme légal* is the political side of the physiocrats' attempt to play down, even to disguise, the powerful implications of their theory for major social and political change.

6.8 Quesnay's 'flaws' and his contribution to classical economics

An analysis of the physiocratic theory of value brings to the fore new features of Quesnay's economics. These elements make it possible to dispose of some popular, but incorrect, opinions about physiocracy, and open the way to a reassessment of its place in the process which led to the formation of economic science. The physiocratic concepts of prices, markets and competition shed light on some ambiguities and inconsistencies in physiocratic theory. But these concepts also provide important insights and clues to the analytical and historical reasons which led Quesnay to make contradictory statements. Thus, instead of 'amending' these 'mistakes', one can try to understand their meaning and their importance in Quesnay's economics. This approach is based on the view that even the 'inconsistencies' of an economic theory help us understand it better. Thus in the history of economic thought the category of 'contradiction' should not be banished from scientific investigation, at least in so far as it helps to unveil new features of past economic theories.

By making full use of the idea of 'contradiction' it is possible to throw new light on interesting aspects of Quesnay's contribution to political economy. First, it clearly emerges that one of the major merits of physiocracy is the fact that it singles out the most important elements of instability and conflict which characterised the transition from feudalism to capitalism in eighteenth-century France. Some of Quesnay's so-called 'mistakes' provide reasons for praising his intuition about the features of the old world which were becoming less and less important, because new economic mechanisms were beginning to operate in the production and circulation of commodities. As a matter of fact, the physiocrats' 'case study' of Louis XV's reign shows the positive aspects of the transition away from feudalism. This is reflected in their constant praise of the cultivators who are the driving force in the process of capital accumulation. But at the same time they are still men of the *ancien régime*, with no intention of changing the old social and political order. Most of their ambiguities derive from this fact. Feudalism and capitalism, therefore, co-exist not only in eighteenth-century France but also in Quesnay's investigation of economic laws; the former dominates the political sphere and the latter begins to show its primacy in the economic one.

This approach to physiocracy shows that although Quesnay singled out some of the most important features of a capitalist economy, he sometimes failed to analyse them in a completely satisfactory way. His thought did not break away from feudalism entirely, but the same was true of the comtemporary French economy. Hence, Quesnay establishes the fact that the main objects of economic analysis are wealth, development and growth; accumulation of capital and technical changes in the process of production are the major means by which wealth and prosperity can be attained. But he does not extend the investigation beyond the primary sector! As far as the problem of the distribution of the net product is concerned, Quesnay shows that society is divided into classes with opposing interests. But he is worried by this 'discovery'; in fact he is not prepared to explicitly accept the permanence of conflicting interests. Thus he tries to limit their effects and to restore harmony between landlords and farmers, and between these two classes and workers.

The physiocratic theory of value, and the analysis of its flaws and contradiction, provide new elements for an evaluation of Quesnay's contribution to theories of surplus, and an examination of the categories he still lacked. We have seen that the physiocrats' distinction between productive and sterile activities does not use the idea of the exploitation of labour according to the features of the capitalist mode of production. If these were added, the surplus would no longer have to be justified by recourse to notions like that of permanent excess demand, but could be fully ascribed to the organisation of the labour processes where capital assists workers. Thus large-scale cultivation would earn a surplus because it would be the only capitalistic activity of economy, and not because of the physical characteristics of the commodities produced, and the lack of competition among wealthy farmers.

Therefore, even if Quesnay did not make full use of his analysis of production to support the theory of the origin of surplus, he showed that the causes of wealth must be found in the process of production of commodities, and not in their exchange. However, for Quesnay the superiority of production over circulation cannot be justified by simply ignoring market phenomena. This would be a very unsatisfactory way of answering the question about the origin of wealth. His analysis of markets, prices and effective demand is an attempt to relate the spheres of production and circulation. The endeavour was only partly successful. However, Quesnay's merit is not so much that he *stated* the primacy of production, but that he showed that, in order to explain why and how wealth springs from production, *it is necessary* to analyse market forces and prices. For Quesnay a theory of surplus and wealth must provide an analysis of all the stages through which a commodity passes; from the study of its inputs to that of its consumption. Thus Quesnay bequeathed to classical economics the idea that a theory of wealth, founded on the notions of surplus and reproduction cannot be isolated from a study of prices and markets.

Coming to the theory of the distribution of income, we have seen that the physiocrats used the concept of profit on alienation (see Chapter 5, 5.2). But this notion of profit does not suit the purpose of securing the accumulation of capital and the process of development, which depends mainly on the state of 'first-hand markets' on the one hand, and on the degree of competition among farmers when the *baux* are renewed on the other. Thus, the analytical framework of physiocracy calls for a different notion of profit. This is the category of a rate of profit on the capital employed in production; a share of surplus which systematically accrues to entrepreneurs in proportion to their advances, and independently of the day-to-day market conditions in sales at first-hand. The fundamental price of agricultural products should then include another net element, profit (together with rent and *taille*), which could constitute a regular and steady source of capital accumulation. The notion of rate of profit on capital invested can obviously be used to reconcile the existence of rent with the possibility of capital accumulation by wealthy farmers, who no longer have to disappear in the 'state of bliss'.[14]

The physiocrats try to relate the problems of value and distribution to that of the production of commodities; this is the task of the notion of fundamental price. By using this concept, Quesnay tries to show that the market value of a commodity depends on its cost of production, and is also influenced by existing class relationships. And classes must be defined with respect to their roles in the process of production. This is another non-trivial way of reaffirming the primacy of production over circulation. But here too we see that Quesnay's economic analysis is limited; in fact one of the most important classes, the merchants, is defined by its role in the process of exchange of commodities. This had for centuries been a well established feature of most economic systems, and left its mark in physiocracy.

However, the physiocrats realise that professional traders are destined to lose more and more power; their share of national output decreases, as is shown by the fact that the retail price tends to be almost equal to the current one. The reduction of the difference between these two prices brings to the fore the fundamental value of commodities and their *bon prix*. These two notions relate the exchange value of commodities to the class structure of the natural order of an agricultural society, where there are only three classes: workers, landlords and farmers, who are the entrepreneurs in the primary sector. Therefore we can see that in physiocracy the role of natural laws is sometimes that of clarifying the growing importance of economic features which are becoming typical. This is the case with the definition of the classes which characterise an economic system where natural laws fully display their effects; this society has a strong resemblance to a capitalist economy.

Quesnay needs the concepts both of *bon prix* and of fundamental price in order to link the theory of value to the question of the accumulation of capital undertaken by an agricultural entrepreneur with a direct interest in the extension and improvement of methods of cultivation. The same task of reconciling the three main features of an economic system, that is to say value, distribution and accumulation, will be tackled by Smith with his concept of natural price. But we must ascribe to Quesnay at least two main merits. First, the concept of fundamental price is a major step forward in the analysis of the dichotomy between natural and market prices. In Quesnay's economics it is clear that the study of prices is precisely an attempt to relate the problem of value to that of the reproduction of the economy. Secondly, Quesnay clearly points out that the theory of value is closely related to the class relationships existing in the economy, and in particular in the production of commodities.

One reason for dissatisfaction with the traditional interpretations of physiocracy is the fact that they either disregard its contradictions, or try to amend them on the basis of mathematical models, whose structures are already fixed before the physiocrats' writings are actually analysed. These schemes cannot adequately detect the problems, issues and doubts which characterise physiocratic thought. In contrast, the approach in this book tries to understand and explain the reasons and motives for Quesnay's failures and limitations. Thus an interpretation emerges which underlines the existence in physiocracy of a different form of consistency, as opposed to the search for a consistency of form stressed by most commentators. Quesnay's economic thought shows flaws and ambiguities because he adjusts all his analytical categories to support the fundamental theme of his work: the idea that France can achieve wealth and prosperity only by means of accumulation of capital in agriculture. This is the physiocrats' answer to the question of the causes of wealth and revenue. In order to achieve an increase in both the *avances annuelles* and *primitives*, Quesnay appropriately models the different parts of his economic investigation. Price concepts and market competition must secure the existence of a value surplus in agriculture and of profits for cultivators, because they are the source of accumulation.

Price categories and the analysis of markets, however, prove inadequate to describe and justify all the features of the physiocratic process of development. Thus since Quesnay lacks the appropriate economic concepts to support his view satisfactorily, he sacrifices formal consistency to the need of establishing accumulation of capital in agriculture. But the very nature of the logical categories missing in physiocracy shows that its flaws and contradictions have to be listed among Quesnay's merits rather than as shortcomings. In fact, his doubts, his questions, and even his wrong answers, set the agenda for later economists and justify his reputation as the founder of the theory of surplus.

Analytically, Smith, Ricardo and Marx will give satisfactory answers to some of the questions posed by Quesnay in his study of the causes of the origin and distribution of surplus. Historically, the capitalist mode of production will be required to fully display its dominance over the old feudal one. However, Quesnay made a fundamental contribution to the formation and definition of the analytical structure of classical political economy.

Notes and References

1. A Reinterpretation of Physiocracy

1. It is assumed here that physiocracy may be regarded as a homogeneous set of doctrines whose core is provided by the work of Quesnay. This assumption is not merely a simplification, but is eminently reasonable, since Quesnay was considered by his followers as the master of the school of *les économistes*, and thus exerted a major influence on the works of the other physiocrats. The writings of his disciples were mostly intended to provide clarifications and to defend the thought and the main ideas introduced by Quesnay. This book will examine, besides the writings of Quesnay, the most important works of Mirabeau, Du Pont de Nemours, *l'Abbé* Baudeau, Mercier de la Rivière and Le Trosne; all these appeared between 1756 and 1777. In 1777, several years after the period of major influence of physiocracy, Le Trosne's *De l'Intérêt Social* was still intended to provide an elucidation of Quesnay's views (see Daire, 1846, vol. II, pp. 880–2).

    Turgot's approach to the problem of the existence of a normal rate of profit represents a major innovation with respect to Quesnay's categories (see Chapter 6, 6.8). However, Turgot cannot be reckoned a disciple of Quesnay (see, for instance, Meek, 1973, p. 311). Although he often supported the policy measures advocated by physiocrats, he was never completely committed to *all* the physiocratic views and contentions. Du Pont remarks several times that Turgot was never really a member of the *secte* of *les économistes* (see Schelle, 1913, vol. II p. 75 note 1; see also Weulersse, 1959, p. 3). On the relationship between Turgot and Quesnay see also Groenewegen, 1977, pp. x, xiii-xiv, xxii-xxiv.
2. Marx bears some responsibility for having emphasised the existence of physical, rather than value, relationships in physiocracy. But it must be noted that he was able to study carefully only one of the physiocrats' writings, the *Analyse de la formule arithmétique du Tableau Economique*, which is the only work to which he consistently refers in his discussion of physiocratic economics. Marx knew Quesnay's works through Daire's 1846 edition (see Marx, 1963, vol. I, pp. 53–4) and Schmalz's *Economie Politique, ouvrage traduit de l'allemand par Henry Jouffroy*, vol. 1, Paris 1826 (see ibid., pp. 308, 484). On Marx's study of the *Analyse* see Kuczynski, 1976, vol. II, pp. 73-5.
3. In Meek, 1962, *The Economics of Physiocracy*, pp. 364–98.
4. Among the more recent works, see for instance the articles and the book by Professor Eltis, which focus in particular on Quesnay's theory of development and growth (Eltis, 1975a, 1975b, 1984, pp. 39 ff).
5. Among the authors who have taken this approach to Physiocracy one must include Meek, with his essay 'Ideas, events and environment – the case of the French Physiocrats', in Eagly, 1968.

6. See for instance Salleron, 1958, pp. 193–4; Ferrara 1850, pp. 804, 837; Hishiyama, 1960, pp. 3, 6; Schumpeter 1954, p. 230. A great stimulus to the study of physiocracy was also provided by publication, in 1955, of Phillips' article 'The *Tableau Economique* as a Simple Leontief Model'.
7. See for instance Walsh and Gram, 1980, *Classical and Neo-classical Theories of General Equilibrium;* and Sraffa, 1960, pp. 93–5.
8. See Cartelier, 1976, pp. 43ff.; Napoleoni, 1975, pp. 9 ff.; Garegnani, 1970, p. 2. This point of view was adopted by Marx (see Marx, 1963, vol. I, p. 44) but was first noticed by McCulloch in his vigorous praise of Quesnay. McCulloch says that he has the merit 'of having first attempted to investigate and analyse the source of wealth, with the intention of ascertaining the fundamental principles of Political Economy, and who thus gave it a systematic form and raised it to the ranks of a science' (McCulloch, 1825, p. 30). Marshall too ascribes to Quesnay 'the first systematic attempt to form an economic science' (Marshall, 1890, p. 625).
9. See Kubota, 1958, p. 169; Deane, 1978, p. 6; Espinas, 1892, pp. 227–8; Meek, 1968, p. 48; Gide and Rist, 1922, pp. 3, 52. Before Quesnay, Petty and Cantillon analysed economic facts in terms of a general system of laws (see Schumpeter, 1954, pp. 209ff. and 216ff.; Roncaglia 1977, pp. 28ff.). One must also remember the less famous Boisguillebert, who contributed to this line of thought with *Le Détail de la France* of 1697 and, in particular, with his last work, *Dissertation sur la nature des richesses de l'argent et des tributs* (see Schumpeter, 1954, pp. 215–17; Cartelier, 1976, pp. 25ff.).

    Among the predecessors of Quesnay who tried to explain economic facts on the basis of general economic laws one must list Locke, Dudley North and Hume. Quesnay's view of the economy as a single system is certainly linked to his belief in the existence of a natural order of societies. Espinas sees this aspect of the physiocrats' philosophical views as deriving from the influence of Locke (see Espinas, 1892, pp. 214–16).
10. See Bénard, 1958, pp. 110–11. In the *Theories of Surplus Value* Marx characterises Quesnay as the first economist who 'transferred the inquiry into the origin of surplus-value from the sphere of circulation into the sphere of direct production' (Marx, 1963, vol. I, p. 45). On the question of Quesnay's emphasis on the process of production of commodities see also Molinier 1958a, p. 48; Zangheri, 1966, pp. xxi, xxix.
11. See Pasinetti, 1977, p. 6; Napoleoni, 1975, pp. 12–13; Ferrara, 1850, p. 809; Marx, 1967, vol. II, pp. 198, 219.
12. See Einaudi, 1958, p. v; Ferrara 1850, pp. 803–4; Cannan, 1929, p. 29. Marx remarks that Quesnay singled out the material aspect of capital: the existence in the annual social product of the commodities which have to be employed in the following period of production (see Marx, 1963, vol. I, p. 44; Marx, 1967, vol. II, pp. 99ff.).
13. Schumpeter underlines the fact that for Quesnay the 'starting point was physical productivity, that is, "creation" of stuff and not of values. He took it for granted that the fact of physical productivity implied value productivity' (Schumpeter, 1954, p. 238). As Dobb remarks, most Russian economists also believed that Quesnay had analysed only the material aspect of production; this view was certainly linked to the fact they

were trying to build up a system of national accounting in purely material terms (see Dobb, 1967, p. 129).

14. According to this view the *Tableau Economique* resembles the corn economy of Ricardo's *Essay on Profits* (see Ricardo 1815, pp. 1ff.). The full title is *An Essay on the Influence of a low Price of Corn on the Profits of Stocks*. Ricardo made the assumption of the homogeneity of output and inputs in agriculture for the specific analytical purpose of determining the rate of profit. For an interpretation of this work (see Sraffa and Dobb 1951, pp. xxx–xlix).

15. See Phillips 1955, p. 141.

Transactions table for the *tableau economique*
(value of real goods in milliards)

| Producing industry | Purchasing industry | | | |
	I *Farmers*	*II* *Proprietors*	*III* *Artisans*	*Total* *production*
I Farmers	2	1	2	5
II Proprietors	2	0	0	2
III Artisans	1	1	0	2
Total purchases	5	2	2	9

This table shows quite clearly the existence of intersectoral relationships between manufacture and agriculture (see also Tsuru, 1942, pp. 366–7).

16. Some followers of the 'fixed prices' view do not think that prices are absolutely invariable; for instance they say that the 'fixed prices' method only implies that prices do not vary 'whenever there is a disequilibrium between the quantities supplied and demanded in the economic system under consideration' (Ridolfi, 1973, p. xxx).

17. This is a very recent interpretation and the authors seem to have arrived quite independently at similar results in the late 1970s.

18. C_c is the quantity of corn used in its own production, C_i is the input of corn in the production of the manufactured commodity, call it 'iron': I_c and I_i are the amount of iron used in the production of corn and iron respectively; C and I are the outputs of agriculture and industry. (Cartelier assumes that the products of industry are used also in their own production: see Cartelier, 1967, p. 57; Candela, 1975, pp. 84–5; also Gilibert, 1977, pp. 66–82.)

19. Of course in the price systems which can be derived from the economic theories of these three authors, surplus is distributed in proportion to the value of the means of production employed in each sector.

20. It is true that the physiocrats ascribed great importance to the *Tableau*: Mirabeau considered it one of the three greatest inventions in the history of mankind, together with writing and money (see Mirabeau, 1764, vol. I, pp. 52–3), a comment to which Smith dedicated a long quotation (see Smith, 1776, vol. II, p. 200).

21. These issues concern the accumulation of capital in agriculture and the role of farmer' investments; the implementation of free trade for wheat; the distinction between productive and sterile activities, the use of modern methods of cultivation, and the existence of a *bon prix* for corn. Clearly, these questions are not examined in the *Tableau;* however they are complementary to it because they constitute crucial elements in Quesnay's general analysis of the causes of wealth and prosperity of nations.

22. Quesnay uses various systems of measurement; the quantities of corn are normally given in *setier*. The *setier* is a unit of capacity equivalent to 156 litres. The unit of measurement of land is the *arpent,* which is equal to 5107 m² (see Weulersse, 1910a, vol. I, p. xxxiv). On the different units of measurement used by the physiocrats, see Groenewegen, 1983, p. xxiv. Quesnay expresses prices in *livres,* according to the following relationship: 1 *livre* = 20 *sous* and 1 *sou* = 12 *deniers.*

23. It has been estimated that by 1740 the total revenues from land were half of their value in 1660 (see Weulersse, 1910a, vol. I, p. 321).

24. At the beginning of the century an attempt to solve the financial problems of France by increasing the supply of money in circulation, in accordance to the principles of John Law, had failed miserably (see Weulersse, 1910a, vol. I, pp. 8–15).

25. The system was based on contracts between the *fermiers généraux* and the administration; the *fermiers généraux* bought the right to collect the taxes. In his *Theorie de l' Impôt* Mirabeau attacked the *fermiers généraux* (see Mirabeau, 1760c, vol. I, pp. 102–8; Beer, 1939, p. 44; Fox-Genovese, 1976, p. 141), who reacted by forcing Louis XV to order the imprisonment of the *marquis* (see Weulersse, 1910 vol. I, p. 74).

26. 'To Quesnay as to Smith, the fundamental economic problem seemed to be that of the nature and causes of the wealth of nations' (Meek, 1962, p. 345).

27. The peak of the crisis was reached at the end of the 1750s, as a result of the military defeats of 1757 and 1758 (see Weulersse, 1910a, vol. I, pp. 60, 67).

28. A different opinion was held by Schumpeter (1954, p. 231) and Espinas (1892, p. 203).

29. This view of the natural order is by no means limited to Quesnay and his school; it is the typical concept of natural law in eighteenth-century France (see Hoselitz, 1968, p. 643). Nature is positive, but it is up to people to detect and to follow its rules. This notion is also adopted, for instance, by the *Abbé* Galiani in his *Dialogues* (see Galiani, 1770, pp. 221–3).

30. It must be noted that the idea of natural order in physiocracy is different from that of Smith and English classical economics (see Taylor, 1930, pp. 226–31). As opposed to Smith's view, in physiocracy there is no 'invisible hand' which guarantees that the natural laws will work 'themselves out, in spite of would be law breakers, and even by means of their hallucinations' (Bonar, 1893, p. 172). For the physiocrats the natural laws only show us the most convenient course of action. Individuals and rulers, however, may violate these laws, even though they would then

incur poverty and ruin (see ibid., p. 140). In contrast, in the nineteenth century natural laws were regarded as overwhelming forces, which could not be avoided by individuals. Socio-economic laws acquire an increasingly stronger resemblance to those of the physical realm, with their deterministic character. Taylor maintains that the physiocrats confused natural and moral laws (see Taylor, 1929, p. 39).

31. According to Neill (1948, pp. 169–70) this fact can be partly explained by the growing influence of Hume in France after his visit to that country from 1763 to 1766 (see Weulersse, 1910a, vol. II, p. 26). Both Mirabeau and Quesnay, and later Turgot, praise the English philosopher in their works (ibid., vol. I, p. 35).

32. See Espinas, 1892, pp. 214–16; Spengler, 1958, p. 57; Schelle, 1901, pp. 179–80. The most direct influence probably came from Malebranche, whose *Recherche de la vérité* Quesnay read in his youth (see Weulersse, 1910a, vol. I, p. 48, vol. II, p. 117; see also Kubota, 1958, pp. 169ff.).

33. See Weulersse, 1910a, vol. II, pp. 121–2. Foley also places Newton among the authors who influenced Quesnay's approach to scientific method (see Foley, 1973, p. 145). Notwithstanding the influence of Descartes, Quesnay criticised the pedantic application of the method of innate ideas in the article *Evidence* (see I.N.E.D., 1958, vol. II p. 409); this article was first published in 1756 in the sixth volume of the *Encyclopédie*. Some of his disciples, particularly Mercier, were much more convinced defenders of the rationalism of Descartes (see Neill, 1949, pp. 538, 541–3).

34. See Mercier, 1767, p. 241, and Mirabeau, 1760c, pp. 24, 107–8; Du Pont 1767, p. 341. Professor Meek has provided a long and detailed analysis of the concept of 'mode of subsistence' in eighteenth-century literature (see Meek, 1976, Ch. I).

35. See also Meek, 1962, p. 376; Cartelier, 1976, p. 48; Weulersse, 1910, vol. II, p. 132; Depitre 1910a, pp. xx-xxi. Mirabeau remarks that the power of the king derives from the coincidence of interests between him and his subjects (see Mirabeau, 1760c, pp. 32, 239). Schelle pushes his interpretation to the point of regarding Quesnay as the first economist who considered economic structure as being at the basis of society (see Schelle, 1907, pp. 329–31).

36. Notwithstanding his materialist approach (and the influence of Descartes), Quesnay did not take up a deterministic attitude in his explanation of social events. He openly defends freedom of will in several works, the most important being the article *Le Droit naturel*. The younger physiocrats took a much more one-sided position, and Neill believes that they completely assimilated social and physical laws (Neill, 1949, pp. 538, 541–3). On the question of Quesnay's attitude to natural right, see also the chapter entitled '*La liberté*' in *Essay physique sur l'oeconomie animale* (1736, in Oncken, 1888, pp. 47ff.) and Part III of *De l'immortalité de l' âme* (ibid., pp. 758ff.).

37. A whole variety of duties had been imposed on land, on its products and on the peasants: there were *taille, dîme, gabelle, aides, capitation* and other less well known taxes (see Beer, 1939, pp. 42–4; McLain, 1977, p. 18). Besides these duties there were the personal obligations, the

famous *corvées,* which regularly took country people away from their fields.

38. See also Mirabeau, 1760b, pp. 260–1 and De Lavergne, 1870, pp. 78–9.
39. The physiocrats were criticised with varying degrees of harshness. Some criticisms took the form of literary disputes, the most famous being that started by Voltaire's pamphlet *L'Homme à 40 écus* (see Weulersse, 1910a, vol II, pp. 657, 693). There were also political attacks from members of the administration, such as those of Terray, who became *contrôleur général* at the end of 1769 (see Weulersse, 1910a, vol. I, pp. 210, 240).
40. See Weulersse, 1910a, vol. I, pp. 27-8; Cannan, 1929, pp. 25-7: in 1751 Gournay had been appointed *intendant du commerce.*
41. For an analysis of the economic contributions of the sixty years that preceded Quesnay's works see Weulersse's introduction (Weulersse, 1910a, vol. I, pp. 1–42).
42. For a study of the English and French publication of the *Essay* see Higgs, 1931, pp. 381ff.; Jevons, 1881, pp. 334–9. 357–9.
43. It is interesting to note that while several of Quesnay's writings on medical subjects took the form of the *traité* (see Sutter, 1958, p. 210), they usually concerned a specific disease and were not a complete exposition of medical science.
44. Quesnay withdrew these works from publication when the government ceased to protect the *Encyclopédie* (see Weulersse, 1910a, vol. I, pp. 46, 108–9). Four articles were written between January 1756 and November 1757 (see I.N.E.D., 1958, vol. II, pp. 427, 459, 511, 579); they examine the most important economic subjects which provide the logical foundations of the *Tableau.*
45. The various versions of the *Tableau* present some relevant formal problems about the consistency of the figures and the assumptions used. Many authors have rectified these 'mistakes', and there are now several amended versions of the *Tableau* (see, for instance, Meek, 1962, pp. 282–6; Woog, 1950, pp. 68ff.; Hishiyama, 1960, pp. 2ff.; Candela and De Niccolò 1982, pp. 610ff.).
46. The first edition of the zigzag appeared at the end of 1758, while the last work in which he used a *Tableau,* in its 'formula' version, was the *Second problème économique,* published in November 1767 in the *Phisiocratie* by Du Pont de Nemours.
47. This is the third version of the zigzag; it was completed at the beginning of 1759 but remained unknown until 1965, when Mrs. Kuczynski discovered and published it. Before Mrs. Kuczynski's discovery it was known that Quesnay had published a third edition of the *Tableau* through a comment of Schelle, who claimed to have found it, although he never gave any precise indication of its location. The search for the third edition is described by Mrs. Kuczynski in Kuczynski and Meek, 1972, section 2, pp. xxv–xxxiv.
48. See, for instance, Marx, 1963, vol. I pp. 308ff., 359; and among other interpreters of physiocracy see Weulersse, 1910a. vol. I, p. 62; Meek, 1962, p. 273, Herlitz, 1961a, p. 46; Bauer, 1895, p. 9.

49. In the *Extrait* appended to the second and third editions of the *Tableau* Quesnay himself defines this work as 'a distribution' (see Kuczynski and Meek (1972) section 3, p. 3 and section 7, p. 3). See also other passages in the *Extrait* of the third edition (ibid., pp. 1–2), and in the *Analyse* (Meek, 1962, pp. 161–2).

50. The *Second problème économique* is a good example of how Quesnay intends to use the *Tableau*. One must set out all the data first, then, on the basis of these data, it is possible to make all the necessary calculations by using the *Tableau*. The *Tableau Economique* is also applied to the problem of taxation in ch. VII of the *Philosophie Rurale*.

51. See also Meek, 1962, pp. 287–9. Eltis regards the *Tableau* as a device for the analysis of three particular causes of disequilibrium, due to alternative modes of expenditure of the revenue, different types of taxation and various trade policies (see Eltis, 1975b, p. 328).

52. In the *Analyse du Gouvernement des Incas du Pérou* Quesnay says that the *Tableau* describes 'a proper order of government' (I.N.E.D., 1958, vol. II, p. 915). All these assumptions refer to particular measures of economic policy, which according to the physiocrats are designed to favour the working of natural laws.

53. This 'half-and-half' expenditure pattern is a permanent characteristic of the *Tableau* and has given rise to several debates (see Boudeville, 1954, pp. 460–1, 470–3).

54. In the excerpt from the *Analyse* Quesnay explicitly mentions the conditions of production among the data. He says that the methods of cultivation are those prevailing in natural laws. Here there is a clear example of Quesnay's methodological sophistication and of the care with which he wants to treat economic matters. He explains that in order to illustrate the properties of the working of the *Tableau* he has chosen a set of data which corresponds to a particular productive situation, large-scale cultivation. If the real French economy does not justify these assumptions, the figures adopted must be different.

55. See also Weulersse, 1910a, vol. II, p. 380. These figures belong to the third edition of the *Tableau* (see Kuczynski and Meek, 1972, section 3). Remember that 300 of the 1500 *livres* annually reproduced in agriculture are interests on the original advances, *avances primitives*, made by the farmers. Therefore the net product amount to 600 *livres*.

56. See Barna 1975, p. 492; Eltis 1975a, p. 169; Cartelier, 1976, pp. 19–21; Gide and Rist, 1922, pp. 23–4 (on this problem see also below, Chapter 4, 4.1).

57. The article *Ferme* was not written by Quesnay but by his disciple Leroy (see Weulersse, 1910a, vol. I pp. 50–51). With chapter VII of *Philosophie Rurale, Grains* and *Fermiers* constitute Quesnay's major attempt to provide a detailed explanation of the phenomenon of production.

58. Quesnay's analysis of production consists of two main aspects. On one hand, he describes the existing conditions of production of various types of primary products. For instance, he shows the type and amount of advances which are necessary to yield a certain quantity of output. On the other hand, he examines the kinds of technical improvements needed

in order to increase the annual output of agriculture and, in particular, he points out the superiority of large-scale over small-scale farming (see Chapter 4, 4.3).

2. Value and Wealth

1. See above, Chapter 1, 1.2; also Rubin, 1929, pp. 125, 148; Malthus, 1798, p. 327; Malthus, 1820, p. 13.
2. Quesnay wrote several commentaries on his *Tableau*. In the first edition there are, besides the *Tableau Economique*, twenty-two *Rémarques sur les variations de la distribution des revenus annuels dune nation*. The second edition has twenty-three maxims with the title *Extrait des oeconomies royales de M. De Sully*. Finally, the third edition is accompanied by the *Extrait* . . . which now has twenty-four maxims and long notes, and by an *Explication du Tableau économique*. On this point see Meek's comment in Kuczynski and Meek 1972, section 1, pp. xviii–xix.
3. Meek translates Quesnay's expression *valeur vénale* as market value (see Meek, 1962, p. 41). This term does not fully capture all the connotations of the French term, but it is probably impossible to find a better translation. *Valeur vénale* could perhaps also be translated as money value, or exchange value, or even market price. The French term in fact has some of the meanings of all these expressions, as well as market value.
4. See Salleron's comment in I.N.E.D., 1958, vol. II, p. 687 note 1; see also Meek, 1962, p. 38.
5. See also *Premier problème économique*, Meek, 1962, p. 179; ibid., pp. 314, 320, 324; Herlitz, 1961a, p. 5.
6. The physiocrats' analysis of the composition of the means of production of the primary sector shows that among the *avances primitives* there are also manufactured commodities. Hence the knowledge of their exchange ratios with primary goods is a necessary step in calculating the difference between inputs and the gross output of agriculture (see below, 2.5 and 2.6).
7. See Weulersse, 1910a, vol. II, pp. 268ff. Before his encounter with Quesnay Mirabeau himself wrote the first three books of *L'Ami des hommes* according to completely *populationnistes* views (see ibid., vol. I, p. 54).
8. See Herlitz, 1961a, p. 4; Smith, 1776, vol. II, pp. 197–8, 199; Marx, 1963, vol. I, p. 45.
9. Quesnay includes in productive activities not only agriculture, but also all the occupations, like fishing, hunting and mining, which make up the primary sector of the economy.
10. Cantillon used the notion of 'prices in the Provinces' (Cantillon, 1755, p. 151), which has slight similarities to Quesnay's 'first-hand price'.
11. See, for instance, Petty's praise of the trading ability of Holland in his *Political Arithmetick*, etc. (see Petty, 1676, pp. 249–68). Another reason for the widespread influence of mercantilist views was that for three centuries they had proved very successful in explaining certain economic events. The most powerful countries, like Holland and England, had a

long tradition of successful performance in foreign trade. In France, mercantilist policies had been put forward by Colbert at the end of the seventeenth century.

12. See Weulersse, 1910a, vol. I, pp. 27–8, 56–60, vol. II, pp. 697–701).
13. The self-interest which rules the exchanges between individuals also guides the trade relationships between different sectors of the economy and, in particular, between agriculture and industry. The two sectors exchange values 'which exist on one side and on the other, before exchange' (*Réponse au Mémoire de M.H.*, I.N.E.D., 1958, vol. II, p. 753). Quesnay believes that in foreign trade exchange is always a transfer of goods of equal value (see ibid., p. 750). A country cannot increase its revenue and welfare by means of policies which artificially turn foreign trade relationships in its favour, because no other country would then be prepared to exchange goods with it. However, Quesnay also took a much more mercantilist attitude towards international trade (see Chapter 4, 4.7).
14. In the *Explication du Tableau Economique* Quesnay writes that trade 'multiplies sales and purchases without multiplying things, and . . . represents nothing but an addition to sterile expenditure' (Kuczynski and Meek, 1972, p. v). This view was by no means restricted to Quesnay and his disciples; indeed it seems to have been widely shared in Paris literary circles. See for instance what the *Abbé* Galiani, one of the physiocrats' fiercest opponents, says in the *Dialogues sur le commerce des bleds* (Galiani 1770, pp. 178–80, 188).
15. See, for instance, the *Lettre de M. Alpha*, in which Quesnay defends himself against the accusation that he was an enemy to traders. He says that trade is '*useful*, often even absolutely *necessary*' (I.N.E.D., 1958, vol. II, p. 946, his italics).
16. The physiocrats remark that there is a direct relationship between the existence of rich merchants and the welfare of a country. But this does not indicate that resale trade is a cause of wealth; on the contrary the growth of trade itself depends on the wealth of the country. The wealthier a nation is, the easier it is for a flourishing commercial activity to develop there (see Baudeau 1767, vol. I, p. 215; *Intérêt de l'argent*, I.N.E.D., 1958, vol. II, p. 766).
17. Harry Johnson maintains that the circulating capital of agriculture also includes commodities of the sterile class; see Johnson, 1975, p. 402.
18. See Herlitz, 1961a, pp. 11–12; Maillet, 1957, p. 344; Spengler, 1945, p. 198.
19. See Eagly, 1969, p. 67; Zagari, 1972, pp. 69–70; Blaug, 1962, p. 27; Marx, 1963, vol. I, p. 331, Napoleoni, 1976, pp. 17–18.
20. Malthus, too, believes that in physiocracy the manufactured goods purchased by the farmers are used both for consumption and as means of production. In a letter to Horner he says that 'the real capital of the farmer which is advanced does not consist merely in raw produce, but in ploughs, waggons, threshing machines, etc. and in the tea, sugar, clothes, etc. etc. used by his labourers' (Malthus, 1815, p. 187).
21. The percentage is 28.59; this figure strongly resembles that given by Bairoch for the decade 1781–90, when domestic product had the following percentage composition: agriculture 42, industry 27, trade 13, others 18 (see Bairoch, 1963, p. 347).

22. Here Mirabeau does not account for the 10 per cent annual interest on the original advances of industry, unlike what happens in the primary sector.
23. Between 1715 and 1750 the production of manufactures began to be organised on the basis of small factories, with some salaried workers depending on an entrepreneur (see Sée, 1967, pp. 126–34). The production of pig-iron underwent an enormous increase in the fifty years after 1740 (see Bairoch, 1963, pp. 313–15). But even if coal and iron can be regarded as special cases, the phenomenon of the concentration of workers in medium-sized factories seems to have been widespread in many types of activities (see Sée, 1967, p. 130).
24. Bairoch lists among the first consequences of agricultural progress 'the (proportionally) remarkable increase in the demand for the products of the steel industry' (Bairoch, 1963, p. 99; see also p. 75). The provinces with a more advanced industrial sector were those in the north of France, Upper Normandy, Picardy and Flanders (see Sée, 1967, p. 128), the very regions presented by the physiocrats as 'models' for French agriculture.
25. The agrarian revolution, whose origins can be traced back to the fourteenth century (see Bloch, 1966, p. 198) did not consist only of the abolition of the system of fallow lands and its substitution with a system of rotation whereby the cultivation of fodder was alternated with that of wheat (see ibid., pp. 213–15). Slicher van Bath, listing the phenomena which characterise a period of agricultural expansion, mentions: 'introduction of new tools (ploughing equipment, farming machines); new special equipment for grain cultivation; the purpose of the new tools is to increase output (ploughs, machines for making furrows)' (Slicher van Bath 1977, p. 56).
26. Alternatively, artisans can be regarded as peasants who have left the cultivation of land and have specialised in the production and repair of houses, stables, implements of cultivation, etc. The essential requisite of all these occupations is the fact that *all* the commodities produced are sold to agriculture and entirely consumed within it. This view seems to be implicit in the writings of many commentators who deny the importance of prices in physiocracy.
27. The problem of the protection of French industry had already been called to the attention of rulers and scholars in the second half of the seventeenth century by Colbert, Louis XIV's minister (see Rubin, 1929, p. 90). Under the influence of a view which went under the name of *colbertisme*, France introduced foreign trade regulations which were intended to favour the industrial sector by limiting imports of foreign manufactures. These measures dominated French trading policy for sixty years (see Bairoch, 1963, p. 329).
28. The idea that artisans do not add any value to the raw materials and the necessaries they use (see Zagari, 1972, pp. 33, 79; Higgs, 1897, p. 43; Zangheri, 1966, p. xxv) is one of the arguments the Physiocrats used to support their contention that only agriculture is productive (see Mercier, 1767, pp. 96–8, 311–13, 320). Artisans only change the form of the goods they receive from the primary sector (see Du Pont, 1764, p. 4 n.; Molinier, 1958a, p. 53; Marx, 1963, vol. I, pp. 46–7).

29. Notice that the interpretation according to which Quesnay assumed a fixed system of relative prices throughout his entire work is in contrast with some major physiocratic contentions. For instance, if one takes the above view of physiocracy, one should also accept that the exchange ratios between the products of land and those of industry are influenced neither by accumulation of capital, nor by technical progress in agriculture, nor by the implementation of free-trade measures for corn, fiscal reforms, etc.

30. Here Le Trosne assumes that the *reprises* are wholly made up of non-agricultural goods, while in the *Analyse* only ⅓ of the means of production must be bought outside the primary sector by the farmers. Even in the latter case a change in relative prices would modify the size of the surplus.

31. This result does not depend on the choice of corn as *numéraire*, but derives from the fact that, by assumption, all the surplus goes to agriculture; hence the unknown S appears only in the first equation.

3. The Theory of Prices in Physiocracy

1. Both Sir James Steuart and Smith (in the 'Glasgow lectures') had the same ideas as Quesnay about the role of the wants of humanity in the economy. This can also be seen from the sequence of economic subjects in their analysis. Both Steuart's *Inquiry* and Smith's *Lectures on Jurisprudence* begin with an analysis of the needs of human beings; see Steuart, 1767, vol. I, book I, chapter VI, XVII, pp. 146, 150–1; Smith, 1762–63, part II 'Of Police', pp. 487–9. On the influence of Physiocracy on Adam Smith's 'Wealth of Nations' see for instance Cannan, 1896, pp. xxvii–xxxi and Scott, 1937, pp. 124–126.

2. In his *Social Science and the Ignoble Savage* Professor Meek has convincingly shown that the view that all the most important features of human societies depend on economic organisation was fairly widespread in the middle of the eighteenth century. The progress of humanity through different stages was explained by the evolution of the mode of subsistence adopted. According to Meek, this idea is one of the major roots of the French and Scottish Enlightenment and was shared by the physiocrats, even if only in a rough form (see Meek, 1976, pp. 91–2, 132; see also Schelle, 1907, pp. 329–1).

3. See also Mirabeau, 1764, vol. II, p. 17; Steuart, 1767, vol. I, pp. 17, 142–4.

4. Quesnay uses the term *valeur usuelle*, but he never adopts the expression *valeur d'échange*; he often speaks of *valeur vénale* and sometimes just uses the word *prix*. But it is easy to see that he has a very clear idea of the difference between the two concepts and his distinction calls to mind the words used by Smith (see Smith, 1776, vol. I, pp. 32–4).

5. See Woog, 1950, p. 26. At the time of physiocracy, the opinion that a commodity had a market value only in so far as it was considered useful by somebody was already widespread (see Sewall, 1901, pp. 76–7). This

view descended from the scholastic tradition. An example of it can be found in Samuel Pufendorf's *De jure natura et gentium – libri octo*, which was a popular textbook in Smith's times (see Pufendorf, 1672, p. 676).

6. It must be remembered that for Quesnay the importance of a commodity refers not only to a particular quality in it, that is to say the particular want it is apt to satisfy. The importance of goods depends also on the specific role that each plays in the economic system. For instance it is true that food is necessary for human subsistence, while diamonds are not. But above all food is one of the many types of commodities which have to be accumulated each year to preserve the productive capacity of the country, and this results from its role in the process of production of wealth. The diamond – water (food) paradox appears for the first time in Locke's *Some Considerations of the Consequences of the Lowering of Interest and Raising the Value of Money* (See Locke, 1691, p. 41). It became a commonplace in the economic literature of the eighteenth century (see Law, 1705, p. 4; Harris, 1757, p. 5).

7. For Quesnay, the market value of a commodity can be occasionally influenced by its use value. When a commodity which is absolutely necessary for the subsistence of people becomes very scarce, as during a famine, then 'it is its value which determines, by chance, its market value. I say by chance because the dearth or scarcity which raises its price is dependent upon causes which have no connection with the use value of the items of wealth concerned' (*Hommes*, Meek, 1962, p. 90). For the physiocrats these causes are either the backwardness of agriculture, or the existence of legal impediments to foreign trade, which have nothing to do with the use value of the products of land.

8. See also Schelle, 1907, p. 373. Not all commentators agree on this point; for instance Roll believes that the physiocrats do not properly distinguish between value in use and value in exchange; see Roll, 1938, p. 129; Schicchi, 1978, p. 25.

9. See also *Maximes Générales*, Meek, 1962, p. 257; *Extrait*, Kuczynski and Meek, 1972, p. 9, note b. The same opinion is presented by Quesnay in a passage in the *Questions intéressantes*, where he asks himself 'whether the opulence of a country consists either in the market or in the use value' (I.N.E.D., 1958, vol. II, p. 661). He examines the case of two countries which produce the same quantities of foodstuffs. But, thanks to free exports, the prices of the products of one country are twice as high as those of the other. Quesnay concludes that, although the two countries have the same goods, their different market values determine the different power of the two sovereigns. The same goods with the same use value in different countries can be exchanged with different quantities of other goods, instruments of war, troops, etc. The wealth and revenue of a country are in proportion to the market value of its products and not to their use values (see ibid., p. 662).

10. None of Quesnay's predecessors seems to have adopted his vigour and determination in presenting the idea that the natural order, which presides over exchanges of commodities, is independent of personal deeds and desires. For instance Boisguillebert insisted that use value is one of the factors affecting the price of commodities (see Boisguillebert,

1707–14, pp. 403–4), even though he certainly did not confuse utility and wealth (see Cartelier, 1976, pp. 29–30).

11. On the factors which influence prices see also *Sur les travaux des artisans*, Meek, 1962, p. 227; *Extrait*, Kuczynski and Meek, 1972, pp. 8–9, note b.; *Du Commerce*, I.N.E.D., 1958, vol. II, p. 819. Notice that when Quesnay wants to stress the role of one of these causes he usually underemphasises the other; in general he mentions only one cause at a time. In such cases Quesnay's statements must be interpreted under the assumption of *ceteris paribus* with regard to the other group of forces.

    Quesnay's analysis of markets has no particular originality; the same forces had already been singled out by previous authors. For instance Sir Francis Hutcheson, Smith's teacher, pointed out the importance of demand and competition in price determination (see Hutcheson, 1754–5, pp. 59–60). Quesnay refers mainly to markets for the products of land, but in most cases his analysis of market forces has a general validity (where this is not so it will be specified).

12. The physiocrats explicitly use the adjective *courant* to indicate the particular price which is influenced by scarcity and competition (see *Réponse au Mémoire de M. H.*, I.N.E.D., 1958, vol. II, p. 752; Mercier, 1767, p. 264).

13. Mirabeau says that in the *Tableau* the overall vaule of annual reproduction is 'calculated by means of the price which occurs among trading countries' (Mirabeau, 1764, vol. I, p. 334).

14. Quesnay's analysis of current and retail price appears in two of his major early works, the articles *Hommes* and *Grains*. This aspect of physiocratic economics was regarded as absolutely crucial by all Quesnay's followers, who often used his concepts of *prix du vendeur* and *prix de l'acheteur*. In particular, Pattullo, in his *Essai sur l'amélioration des terres* of 1758, presents the same tables used by Quesnay: he defines the notion of current and retail price in exactly the same way (see Pattullo, 1758, pp. 231–6). Six years later, in his *De l'exportation et de l'inportation des grains*, Du pont de Nemours uses the same notions of price.

    For a definition of the different measures of area and of volume, and the weights and currency used by Quesnay see, for instance, Groenewegen, 1983, pp. xxiii–xxv.

15. Of course these figures must represent the quantities *actually sold* by the producers. If they only indicate the output, without saying anything about its actual sale, it would be completely meaningless to envisage a relationship between them and the first-hand prices. Forbonnais criticised as unrealistic Quesnay's account of the range of variation of wheat prices in France (see Forbonnais, 1767, vol. II, pp. 3–33). The huge instability of the level of output is the result of technological backwardness in the primary sector and its lack of advances; from this situation derives the use of old-fashioned methods of cultivation which still employ oxen, instead of horses, in the ploughing of soil (see *Fermiers*, Groenewegen, 1983, p. 1).

    The amount of land is fixed in terms of *arpents*, therefore a different productivity per unit of land corresponds to different overall outputs of corn.

16. The figures in the first two columns can be used to describe the relationship between the price of a commodity and the quantity sold on the first-hand market. However, these two tables can in no way be taken as a proxy for demand schedules. This term could give the impression that in physiocracy there is an anticipation of the marginalistic analysis of individual preferences. But it must be clear that Quesnay explains the idea that when the market value of corn is high a lower quantity is actually sold, and *vice versa*, in terms which have nothing to do with the marginalistic theory. First, the level of prices does not depend on the preferences of individuals, but is related to the social features of the economy, such as the state of trade, the transportation system, the number of merchants and producers, and the laws which rule commerce (see 4.4–4.6) which are historically given phenomena. These characteristics determine a relationship between price and quantity, which is usually different from good to good and from country to country.

    Secondly, it is not possible to maintain that Quesnay intended to join these five numbers as points on a single curve which depicted a continuous downward sloping relationship between the demand for corn and its price. Quesnay was not interested in the calculation of marginal changes in utility; he only wanted to say that, at any given time, and for any current price, there was a definite quantity of a commodity which could be actually sold on the market. Historical experience showed that larger quantities of corn were in fact purchased when the current price was lower and *vice versa*.

17. In *Grains*, Quesnay gives two figures: the total amount of land cultivated in France, 36 million *arpents*, and the lands which are exploited with large-scale cultivation, 6 million *arpents*. The tables he presents in this article are in a section with the heading '*Etat de la grande culture des grains*', hence he seems to refer here to the 6 million *arpents*. The average annual output of corn is estimated as 45 million *setiers*, but according to Quesnay this figure includes, with *blé*, also '*avoine et autres grains de mars*' (*Grains*, I.N.E.D., 1958, vol. II, pp. 461–2). In *Hommes* he gives only the figure of 45 million *setiers*, but this number at one point indicates the total corn output of French agriculture, and at another refers to output of large-scale cultivation only (*Hommes*, ibid., 533–4, note 5). The only figure he gives in *Hommes* for the amount of land is '15 million of properly cultivated land' (ibid., p. 534, note 5).

18. Quesnay explains that the term *commun* is used to indicate an average value of prices over several years; he speaks of 'the common prices regulated . . . on the different prices of different years' (ibid.).

19. Note that, even in this case, the relationship between prices and outputs depends on the social and structural characteristics of the country, and not on the psychology and feelings of individuals.

20. Of course Quesnay does not think that the retail price of corn never changes at all. The tables are just stylised examples to show that in the French economy there are built-in forces and mechanisms which tend to provoke a relative stability in the price of corn when it is finally resold, while leaving a highly unstable selling price for farmers.

21. Here we examine Quesnay's notion of market competition between buyers and sellers, that is to say, competition in the sphere of circulation

of commodities. His view of competition among producers is examined in Chapter 5, 5.6.

22. The physiocrats include among the positive effects of competition the fact that it reconciles the opposing interests of individuals. In this case markets work according to natural laws which prevent people from taking advantage of their trading partners (see *Lettre de M. Alpha*, I.N.E.D., 1958, vol. II, pp. 939, 947; see also Mercier, 1767, p. 207).

23. In the same article Quesnay says that the international prices of primary commodities are the upper limit for domestic ones (see *Grains*, I.N.E.D., 1958, vol. II, p. 86).

24. If the rulers introduce 'unsound regulations', they cause great damage to the country. In fact, these measures lead to 'a price out of harmony with the price which is general and common among other nations and this fact wipes out the revenue of the kingdom' (*Hommes*, Meek, 1962, p. 91).

25. Le Trosne writes that 'the clear intention of Providence which alternately favours different countries with abundance, has been that the excess wheat in some of them should make up what is lacking in others' (Le Trosne, 1777, p. 988).

26. A similar table exists in *Grains*, I.N.E.D., 1958, vol. II, p. 474:

Table 4

Annees	Setiers	Prix du setier	Total par arpent	Frais par arpent	Reste
Abondante	8 *liv.*	16 *liv.*	128 *liv.*		62 *liv.*
Bonne	7	17	119	66 *liv.*	53
Moyenne	6	18	108		42
Faible	5	19	95		29
Mauvaise	4	20	80		14
Total	30	90			200

27. Le Trosne says that all trading countries should benefit from free international trade, because 'they cannot establish their prosperity on the ruin of their neighbours' (Le Trosne, 1777, p. 1010). But the advantages are particularly relevant for France, which should venture into a free trading policy whatever the attitude of other countries (see ibid., pp. 1009–10). In fact France has the advantage of a large and fertile territory, thus it is more likely to play the role of seller than that of buyer in the international trade in foodstuffs (see ibid., p. 988, and Chapter 4, 4.7).

28. See for instance Pufendorf, 1672, p. 687. The debate about the notion of just price derives directly from St. Thomas and the scholastic tradition (see Schumpeter, 1954, pp. 93, 98–9); the origin of this notion can be traced back to Aristotle (see ibid., pp. 60–1).

29. See Schelle, 1907, pp. 180–1; he says that this term was first used by Dupré de Saint Meur in his *Essai sur les monnaies* (1746).

30. It must be noted that some authors who focused attention on the cost of production also shared the widespread belief that the forces of 'supply' and 'demand' provided an explanation of the value of commodities and not just of its variations (see for instance Pufendorf, 1672, pp. 688–9). Therefore the idea that the expenses of production play a major role in the determination of prices goes together with the view that 'the prices of things will be in a compound proportion of the *demand* for them, and the *difficulty* in acquiring them' (Hutcheson, 1753, p. 199, his italics; see also Taylor and Robertson, 1957, pp. 183–86). On the different price concepts in Smith's predecessors see Taylor, 1965, pp. 63–70.

31. Cantillon was well known by both Quesnay and Mirabeau, who intended to make an edition of his *Essai* (see Routh, 1975, p. 70). Petty apparently influenced physiocracy through his impact on Cantillon. For an analysis of the difference between these two authors' value theories see Candela and Palazzi, 1979, pp. xxvii–ff. It has also been suggested that Quesnay's analysis of price determination is almost identical to Cantillon's theory of *valeur intrinsique* (see Gilibert, 1977, pp. 76–7).

32. Cantillon and Petty assume the existence of a subsistence wage rate (see Cantillon, 1755, pp. 23–5, 33–9; Petty, 1676, p. 267). This is by no means a necessary hypothesis. Even if workers also receive products which are not part of their necessary consumption it is still possible to calculate the quantity of land directly and indirectly embodied in wages, provided that their physical composition in terms of primary commodities is known.

33. See also *Réponse au Mémoire de M. H.*, I.N.E.D., 1958, vol. II, p. 753, where Quesnay examines the value of a pair of shoes, which is equal to the costs undertaken by the cobbler. The fact that in physiocracy the price of manufactured commodities in given by their cost of production is a well known and accepted result (see for instance Marx, 1970, vol. I, pp. 185–6, note 1; Cannan, 1893, p. 16). Note that Quesnay does not mention the existence of fixed capital among the costs of the manufacturer. Le Trosne and Mercier provide a similar analysis of the items which make up the value of the products of industry, for which they use the term *prix nécessaire* (see Le Trosne, 1777, p. 953; Mercier, 1767, pp. 309). Le Trosne speaks also of *prix indispensable* (see Le Trosne, 1777, p. 952). On the fundamental price of manufactured commodities see also Steuart, 1767, vol. II, p. 340.

34. When Quesnay examines the costs of cultivation he generally uses the term *frais* instead of 'raw materials' (see for instance *Grains*, Meek, 1962, p. 72, and *Hommes*, ibid., p. 89).

35. See Gilibert, 1977, pp. 66ff.; Cartelier, 1976, pp. 110ff. Note that the 'physical costs' and the 'land theory' interpretations provide very similar explanations of the determination of relative prices. All that is needed for a complete overlapping of the two views is a wage rate given in terms of physical quantities of commodities.

36. The second element of the definition of fundamental price does not modify the component parts of this category in the case of manufactures. The artisans sell their products to the merchants, and when the current price is lower than the sum of wages and raw materials, which constitute their costs of production, they make a loss. Thus the two features of the

prix fondamental coincide in the value of the products of the industrial sector.

37. One of the few commentators who recognises the existence of rent in the fundamental price of primary commodities is Herlitz (see Herlitz, 1961b, pp. 139–40).

38. The idea that the fundamental price is the minimum price the cultivator can accept without making a loss was widespread among the physiocrats (see *Hommes*, I.N.E.D., 1958, vol. II, p. 587). This view was also adopted by Turgot in a passage of his *L'impôt. indirect. Observations sur les Mémoires Récompensés par la Société d' Agriculture de Limoges*, in the section where he comments on Saint-Péravy's work (see Turgot, 1767a, pp. 655–6, note 1).

39. Note that this monetary obligation of the farmer towards the landlord was typical of the provinces of France where large-scale farming, carried out by wealthy producers, was the dominant method of cultivation of soil (see Sée, 1967, p. 26), as the physiocrats always advocated. These provinces were Normandy, Picardy, Flanders and Orléanais (see Groenewegen, 1983, p. 29). Of course *fermage* was not the only type of contract of cultivation in France in the middle of the eighteenth century. *Métayage* (share-cropping) was still widely in use, particularly in the southern provinces; it entailed the payment to the landlord of a share of the output in kind, instead of a fixed amount of money.

    A description of the relationships between the proprietor and the cultivator also appears in Turgot's *Sur la grande et la petite culture*. He writes that 'the landlords look for *farmers* who give them a constant revenue and purchase the right from them to cultivate it (land) for a certain number of years (see Turgot, 1767b, p. 28, italics in the original).

40. Boudeville also includes tithes, *dîme* (taxes which were due to the clergy) in the fundamental price (see Boudeville, 1954, pp. 476–7), but there is little evidence that Quesnay and his disciples agreed with this view.

    There is an important difference between the inclusion of rent and that of taxes in the fundamental price. In fact Quesnay strongly opposes all the types of taxes which fall on the farmers, because this kind of taxation does not follow the natural order of society. In contrast he considers the payment of rent to landowners as being perfectly in harmony with the general laws of the natural order.

41. See Du Pont, 1764, p. 18; *Questions intéressantes*, I.N.E.D., 1958, vol. II, p. 642. In France at the time of the physiocrats there were several types of *taille* (see Dakin, 1939, pp. 149–76; Palgrave, 1899, vol. III, pp. 512–13).

42. As Oncken first noted, Quesnay makes a mistake and calculates a total amount of 3220 *livres* (see Oncken, 1888, p. 178).

43. This is a further proof that Quesnay's price categories must be studied as a coherent set of concepts, since they are clearly intended to describe and explain the mechanism of price formation according to the systematic laws of the market.

44. See *Grains*, p. 462; in a similar table for England the heading becomes *Prix, taille et fermage par arpent chaque année*, (see *Hommes*, p. 533).

45. We have seen that the cultivators cannot fix the price in the sales at first-

hand, but can always decide that a certain price is too low to justify continuing to cultivate.

46. The problem of whether or not Quesnay regarded the profits of farmers as part of the net product of the economy, will be examined in Chapter 5.

47. Quesnay makes a mistake in his calculations; the sum of rent and *taille* gives 13 *liv*. 17 *s*. 1 *d*., hence the expenses of the farmers are 73 *liv*. 17 *s*. 1 *d*., which gives 14 *liv*. 15 *s*. 5 *d*. as the cost of production of each *setier* of corn to the cultivator.

48. Quesnay also uses the term *prix naturel*, by which he refers to the state of prices in an economy where natural laws have displayed their effects fully. In order to have a natural level of prices rulers must make economic policy conform to the indications of physiocracy. In particular, free competition in foreign trade is the most important policy measure for the establishment of 'the natural state of price' (*Du Commerce*, I.N.E.D., 1958, vol. II, p. 829; see also Le Trosne, 1777, p. 955). The existence of natural prices is the outcome of free and unobstructed competition.

According to the physiocrats the French economy has two specific characteristics which prevent the existence of natural prices. The first results from all types of indirect taxation; prices are distorted by commercial prohibitions, constraints and 'surcharges' on the natural price; Quesnay speaks of 'the additional burden of taxes on the natural price' (*Extrait*, Kuczynski and Meek, 1972, p. 6, note a; see also Du Pont, 1774, p. 3). Tolls and other exises artificially increase first-hand prices, thus discouraging buyers. By preventing the establishment of natural prices indirect taxation represents an obstacle to the reproduction of output (see Le Trosne, 1777, p. 901). The negative effects of taxes which are interposed between the natural price and the market value of products are due to the fact that these impositions rest on farmers. In fact, when Quesnay refers to the natural state of current prices, he writes: 'indirect taxes weigh upon the prices received in sales at first-hand' (*Second problème économique*, Meek, 1962, p. 195; see also Le Trosne, 1777, p. 990).

But the retail price too can be far from its natural level; this happens when the costs of transportation exceed what is strictly required to bring the products to market. There are 'some natural and indispensable expenses of trade, transportation and storage' (Du Pont, 1774, p. 8), which are as necessary as the costs of cultivation, and can be regarded as part of the overall cost of production (see Mirabeau, 1764, vol. I, p. 347). But 'an additional burden of expenses of transportation' (*Hommes*, I.N.E.D., 1958, vol. II, p. 546) distorts the value of the retail price.

Transport costs and exises play a similar role; both items are interposed between the price received by the direct producers and the retail price. Of course the expenses of transportation are incurred by the merchants, who can add them to the current price paid to cultivators. Prices are not at their natural level if tradesmen make a profit by speculating on the costs of transportation.

Note that Quesnay's concept of natural price does not refer either to a specific price level or to a concept which has a definite relationship with

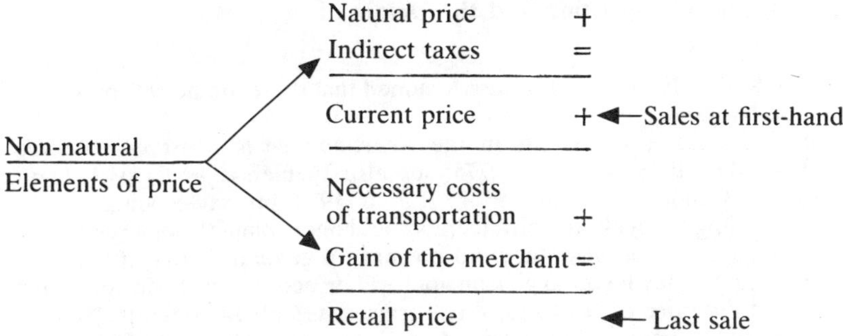

some quantifiable feature of the economy. The physiocrats stress the qualitative feature of the 'natural' value of commodities which is always contrasted to a situation dominated by excises, duties and other obstacles to trade. These impediments and barriers can be the result of unwise policy measures, which prevent natural laws from displaying their effects.

49. A similar dichotomy in the analysis of rent can be found in Smith's *Wealth of Nations*, where rent is sometimes regarded as a revenue whose size depends on the level of prices (see Smith, 1776, vol. I, p. 93), and in other places is treated as a cost (see ibid., pp. 56, 71). Of course, this ambiguity in the analysis of rent disappears in Ricardo's theory, where rent cannot be regarded as a cost (see for instance Ricardo, 1821, p. 77–8, and Ricardo, 1820, pp. 42–3, 72–3).

50. According to Bauer the 'three rents approach' can be traced back to John Bellers' *An Essay Towards the Improvement of Physick, etc.* of 1714; see Bauer, 1895, pp. 5–6, note 1. As Professor Groenewegen has pointed out to me, the 'three rents' doctrine was widespread in eighteenth-century economic literature. It occurs in Charles King's *The British Merchant* (King, 1721, vol. I, pp. 190–1) and in many writings in agricultural economics (see for instance John Mortimer, *The whole art of husbandry*, 1761, vol. I, pp. 310–11).

51. Turgot used the concepts of current and fundamental price in a way quite similar to Quesnay (see Groenewegen, 1970, pp. 181–2, 195). In the *Réflexions sur la formation et la distribution des richesses* the current price is regarded as an average value between the supplies and the demands of individuals; buyers and sellers must ultimately accept the fact that this average market value regulates their exchanges (see Turgot, 1766, pp. 136–7). Turgot examines the market mechanisms which lead prices to an average value in *Valeurs et monnais* (see Turgot, 1769, pp. 89–93). Moreover, in a letter to Hume of March 1767, Turgot says that the fundamental price is the permanent and stable level of market value of commodities, below 'which the current price cannot sink' (in Rotwein, 1955, p. 211; see also Turgot, 1767a, pp. 655–6, note 1).

4. Capital, Competition and the Origin of Surplus

1. See Sraffa, 1960, p. 8. It is also assumed that there are no self-producing non-basics; see ibid., pp. 90–1.
2. See Quesnay's comments in the *Répétition de la question proposée*, I.N.E.D., 1958, vol. II, p. 775; see also Weulersse 1910a, vol. I, pp. 256–8; Candela, 1975, pp. 91–2; Ridolfi, 1973, pp. xxv–xxviii.
3. According to Meek, the physiocrats could not explain the emergence of a value surplus, because they did not have a general theory of value. In particular, they failed to give an appropriate account of the factors which affect the price of land and of its services (see Meek, 1962, p. 388).
4. Among the people who criticised physiocracy are Veron de Forbonnais, in his *Principes et Observations Oeconomiques* (1767), and Voltaire, particularly in the pamphlet *L' Homme à 40 écus*. Here Voltaire makes fun of Quesnay's praise of the prosperity of France at the time of Henry IV (see Voltaire, 1767, pp. 401–2, 412–6). Voltaire also criticises Quesnay's contributions to the *Encyclopédie* (see Voltaire, 1770, pp. 143–59).

   In Italy Quesnay's *Encyclopédie* articles were approvingly quoted by Cesare Beccaria, in the *Elementi di Economia Pubblica* (see Beccaria, 1769–70, pp. 447–52). This work was written in 1769–70, in the form of lecture notes for students, and was first published in 1804 (see ibid., p. xiii).

   Higgs gives a description of the opponents of physiocracy (see Higgs, 1897, pp. 102–22).
5. See Ronchetti, 1978, p. 43. Galiani was secretary in the Embassy of the Kingdom of Naples in Paris from 1759 to 1769, with a short intermission between 1765 and 1766. Diderot was a great admirer of Galiani and wrote an *Apologie de l'Abbé Galiani*, in order to defend his views from the attacks of the physiocrats (see Diderot, 1770, pp. 69ff.).
6. A fierce attack on Quesnay's view of the sterility of industry can also be found in Arthur Young's *Political Arithmetic* of 1774 (see Young, 1774, pp. 254–7).
7. See also ibid. pp. 232–3; *Premier problème économique*, ibid., p. 169, note 1.
8. The beneficial effects of large-scale farming were also underlined by Turgot in his *Sur la grande et al petite culture* of 1767 (see Turgot, 1767b, pp. 28–9). By contrast, Forbonnais attacked physiocracy precisely on the issue of the superiority of horses; this was part of a long discussion of the different types of cultivation (see Forbonnais, 1767, vol. II, pp. 33–112).
9. The differences between the two methods of cultivation are clearly singled out by Groenewegen; he correctly remarks that Quesnay put the 'emphasis on discontinuous choice of techniques' (Groenewegen, 1983, p. xiv). Indeed, the use of horses required qualitative changes in the cultivation of the soil, and not just an expansion of cultivated lands. Modern methods of cultivation were used in English agriculture (see Bauer, 1890, p. 102).
10. For Quesnay there can be a gain over costs in all occupations which

require particular skill and talent. Pre-eminent artists provide an example, 'since there are so few of them that competition between them does not force them to lower the price of their labour' (*Sur les travaux des artisans*, Meek, 1962, p. 210.

11. The demographic conditions of France explained the existence of poor people, who were prepared to become artisans for a low salary in order to obtain the necessaries (see, for instance, *Sur les travaux des artisans*, Meek, 1962, pp. 212–13).

12. French industry experienced a major crisis between 1750 and 1760, which resulted in high unemployment among workers in the biggest factories (see Weulersse, 1910a, vol. I, pp. 283–4).

13. However, for Quesnay there is at least one case in which there are profits in industry, although there is no lack of competition between the manufacturers. This happens 'in countries where manufacturing labour is cheap because of the low price of the produce which serves for the subsistence of the workers' (*Extrait*, Kuczynski and Meek, 1972, p. 12, note b). Thus the master manufacturer makes a profit because the cost of reproduction of labour is lower at home than in other countries producing the same commodities.

14. In England agricultural output is abundant and the country is much less prone to famines; moreover, the value of net product is higher than in France.

15. Note that Quesnay's statements in no way anticipate Say's law of markets (see Semmel, 1964–65, p. 535). In fact, Quesnay refers only to an increase of population raising the number of potential consumers. For Quesnay the increase of agricultural output does not necessarily imply an equal rise in the revenues of people, and hence in the effective demand for the products of land. In physiocracy there is no automatic mechanism which guarantees that the entire production will be sold. It is demand which sets the pace of production and not vice-versa (see 4.6).

16. See *Extrait*, Kuczynski and Meek, 1972, p. 12; see also the sixteenth remark in the *Remarques sur les variation de la distribution des revenues annuels d'une nation*, which is part of the first edition of the *Tableau* (ibid., Appendix A). Similar statements can also be found in Baudeau's *Principes de la science morale et politique* (see Baudeau, 1767, p. 27; see also Spengler, 1942, pp. 184–5). For an analysis of the effects on revenue of different patterns of expenditure by the landlords, see for instance Eltis, 1975a, pp. 169, 190 and Eltis, 1975b pp. 329–35. The role of consumption and expenditures in physiocracy is also emphasised in Spengler, 1945, pp. 317–9 and in Johnson, 1966, pp. 627–9.

17. Quesnay and Mirabeau are so·convinced of the primacy of expenditure in determining the level of activity of the economy, that they strongly oppose saving by proprietors and by wealthy people in general. They 'must not indulge in sterile savings, which remove part of their revenue from circulation and distribution' (Mirabeau, 1764, vol. II, p. 343; see also *Extrait*, Kuczynski and Meek, 1972, p. 4). Landlords who save part of their revenues damage the nation, because they subtract – *retranche* – these incomes from circulation and reproduction. This behaviour reduces

the overall level of activity and general welfare, because it implies a reduction in the aggregate effective demand of the country and is therefore a sterile way of using revenue.

18. Quesnay seems to believe that if final consumers are wealthy enough to afford a high retail price for wheat, there will be strong competition among merchants. They try to purchase large amounts of products on first-hand markets, since they are sure to be able to resell them profitably on retail markets.

19. The physiocrats are so concerned about the lack of effective demand that in this case they even oppose projects which would raise the output of agriculture. In a letter of 1760 to the *Intendant* of Soissons Quesnay opposes improvements in cultivation: 'it is like putting the cart before the oxen; as long as the cultivation of wheat will be restricted to domestic consumption one must not increase harvests' (quoted in Weulersse, 1910, vol. I, p. 460). As long as the effective demand for corn does not increase, French production *must not* be improved; if the output is increased it is possible to sell it only by lowering the current price of corn below its unit cost of production. Primary products become *non-valeurs*, they lose their quality of being part of the wealth of the country. Of course in general Quesnay welcomed all technical improvements which might eventually lower the physical cost of production of agricultural products (see ibid; and 4.3). But with given methods of production and without appropriate effective demand, an increase in output could be harmful to French agriculture. This is a good example of Quesnay's care in applying his analytical conclusions to the actual economic situation of France. Because one of the conditions which define the natural order of society, free export of the products of soil, is lacking, he does not hesitate to oppose one of his favourite contentions: the need to increase agricultural output.

20. Mercier says that free trade is a way of securing 'a great competition among the buyers of national products' (Mercier, 1767, p. 327).

21. Quesnay uses the expression *laissez-faire et laissez-passer* only once, in the *Lettre de M. Alpha* (see I.N.E.D., 1958, vol. II, p. 940), where it is quoted with no comment or explanation. On the origin of this expression see Oncken's footnote in his edition of Quesnay's works (see Oncken, 1888, pp. 671–2). Samuels, 1962, provides a clear analysis of the role of free trade in physiocracy and of the argument for state intervention in economic affairs; see in particular pp. 148–54. See also Semmel, 1964–65, pp. 526–28. On the development of free trade views in England see Beer, 1938, pp. 198–ff.

22. Foreign trade requires higher transport costs than internal trade. These expenses are detrimental to both consumers and producers, because they increase the retail price, and tend to depress the current one (see Chapter 3, 3.4, note 48). Mercier writes, that the interest of consumers is that of being close to the place of production (see Mercier, 1767, p. 266).

23. 'Not all nations can be agricultural countries', wrote M. Toutain de Frontebosc in a *Mémoire à la Societé d' Agriculture de Rouen* (quoted in Weulersse, 1910a, vol. I, p. 251, note 7).

24. Groenewegen points out that, in the *Observation sur le mémoire de M. de Saint-Péravy*, Turgot gives a déscription of the working of competition which is similar to Smith's (see Groenewegen, 1970, pp. 181–2).
25. For the physiocrats a lack of wealthy artisans co-exists with the fact that the degree of competition in manufacturing activities is much higher than among agricultural entrepreneurs. The average techniques of industrial production require much smaller advances than those of agriculture, and there is no rent to be paid. Less money, therefore, is required to become an artisan, and industrial output can rise more easily and more quickly than that of agriculture.
26. On Quesnay's analysis of capitalist production, and in particular on the role of machinery, see Chapter 6, 6.2; see also Vaggi, 1982, pp. 62–5.
27. Steuart carefully describes the many ways in which the concept of demand can usefully be used in analysing of the price mechanism (see Steuart, 1767, vol. I, pp. 151ff.).
28. See *Hommes*, I.N.E.D., 1958, vol. II, p. 528 and also the same article in Meek, 1962, p. 92. Quesnay's term *prix actuel* does not exactly mean 'current price'; it could also be translated by terms like 'present price', 'actual price' or 'ruling price'.

5. The Theory of Distribution

1. 'The Physiocratic concept of profit', *Economica*, February 1959, republished in Meek, 1962. Before Meek, Weulersse had already maintained that according to the Physiocrats farmers' competition puts profits into rent (Weulersse, 1910a, vol. II, p. 442; see also Boudeville, 1954, p. 460). However, Meek was the first to adapt this idea into a complete interpretation of the Physiocratic theory of distribution.
2. See Eltis, 1975a, pp. 178–9; Cartelier, 1976, pp. 80–2; Gilibert, 1972, p. 71. Profits have been regarded either as a 'disequilibrium phenomenon' (see Salvati, 1980, p. 44), or as an element of surplus which cannot be separated from rent (see Candela, 1975, p. 76).
3. The net product also includes the tithe or *dîme* for the church (see *Analyse de la Formule Arithmétique du Tableau Economique*, Meek, 1962, p. 150 and *Grains*, I.N.E.D., 1958, vol. II, p. 463), but Quesnay sometimes forgets it (see ibid., p. 475). For the sake of simplicity, we shall refer to rent and *taille* only.
4. On the different types of *taille* existing in France in the eighteenth century see, for instance, Dakin, 1939, pp. 279–300.
5. From Quesnay's calculations concerning the corn trade in England, it emerges that there rent takes half of the net product, while *taille* and farmers' profit take a quarter each (see *Grains*, I.N.E.D., 1958, vol. II, p. 475. The share of rent in net output is still higher than that of profits, but Quesnay remarks that with the introduction of large-scale cultivation the ratio of profit to rent increases from 36 per cent to 41 per cent (see ibid, p. 478).
6. Quesnay also mentions the existence of profits in cattle breeding, in the

Extrait des Economies Royales de M. de Sully which appeared with the *Tableau Economique* (see Kuczinsky and Meek, 1972, p. 11).

7. See also Mirabeau, 1760b, pp. 72, 195; Weulersse, 1910b, p. 55

8. The *prix commun de vendeur* is the current price (see Chapter 3, 3.3). On the relation between this price and the fundamental one see Chapter 3, 3.7.

9. Quesnay calculates the losses to farmers in years in which the crop is plentiful; they are 3 *liv.* 18 *s.* 6 *d.* and 1 *liv.* 18 *s.* 6 *d.* These figures are almost identical to those of 4 and 2 *livres* respectively that we have arrived at (see *Grains*, I.N.E.D., 1958, vol. II, p. 463).

10. Of course the *annual* fundamental price is also affected by output variations, because Quesnay assumes that the costs of cultivation, including rent and *taille*, are fixed per *arpent*. But this is not the case for the *average* fundamental price, which is not influenced by good and bad harvests.

11. Groenewegen believes that in the article *Fermiers* this interest could be regarded as a 'minimum supply price of capital' (Groenewegen, 1983, p. xvi), because in his *Essai sur l'amélioration des terres* Pattullo interprets the magnitude as an 'interest on the money advanced' (Pattullo, 1758, p. 95). However, there is no such remark in Quesnay's own writings.

12. See also *Impôts*, INED, 1958, vol. II, p. 616. Of course while the amounts of rent, *taille* and other duties are fixed in terms of money, their shares in the surplus vary, depending on annual variations in the value of net product.

13. See *Grains*, I.N.E.D., 1958, vol II, p. 482–3; Herlitz, 1961b, pp. 130–1; and Meek, 1962 pp. 268–9, 301.

14. Cantillon speaks of the *valeur intrinsique* of commodities (see above Chapter 3, 3.8, but does not use this notion consistently in dealing with the question of the origin of profits (see Herlitz, 1961b, p. 130).

15. Steuart may have been familiar with the works of the physiocrats (see Groenewegen, 1983, p. XIX, note 50 and Skinner, 1966, p. xxxvii, note 79 and pp. lxix–lxx). His theory of profit differs from that of Quesnay on at least two points. First, he recognises the existence of profits in the production of any commodity and not only in the cultivation of the soil. Secondly, he concedes much more explicitly the possibility that profits could be consolidated within the intrinsic value of commodities, thus 'becoming in a manner necessary to the existence of goods', even if he regards this fact as being harmful to the nation (see Steuart, 1767, vol. I. pp. 193–5, 240).

16. The *bon prix*, then, has the remarkable quality of priming economic mechanisms which raise the annual output of the country, its population and particularly the incomes of all classes (see *Hommes*, I.N.E.D., 1958, vol. II, p. 525). Moreover, Quesnay reassures the lower classes, *le bas peuple*, that the increase in the price of corn is not detrimental to their standard of living, because wages rise in the same proportion. He also maintains that workers could benefit from a high price for wheat, 'because it increases the expenditures which procure wheat to people' (ibid., p. 535). Earlier in the same article Quesnay seems to suggest that

the incomes of the dominant social groups can rise without reducing those of the poorer people. The profits of cultivators and the revenues of landlords, of the Church and of the State increase more than the price of corn, hence these four classes are better off, while the lower classes maintain their previous purchasing power, because wages 'will increase in proportion' to the rise in prices (ibid., p. 509).

17. A clear example of the physiocrats' different attitudes towards the elements making up the surplus can be found in Du Pont's *De l'Exportation et de l'Inportation des Grains*, in a *tableau* where he describes the way in which an increase in the current price of corn raises both advances and output (see Du Pont, 1764, pp. 20-21). The immediate effect of the price rise is to increase the value of the net product, which is then divided between revenues and investments in the original and annual advances. (For a detailed analysis of this *tableau* see Appendix A of this Chapter.) The net product is shared between profits and rent, but only the latter, together with tithe and *taille*, is a completely disposable revenue; profits have to be used to increase the stock of capital.

18. The physiocratic insistence on the different ways of spending the two parts of the net product are reminiscent of the Keynesian distinction between consumption and investment. However, Quesnay's analysis is based on a scheme of reproduction where part of the output has a fixed destination, because it must necessarily replace the means of production which have been used up. Therefore he discusses the problem of the expenditure of surplus, but does not directly face the question of the employment of the whole social product.

19. See also Meek, 1962, p. 384; Eagly, 1969, p. 75; Deane, 1978, pp. 30–1.

20. As Weulersse says, 'The physiocrats did not believe that it was possible to find a sufficient number of proprietors who were learned enough, interested enough in matters of cultivation, and, at the same time rich enough, to guarantee by themselves, by their means alone, the improvement of agriculture' (Weulersse, 1910a, vol. I, p. 407; see also Fox-Genovese, 1976, p. 132).

21. Meek points out that the later physiocrats – Baudeau, Mercier de la Rivière, Le Trosne – faced the question of profits much more decisively than Quesnay and Mirabeau, indeed innovating in their analysis to some extent (see Meek, 1962, pp. 289, 307ff.). However, the idea of profits as the source of accumulation permeates the whole of Quesnay's work, from the first articles of the *Encyclopédie* to the last ones in the *Ephémérides*.

22. See also Spengler, 1958, p. 61; *Analyse de la Formule Arithmétique du Tableau Economique*, Meek, 1962, p. 164 note 1; Mercier, 1767, p. 289.

23. These stages, particularly the last two, are clearly described by Du Pont in his *tableau* in *De l'Exportation et de l'Inportation des Grains* (see Du Pont, 1764, pp. 19ff.).

24. See Mercier, 1767, p. 289; Salleron, I.N.E.D., 1958, vol. II, pp. 509–10, note. 28; Spengler, 1958, p. 61: Depitre, 1911, pp. xxiii–xxiv.

25. According to Meek, Quesnay considered the farmer's income 'as a sort of superior wage-of-management-plus-payment-for-risk-bearing rather than a "net profit"' (Meek, 1962, p. 280).

26. See Weulersse, 1910a, vol. I, pp. 404–6, and vol. II, p. 342–44. The two questions are related because the *baux* were quite often used as the base for an estimate of the net product accruing to proprietors, and hence of their taxable income (see ibid., vol. II, p. 337).
27. See, for instance, Weulersse, 1910a, vol I, pp. 357–8; 1910b, pp. 37-8. Baudeau, 1767, p. 200; Baudeau, 1767–70, vol. XII, pp. 152ff., 170–1).
28. 'Poor peasants, poor Kingdom' writes Quesnay in the *Extrait des Economies Royales de M. de Sully* (Kuczynski and Meek, 1972, p. 10, note b).
29. In the *Journal de l'Agriculture* of February 1768, a critic of physiocracy remarked with some suspicion that in England 'the farmer makes more revenue from land than the same proprietor' (Weulersse, 1910a, vol. II, p. 344).
30. See Fling, 1908, pp. 118–19; Loménie, 1879, pp. 221–6.
31. See Weulersse, 1910a, vol. I, p. 79. In the *Ephémérides* of 1769, Du Pont remembers this period with a famous expression: 'the progress of enlightenment has necessarily been delayed by *two and a half years* (in Loménie, 1879, p. 244, Du Pont's italics).
32. This argument was also used by such opponents of physiocracy as Forbonnais and Terray (see Weulersse, 1910a, vol. II, p. 441).
33. This article appeared in the *Journal de l' agriculture, du commerce et des finances* of August 1766 and was Quesnay's main effort to reduce the reasons for confrontation between landlords and farmers.
34. Both works were greatly influenced by Quesnay; part of the *Phylosophie Rurale* is traditionally ascribed directly to him (see I.N.E.D., 1958, vol. II, p. 687 note 1; Meek, 1962, p. 38). Mirabeau and Du Pont wrote two *tableaux* (Du Pont, 1674, pp. 20–1; Mirabeau, 1764, vol. I; pp. 36–7) explicitly to show the mechanisms which will give the surplus to the proprietors. It must be remarked that, despite competition among farmers, both authors clearly show that the profits maintain the characteristic of being the *only* form in which surplus is transformed into advances. The two *tableau* are extensively analysed in Appendix A of this chapter.
35. In the 1750s Quesnay also mentions competition among cultivators, in the article *Hommes* of 1756 (see I.N.E.D., 1958, vol. II, pp. 560). Note that although *Impôts* and *Hommes* were certainly known at the time of the physiocrats, they were not published until the beginning of the twentieth century; *Impôts* appeared in 1902 in the *Reveu d'histoire des doctrines économiques et sociales*, edited by Gustave Schelle (see ibid., p. 579, note 1); *Hommes* was published in the same journal in 1908 by Etienne Bauer (see ibid., p. 511, note 1).
36. Le Trosne clearly states that the entire output belongs to farmers, who then give the landlords part of the surplus over technical expenses, according to the agreements they have made to rent the land (see Le Trosne, 1777, p. 927, 932).
37. In 1770, in one of his *Lettres au contrôleur général (abbé Terray) sur le commerce des grains*, Turgot uses this argument to show that cultivator will always retain part of the surplus (see Turgot, 1770, pp. 301–4).
38. See Groenewegen, 1971, pp. 333–4, 337–9; Groenewegen, 1969, pp. 285–6; Meek, 1954, pp. 138–42.
39. Professors Meek and Barna have already examined some of the prob-

lems related to this *tableau* (see Meek, 1962, pp. 142–5; Barna 1976, pp. 326–30).

40. PN_t/AA_t can hardly be regarded as a purely technical ratio, as Du Pont seems to consider it. In fact the two magnitudes are expressed in value terms and not in physical ones; in particular the net product is influenced by variations in the value of output X caused by changes in prices. The figures for physical production for the ten years are as follows (*setiers* of corn): 266.6, 266.6, 262.8, 287.6, 301.7, 315.2, 327.4, 337.4, 344.4, 348.

41. It is assumed that the *baux* are renewed in the middle of the year; therefore half the net product of that year accrues to landlords and half to cultivators. This device avoids the formal discrepancies which arise when the surplus accrues to proprietors either at the end or at the beginning of the year.

42. The sum of the first $n - 1$ natural number is $\sum_{0}^{n-1} {}_t\, t = \frac{n\,(n-1)}{2}$, and by substituting this expression in equation 12, one obtains:

$$\frac{n + (n-1)\,n}{2} = \frac{n^2}{2}.$$

The same is true for equation 13.

6. Physiocracy and the Origin of Political Economy

1. A study of the physiocrats' analysis of the old and new features of the French economy can be found in Tribe, 1978, pp. 99–101; Lüthy, 1970, pp. 147ff.

2. If, with a given *bon prix*, the unit cost of production falls, when the *baux* are renewed both farmers' profits and rent can be higher than before, because the fundamental price diminishes less than in proportion to the unit cost of production. For Quesnay, the reduction of *frais* has the same effect as an increase in the current price, and entails a higher value of the net output (see *Hommes*, I.N.E.D., 1958, Vol. II, p. 563). If the unit cost of production falls, even a decrease in the current price is compatible with a rise in surplus. On the relationships between relative prices and income distribution in physiocracy see Vaggi, 1985, pp. 929ff.

3. Graslin criticised the physiocrats because they did not assign the quality of productive to labour alone (see Weulersse, 1910a, vol. II, 676–80). Mirabeau says that labour is the *second* principle of wealth (see Mirabeau, 1760c, p. 45).

4. Quesnay realises the weakness of his argument. In some of his later dialogues he assumes both the role of the defender and that of the opponent of physiocracy; but the comments and remarks of the opponent (*M.H.*) are much clearer and more powerful than those of the physiocrat (*M.N.*). As *M.H.* Quesnay poses important questions about his theory, but the answers are much weaker than the doubts and criticisms.

5. Referring to the case of international trade between a colony and the

metropolis Quesnay says: 'the traders of a nation make a profit almost entirely at the expense of the nation itself; in particular if the government grants them some exclusive privileges' (*Remarques sur l'opinion de l'auteur de l'esprit des lois*, I.N.E.D., 1958, vol. II, p. 787.)

6. Therefore the natural order, which secures wealth and prosperity for France, does not benefit its commercial partners. On the contrary, they are damaged by the type of free international trade advocated by the physiocrats (see Chapter 4, 4.7).

7. In the 1760s the price of corn in France rose considerably, but this fact must not be ascribed wholly to the influence of free exports. In particular, in the second half of the decade there were also very poor harvests (see Weulersse, 1910a, vol. II, pp. 230–31).

8. The physiocrats praise the 'new proprietors', who purchase land from a noble man and then decide to take charge of cultivation themselves. This class of 'commoner landowners' (Ware, 1931, p. 618) will greatly benefit from the implementation of physiocratic economic policy. Such new proprietors share the characteristics of both landlords and farmers. Juridically they own the soil, and economically they control the process of production in which they risk their own money. There are striking differences between these commoner landowners and the old proprietors; not only have the former a *bourgeois* mentality (see ibid., pp. 608–9), but their title of possession 'derives only from the money used to buy their estates' (Weulersse, 1910a, vol. II, p. 695).

9. In the last decades of the *ancien régime* seigneural rights became more and more burdensome both for the cultivators and for the people (see Sée, 1967, pp. 28–30).

10. See Salleron, 1958, pp. 26, 33; Cartelier, 1976, pp. 144–55; Meek, 1962, pp. 303–4.

11. The physiocrats were aware of the differences in rents due to the varying fertility of the soil (see Weulersse, 1910a, vol. II, p. 635), but they had to justify the existence of surplus in one sector and not differential rents. Note that McCulloch denied the existence of rent in physiocratic analysis for the reason that, according to him, with only the best lands being cultivated there could be no rent (see McCulloch, 1853, pp. xliii, 305, note 1).

12. A few months after the *Analyse* Quesnay wrote the *Premier problème économique* in which he uses a similar *tableau* to illustrate the consequences of an increase in the price of corn (see Meek, 1962, pp. 168–73). The following year, in the *Second problème économique*, he applies the 'formula' to analyse the effects of direct and indirect taxation (see ibid., pp. 186–9).

13. Du Pont calls the sovereign the *autorité tutélaire* (see Du Pont, 1767, p. 363; Du Pont, 1772, p. 377).

14. The view that profits accrue to the owners of capital in proportion to the financial resources invested represents one of Turgot's major innovations with respect to physiocracy (see, for instance, Turgot 1766, p. 541, 568–70, 592). On this problem see also Meek, 1973, pp. 22–6; Groenewegen 1971, pp. 333–4, 338–9.

Bibliography

BAIROCH, P. (1963) *Révolution industrielle et sous-développement.* Société d'Edition d'Enseignement Supérieur, Paris.

BARNA, T. (1975) 'Quesnay's *Tableau* in Modern Guise', *Economic Journal*, vol. 85.

BARNA, T. (1976) 'Quesnay's Model of Economic Development', *European Economic Review*, 8.

BAUDEAU, N. (1767) 'Principes de la Science Morale et Politique sur le Luxe et les Lois Somptuaires', in *Collection des Economistes et des Réformateurs Sociaux de la France*, 1912, Librairie Paul Geuthner, Paris. First published in *Ephémérides du citoyen, ou Bibliothèque raisonnée des sciences morales et politiques*,1767, vols I, III.

BAUDEAU, N. (1767–70) 'Explication du *Tableau Economique* à Madame de *** par l'auteur des Ephémérides', in *Ephémérides*, 1767, vol. XI and XII; 1768, vol. III; 1770, vol. II.

BAUER, S. (1890) 'Studies in the Origin of the French Economists', *Quarterly Journal of Economics*, October.

BAUER, S. (1895) 'Quesnay's *Tableau Economique*', *Economic Journal*, March.

BECCARIA, C. (1769–70) '*Elementi di Economia Pubblica*', in S. Romagnoli, *Cesare Beccaria Opere*, 1958, vol. I. Sansoni, Florence.

BEER, M. (1938) *Early British Economics*. Allen and Unwin, London.

BEER, M. (1939) *An Inquiry into Physiocracy*. Allen and Unwin, London.

BÉNARD, J. (1958) 'Marx et Quesnay', in I.N.E.D. (1958), vol. I.

BLAUG, M. (1962) *Economic Theory in Retrospect*. 1970, Heinemann Educational Books, London.

BLOCH, M. (1966) *French Rural History – An Essay on its Basic Characteristics*. Routledge and Kegan Paul, London.

BLOOMFIELD, A. J. (1938) 'The foreign trade doctrine of the Physiocrats', *American Economic Review*, vol. XXVIII.

BOISGUILLEBERT, Pierre Le Pesant (1707–14) '*Dissertation sur la nature des richesses, de l'argent et des tributs*', in *Economistes et Financiers du dix-huitième siècle*, E. Daire (ed.). 1843, vol. I. Guillaumin, Paris.

BONAR, J. (1893) *Philosophy and Political Economy*. 1967, Allen and Unwin, London.

BOUDEVILLE, J. R. (1954) 'Les Physiocrates et le Circuit Economique', *Revue d'Economie Politique*, May–June.

BOWLEY, M. (1973) *Studies in the History of Economic Theory before 1870*. Macmillan, London.

CANDELA, G. (1975) 'Il modello economico di Francois Quesnay', *Giornale degli economisti e annali di economia*, January–February.

CANDELA, G. and DE NICCOLO', V. (1982) 'Coerenza statica ed incoerenza dinamica dei "Tableu Economique"', *Giornale degli economisti e annali di economia*, 9/10, September–October.

CANDELA, G. and PALAZZI, M. (1979). *Dibattito sulla Fisiocrazia*. La Nuova Italia, Firenze.

CANNAN, E. (1893) *A History of the Theories of Production and Distribution in English Political Economy from 1776 to 1848*. 1967, Augustus M. Kelley, Reprints, New York.

CANNAN, E. (1896) Introduction to *Lectures on Justice, Police, Revenue and Arms, delivered in the University of Glasgow by Adam Smith*. 1956, Kelley–Millman, New York.

CANNAN, E. (1904) Introduction to *An Inquiry into the Nature and Causes of the Wealth of Nations*. 1961, Methuen, London.

CANNAN, E. (1929) *A Review of Economic Theory*. 1971, Augustus M. Kelley, New York.

CANTILLON, R. (1755) *Essai sur la Nature du Commerce en Général*, H. Higgs (ed.), 1959, Frank Cass, London.

CARTELIER, J. (1976) *Surproduit et Reproduction – La formation de l' économie politique classique*. Presse Universitaire de Grenoble.

CONAN, J. (1958) *Une Fantasie Démographique du Docteur Quesnay*, I.N.E.D. (1958), vol. I.

DAKIN, D. (1939) *Turgot and the Ancien Régime in France*, Methuen, London.

DAIRE, E. (1846)*Physiocrates – Quesnay, Du Pont de Nemours, Mercier de la Rivière, l' Àbbé Baudeau, Le Trosne*. Librairie de Guillaumin, Paris.

DEANE, P. (1978) *The evolution of economic ideas*. Cambridge University Press, Cambridge.

DE LAVERGNE, L. (1870) *Les Economistes Français du dixhuitième siècle*. Librairie de Guillaumin, Paris.

DEPITRE, E. (1910a) 'Notice on Mercier de la Rivière's *L'Ordre naturel et essentiel des Sociétés politiques*', in *Collection des Economistes*. Paul Geuthner, Paris.

DEPITRE, E. (1910b) Introduction to A. J. Herbert's *Essai sur la police générale des grains*, in *Collection des Economistes*. Paul Geuthner, Paris.

DEPITRE, E. (1911) Introduction to Du Pont de Nemours' *De l'Exportation et de l'Inportation des Grains*. Paul Geuthner, Paris.

DIDEROT, D. (1770) *Apologie de l'Abbé Galiani*, in *Oeuvres Politiques*, P. Vernière (ed.), 1963, Garnier Frères, Paris.

DOBB, M. H. (1963) *Studies in the Development of Capitalism*. Routledge and Kegan Paul, London.

DOBB, M. H. (1967) *Papers on Capitalism, Development and Planning*. Routledge and Kegan Paul, London.

DOBB, M. H. (1973) *Theories of Value and Distribution Since Adam Smith*. Cambridge University Press, Cambridge.

DU PONT de NEMOURS, P. S. (1764) '*De l'Exportation et de l'Inportation des Grains*', in *Collection des Economistes*. 1911, Paul Geuthner, Paris.

DU PONT de NEMOURS, P. S. (1767) *De l'Origine et du Progrès d'une Science Nouvelle*, in Daire (1846) vol. I.

DU PONT de NEMOURS, P. S. (1772) '*Abregé des Principes de l'Economie Politique*', in Daire (1846) vol. I. 1st publ. in *Ephémérides du citoyen*.

DU PONT de NEMOURS, P. S. (1774) *On Economic Curves*, a letter reproduced in English translation with the original diagram, by H. W. Spiegel. 1955, Johns Hopkins Press, Baltimore.

EAGLY, R. V. (1961) 'Sir James Steuart and the "Aspiration Effect"', *Economica* 109.

EAGLY, R. V. (1968) *Events, Ideology and Economic Theory*. Wayne State University Press, Detroit.

EAGLY, R. V. (1969) 'A Physiocratic Model of Dynamic Equilibrium', *Chicago Journal of Political Economy*, January–February.

EINAUDI, L. (1958) Preface to the I.N.E.D. edition of Quesnay's writings, in I.N.E.D. (1958), vol. I.

ELTIS, W. A. (1975a) 'Francois Quesnay: a Reinterpretation. 1. the *Tableau Economique*', *Oxford Economic Papers*, vol. XXVII, 2.

ELTIS, W. A. (1975b) 'Francois Quesnay: a Reinterpretation. 2. The Theory of Economic Growth', *Oxford Economic Papers*, vol. XXVII, 3.

ELTIS, W. A. (1984) *The Classical Theory of Economic Growth*. Macmillan, London.

ENGELS, F. (1878) *Herr Eugen Dühring's Revolution in Science (Anti-Dühring)*. 1943, Lawrence and Wishart, London.

ESPINAS, A. (1892) *Histoire des Doctrines Economiques*. Armand Colin, Paris.

FERRARA, F. (1850) 'Nota Sulla Dottrina Dei Fisiocratici', *Biblioteca dell'economista*, vol. 1. Pomba, Torino.

FLING, F. M. (1908) *Mirabeau and the French Revolution*, vol. 1. Putnam, New York.

FOLEY, V. (1973) 'An Origin of the *Tableau Economique*', *History of Political Economy*, Spring.

FORBONNAIS, Francois Veron de (1767) *Principes et Observations Oeconomiques*, Marc Michel Rey, Amsterdam, 2 vols. Reprinted 1980, Kraus Thomson, Munich.

FOX-GENOVESE, E. (1976) *The Origins of Physiocracy. Economic Revolution and Social Order in Eighteenth-Century France*. Cornell University Press, Ithaca and London.

GALIANI, F. (1770) *Dialogues sur le commerce des bleds*. 1958, Riccardo Ricciardi, Milan, Naples.

GAREGNANI, P. (1960) *Il Capitale nelle Teorie della Distribuzione*. Giuffré, Milan.

GAREGNANI, P. (1970) *Appunti sulla Teoria della Distribuzione e del Valore negli Economisti Classici*. Appunti Dalle Lezioni, Florence.

GIACOMIN, A. (1979) 'Un modello fisiocratico di accumulazione'. *Ricerche Economiche*, n. 1.

GIDE, C. and RIST, C. (1922) *Histoire des Doctrines Economiques*. Librairie de la Société du Recueil Sirey, Paris.

GILIBERT, G. (1972) 'Una Formulazione Algebrica del Tableau Economique', *Studi Economici*, 1–6.

GILIBERT, G. (1977) *Quesnay – la costruzione della 'macchina della prosperità'* Etas Libri, Milano.

GROENEWEGEN, P. D. (1969) 'Turgot and Adam Smith', *Scottish Journal of Political Economy*, November.

GROENEWEGEN, P. D. (1970) 'A Reappraisal of Turgot's Theory of Value, Exchange, and Price Determination', *History of Political Economy*, Spring.

GROENEWEGEN, P. D. (1971) 'A Re-interpretation of Turgot's Theory of Capital and Interest', *Economic Journal*, June.

GROENEWEGEN, P. D. (1977) *The Economics of A.R.J. Turgot*, The Hague.

GROENEWEGEN, P. D. (1983) *Quesnay: Farmers 1756 and Turgot: Sur la Grande et la Petite Culture.* Reprints of Economic Classics, Series 2, no.2, University of Sydney, Sydney.

HARRIS, J. (1757) 'An Essay Upon Money and Coins. part I', in *The Theories of Commerce, Money and Exchanges*, G. Hawkins, London.

HECHT, J. (1958) 'La vie de François Quesnay', in I.N.E.D. (1958), vol. I.

HERLITZ, L. (1961a) 'The *Tableau Economique* and the Doctrine of Sterility', *Scandinavian Economic History Review*, 1.

HERLITZ, L. (1961b) 'Trends in the Development of Physiocratic Doctrine', *Scandinavian Economic History Review*, 2.

HIGGS, H. (1897) *The Physiocrats – Six Lectures on the French Economistes of the eighteenth century.* Macmillan, London.

HIGGS, H. (1931) 'Life and Work of Richard Cantillon', in Cantillon's *Essai sur la Nature du Commerce en Général.* 1959, Frank Cass, London.

HISHIYAMA, Í. (1960) 'The *Tableau Economique* of Quesnay. Its analysis, reconstruction and application', *Kyoto University Economic Review*, April.

HOLLANDER, S. (1973) *The Economics of Adam Smith.* University of Toronto Press, Toronto.

HOSELITZ, B. F. (1968) 'Agrarian Capitalism, the Natural Order of Things: François Quesnay', *Kyklos*, 4.

HUTCHESON, F. (1753) *A short introduction to moral philosophy, in three books containing the elements of Ethics, and the Law of Nature*, 2nd ed. Robert and Andrew Foulis, Glasgow.

HUTCHESON, F. (1754–5) *A system of moral philosophy, in three books, published from the original manuscript by his son F. Hutcheson.* Robert and Andrew Foulis, Glasgow.

I.N.E.D. (1958) *Francois Quesnay et la Physiocratie*, Institut Nationale d'Études Démographiques. Presses Universitaires de France, Paris.

JEVONS, W. S. (1881) Richard Cantillon and the Nationality of Political Economy, in R. Cantillon (1755). First published in *Contemporary Review*, January.

JOHNSON, A. J. (1937) *Predecessors of Adam Smith – The Growth of British Economic Thought.* Prentice Hall, New York.

JOHNSON, H. G. (1975) 'Quelques Réflexions sur le Tableau Economique de Quesnay', *Revue d'Economie Politique*, May–June.

JOHNSON, J. (1966) 'The Role of Spending in Physiocratic Theory', *Quarterly Journal of Economics*, November.

KING, C. (1721) *The British Merchant or Commerce Preserved.* John Darby, London.

KUBOTA, A. (1958) 'Quesnay, disciple de Malebranche', in I.N.E.D. (1958), vol. I.

KUCZYNSKI, M. and MEEK, R. (1972) editors, *Quesnay's Tableau Economique* with the *Extrait des Economies Royales de M. De Sully* and the *Explication du Tableau Economique*. Macmillan, London.

KUCZYNSKI, M. (ed.) (1976) *François Quesnay, Oekonomische Schriften*, 2 vols. Akademie Verlag, Berlin.

LANDRY, A. (1958) 'Les idées de Quesnay sur la population', in I.N.E.D. (1958), vol. I.

LAW, J. (1705) *Money and Trade Considered with a Proposal for Supplying the Nation with Money*. Heirs and Successors of Andrew Anderson, Edinburgh; 1966, Augustus M. Kelley, New York.

LEONTIEF, W. (1951) *The Structure of the American Economy*, 1919–1939 2nd edn. Oxford University Press, Oxford.

LE TROSNE, G. F. (1777) *De L'Intérêt Social, par rapport à la Valeur, à la Circulation, à l'Industrie et au Commerce intérieur et extérieur*, in Daire (1846), vol. II.

LOCKE, J. (1691) *'Some considerations of the consequences of the lowering of interest and raising the value of money'*, in *The Works of John Locke*, T. Tegg, 1823, London, vol. V.

LOMÉNIE, L. de (1879) *Les Mirabeau – Nouvelle Etudes sur la Société Française au XVIII siècle*, vol. II. Dentu, Paris.

LÜTHY, H. (1970) *From Calvin to Rousseau*. Basic Books, New York.

McCULLOCH, J. R. (1825) *Principles of Political Economy*. 1870, John Murray, London.

McCULLOCH, J. R. (1853) Introductory Discourse to Smith's *An Inquiry into the Nature and Causes of the Wealth of Nations*. Adam and Charles, Edinburgh.

McLAIN, J. J. (1977) *The Economic Writings of Du Pont de Nemours*. Associated University Presses, London.

MAILLET, P. (1957) 'L'economie française vue à travers le Tableau Economique', *Revue d'Economie Politique*, May–June.

MAITAL, S. (1972) 'The *Tableau Economique* as a Simple Leontief Model: an Amendment', *Quarterly Journal of Economics*, August, vol. LXXXVI.

MALTHUS, T. R. (1798) *An Essay on the Principle of Population*. 1965, Augustus M. Kelley, New York.

MALTHUS, T. R. (1815) Letter to Horner, 14 March 1815, in *The Works and Correspondence of David Ricardo*, P. Sraffa and M. H. Dobb, (eds.) vol. VI. 1962, Cambridge University Press, Cambridge.

MALTHUS, T. R. (1820) *Principles of Political Economy*, in *The Works and Correspondence of David Ricardo*, P. Sraffa and M. H. Dobb (eds), vol. II, 1951, Cambridge University Press, Cambridge.

MARSHALL, A. (1890) *Principles of Economics*, 8th edn. 1972, Macmillan, London.

MARX, K. (1970) (1967) *Capital – A Critique of Political Economy*, vol. I. Lawrence and Wishart, London, 1970; vols II and III, 1967, International Publishers, New York.

MARX, K. (1963) *Theories of Surplus Value, Vol. IV of Capital*. Lawrence and Wishart, London.

MEEK, R. L. (1954) 'Adam Smith and the classical concept of profit'. *Scottish Journal of Political Economy*, vol. I.

MEEK, R. L. (1962) *The Economics of Physiocracy – Essays and Translations*. Allen and Unwin, London.

MEEK, R. L. (1967) *Economics and Ideology and Other Essays*. Chapman and Hall, London.

MEEK, R. L. (1968) 'Ideas, Events and Environment – The case of the French Physiocrats', in Eagly (1968).

MEEK, R. L. (1973) Introduction to *Turgot on Progress, Sociology and Economics*. Cambridge University Press, Cambridge.

MEEK, R. L. (1976) *Social Science and the Ignoble Savage*. Cambridge University Press, Cambridge.

MERCIER DE LA RIVIÈRE, P. F. J. H. (1767) *L'Ordre Naturel et Essentiel des Sociétés Politiques*, in *Collection des Economistes*. 1910, Paul Geuthner, Paris.

MIRABEAU, V. R. (1758) 'Precis de l'Organisation, ou Mémoire sur les états provinciaux', in *L'Ami des Hommes ou Traité de la Population*, vol. II, part IV, 1758, Reprinted 1970, Scientia Verlag, Aalen, from the 1758–60 edition of Avignon.

MIRABEAU, V. R. (1760a) 'Réponse à l'Essai sur les Ponts chaussées, la Voierie et les Corvées', in *L'Ami des Hommes*, vol. II, part II.

MIRABEAU, V. R. (1760b) '*Tableau Economique* avec ses explications par François Quesnay', in *L'Ami des Hommes*, vol. II, part VI.

MIRABEAU, V. R. (1760c) *Théorie de l'Impôt – Pour servir de Suite ou Traité intitulé L'Ami des Hommes*, Benjamin Gibert, The Hague. Reprinted 1772, Scientia Verlag, Aalen.

MIRABEAU, V. R. (1760d) 'Mémoire sur l'agriculture', in *L'Ami des Hommes*, vol. II, part V.

MIRABEAU, V. R. (1764) *Philosophie Rurale, ou Economie Générale et Politique de l'Agriculture*. Chez Les Libraires Associés, Amsterdam. Reprinted 1972, Scientia Verlag, Aalen.

MIRABEAU, V. R. (1769) 'Suite de la Seizième lettre de M.B. A M *** et la Quatrième sur la Stabilité de l'Ordre Légal', in *Ephémérides du citoyen*, 1769, vol. II.

MOLINIER, J. (1958a) *Les Métamorphoses d'une théorie économique. Le Revenu National chez Boisguilbert, Quesnay et Jean-Baptiste Say*, Armand Colin, Paris.

MOLINIER, J. (1958b) 'Le système de comptabilité nationale de François Quesnay', in I.N.E.D. (1958), vol. I.

MONTCHRÉTIEN, A. (de) (1615) 'Traité de l'Oeconomie Politique', *Collection des economistes* vol. 14, T. Funck Brentano (ed.), Marcel Rivière, Paris.

MORTIMER, J. (1716) *The Whole Art of Husbandry*. Mortlock and Robinson, London.

NAPOLEONI, C. (1975) *Smith, Ricardo, Marx*. Basil Blackwell, Oxford.

NAPOLEONI, C. (1976) *Valore*. ISEDI, Milano.

NEILL, T. P. (1948) 'Quesnay and Physiocracy', *Journal of the History of Ideas*, April.

NEILL, T. P. (1949) 'The Physiocrats' Concept of Economics', *Quarterly Journal of Economics*, November.

ONCKEN, A. (1888) Introduction to *Oeuvres Economiques et Philosophiques de François Quesnay*. Jules Peelman, Paris.

PALGRAVE, I. H. R. (1894–99) *Dictionary of Political Economy*, H. Higgs (ed.), 3 vols. 1963, M. Kelley, New York.

PASINETTI, L. L. (1977) *Lectures on the theory of production*. Macmillan, London.

PATTULLO, H. (1758) *Essai sur l'amélioration des terres*. Durand, Paris.

PETTY, W. (1662) *A Treatise of Taxes and Contributions*, in *The Economic Writings of Sir William Petty*, C. H. Hull (ed.), vol. 1. 1899, Cambridge University Press, Cambridge.

PETTY, W. (1676) *Political Arithmetick*, in *The Economic Writings of Sir William Petty*, in C. H. Hull (ed.), vol. 1, 1899, Cambridge University Press, Cambridge.

PHILLIPS, A. (1955) 'The *Tableau Economique* as a simple Leontief Model', *Quarterly Journal of Economics*, February.

PUFENDORF, S. (1672) *De jure naturae et gentium – libri octo*, Translation from the 1688 edition by C. H. and W. A. Oldfather. 1934, Clarendon Press, Oxford.

QUESNAY, François. The works of Quesnay are published in I.N.E.D. (1958); Meek (1962); Kuczynski-Meek (1972); Groenewegen (1983).

RICARDO, D. (1815) *An Essay on the Influence of a low Price of Corn on the Profits of Stock*, in *The Works and Correspondence of David Ricardo*, P. Sraffa and M. H. Dobbs (eds.), vol. IV, 1951, Cambridge University Press, Cambridge.

RICARDO, D. (1820) *Notes on Malthus's Principles of Political Economy*, in *The Works and Correspondence of David Ricardo*, P. Sraffa and M. H. Dobbs (eds.), vol. II, 1951, Cambridge University Press, Cambridge.

RICARDO, D. (1821) *On the Principles of Political Economy and Taxation*, in *The Works and Correpondence of David Ricardo*, P. Sraffa and M. H. Dobbs (eds.), vol. I, 1951, Cambridge University Press, Cambridge.

RIDOLFI, M. (1973) *Quesnay, il tableau économique ed altri scritti di economia*. ISEDI, Milan.

ROLL, E. (1938) *A History of Economic Thought*. 1961, Faber and Faber, London.

RONCAGLIA, A. (1977) *Petty – la nascita dell'economia politica*. Etas Libri, Milan.

RONCHETTI, E. (1978) Introduction to F. Galiani, *Dialoghi sul Commercio dei Grani*. Editori Riuniti, Rome.

ROTWEIN, E. (1955) *David Hume: Writings on Economics*. Thomas Nelson and Sons, Edinburgh.

ROUTH, G. (1975) *The Origin of Economic Ideas*. Macmillan, London.

RUBIN, I. I. (1929) *A History of Economic Thought*. 1979, Ink Links, London.

SALLERON, L. (1958) 'Le produit net des Physiocrates', in I.N.E.D. (1958), vol. I.

SALVATI, M. (1980) 'François Quesnay: lavoro produttivo e lavoro sterile', *Note Economiche*, 2.

SAMUELS, W. J. (1961) 'The Physiocratic Theory of Property and State', *Quarterly Journal of Economics*, February, vol. LXXV.

SAMUELS, W. J. (1962) 'The Physiocratic Theory of Economic Policy', *Quarterly Journal of Economics*, February, vol. LXXVI.

SAUVAIRE-JOURDAN, J. F. (1903) 'Isaac de Bacalan et les idées libre-échangiste en France vers le milieu du XVIII siècle', *Revue d' Economie Politique*, July–August.

SCHELLE, G. (1907) *Le Docteur Quesnay*, Felix Alcan Editeur, Paris.

SCHELLE, G. (1913–23) 'Turgot sa Vie et ses Oeuvres', in *Oeuvres de Turgot et documents le concernant*, 5 vols, G. Schelle (ed.) Librairie Felix Alcan, Paris. Reprinted 1972, Verlag Detlev Auvermann, Glashütten im Taunus.

SCHICCHI, S. (1978) *Quesnay e Marx*. Bonanno Editore, Catania.

SCHUMPETER, J. A. (1954) *History of Economic Analysis*. Allen and Unwin, London.

SCOTT, W. R. (1900) *Francis Hutcheson*. Cambridge University Press, Cambridge.

SCOTT, W. R. (1937) *Adam Smith as Student and Professor*. Jackson, Glasgow.

SÉE, H. (1967) *La France Economique et Sociale au XVIII Siècle*. Librairie Armand Colin, Paris.

SEMMEL, B. (1964–65) 'Malthus: "Physiocracy" and the Commercial System', *Economic History Review*, vol. 17, April.

SEWALL, E. (1901) 'The theory of value before A. Smith', *American Economic Association Publications*, vol. III, 3rd series.

SKINNER, A. (1966) Analytical Introduction to Sir James Steuart's *An Inquiry into the Principles of Political Oeconomy*. Oliver and Boyd, Edinburgh.

SLICHER VAN BATH, B. H. (1977) 'Agriculture in the vital revolution', in *Cambridge Economic History*, vol. V. Cambridge University Press, Cambridge.

SMITH, A. (1762–63) *'Lectures on Jurisprudence' or Notes from the Lectures on Justice, Police, Revenue and Arms*, R. L. Meek, D. D. Raphael and P. G. Stein (eds). 1978, Oxford University Press, Oxford.

SMITH, A. (1776) *An Inquiry into the Nature and Causes of The Wealth of Nations*, E. Cannan (ed.). 1961, Methuen, London.

SPENGLER, J. J. (1942) *French Predecessors of Malthus* Duke University Press, Durham, North California.

SPENGLER, J. J. (1945) 'The Physiocrats and Say's Law of Markets', *Journal of Political Economy*, September–December.

SPENGLER, J. J. (1958) 'Quesnay Philosophe. Empiriste, Economiste', in I.N.E.D. (1958), vol. I.

SRAFFA, P. and DOBB, M. H. (1951) Introduction to *The Works and Correspondence of David Ricardo*, vol. I. Cambridge University Press, Cambridge.

SRAFFA, P. (1960) *Production of commodities by means of commodities* 1972, Cambridge University Press, Cambridge.

STEUART, J. (1767) *An Inquiry into the Principles of Political Oeconomy*. 1966, Oliver and Boyd, Edinburgh.

SUTTER, J. (1958) *Quesnay et la médicine*, in I.N.E.D. (1958), vol. I.

TAYLOR, O. H. (1929) 'Economics and the Idea of Natural Laws', *Quarterly Journal of Economics*, November.

TAYLOR, O. H. (1930) 'Economics and the Idea of *Jus Naturale*', *Quarterly Journal of Economics*, February.

TAYLOR, W. L. and ROBERTSON, H. M. (1957) 'Adam Smith's approach to the theory of value', *Economic Journal*, June.

TAYLOR, W. L. (1965) *Francis Hutcheson and David Hume as Predecessors of Adam Smith*. Duke University Press, Durham, North Carolina.

TRIBE, K. (1978) *Land, Labour and Economic Discourse*. Routledge and Kegan Paul, London.

TSURU, S. (1942) 'On reproduction schemes', in Sweezy P. M. *The theory of capitalist development* 1968, Modern Readers Paperback, New York and London.

TUCKER, G. S. L. (1960) *Progress and Profits in British Economic Thought 1650–1850* Cambridge University Press, Cambridge.

TURGOT, A. R. J. (1766) *Réflexions sur la Formation et la Distribution des Richesses*, in Schelle (1913–23), vol. II.

TURGOT, A. R. J. (1767a) *Observations sur le Mémoire de Saint-Péravy*, in Schelle (1913–23) vol. II.

TURGOT, A. R. J. (1767b) *Sur la Grande et la Petite Culture* in Groenewegen (1983), First published in *Ephémérides du citoyen*.

TURGOT, A. R. J. (1769)*Valeurs et Monnais*, in Schelle (1913–23), vol. III.

TURGOT, A. R. J. (1770) *Lettres au Contoleur général (abbé Terray) sur le commerce des grains*, in Schelle (1913–23), vol. III.

VAGGI, G. (1982) 'Surplus and Effective Demand in Physiocracy', *Studi Economici*, 18.

VAGGI, G. (1983) 'The Physiocratic Theory of Prices', *Contributions to Political Economy*, 2.

VAGGI, G. (1985) 'A Physiocratic Model of Relative Prices and Income Distribution', *Economic Journal*, vol. 95, December.

VOLTAIRE, F. M. (1767) *L'homme aux quarante écus*, in *Oeuvres Complètes de Voltaire*, vol. 59. 1826, Paris, Baudouin.

VOLTAIRE, F. M. (1770) *Questions sur l'Encyclopédie*, in *Oeuvres Complètes de Voltaire*, vol. 51. 1825, Paris, Baudouin.

WALSH, V. and GRAM, H. (1980) *Classical and Neoclassical Theories of General Equilibrium*. Oxford University Press, Oxford.

WARE, N. J. (1931) 'The Physiocrats: a study in Economic Rationalization' *American Economic Review*, December.

WEULERSSE, G. (1910a) *Le mouvement physiocratique en France (de 1756 à 1770)*, 2 vols, Editions Mouton, Paris, 1968. First published, Felix Alcan éditeur, Paris.

WEULERSSE, G. (1910b) *Les Manuscrits Economiques de François Quesnay et du Marquis de Mirabeau aux Archives Nationales*. Paul Geuthner, Paris.

WEULERSSE, G. (1950) *La Physiocratie sous les ministères de Turgot et de Necker (1774–1781)*. Presses Universitaires de France, Paris.

WEULERSSE, G. (1959) *La Physiocratie à la fin du Règne de Louis XV (1770–1774)*. Presses Universitaires de France, Paris.

WOOG, H. (1950) *The Tableau Economique of François Quesnay*. A. Franckle Verlag, Berne.

YOUNG, A. (1774) *Political Arithmetic*. W. Nicoll, London.

ZAGARI, E. (1972) *Una reinterpretazione della teoria fisiocratica*. Jovene, Napoli.

ZANGHERI, R. (1966) *François Quesnay – Scritti Economici*. A. Forni Editore, Bologna.

Index